The Master Musicians Series

HANDEL

Series edited by
Stanley Sadie

THE MASTER MUSICIANS SERIES

HANDEL

Percy M. Young

J. M. DENT & SONS LTD
London, Toronto and Melbourne

Printed in Great Britain
by
Biddles Ltd, Guildford, Surrey
and bound at the
Aldine Press, Letchworth, Herts
for
J. M. DENT & SONS LTD
Aldine House, Welbeck Street, London

First published 1947
First paperback edition 1975
Last revised 1979

Hardback ISBN: 0 460 03161 9
Paperback ISBN: 0 460 02165 6

CONTENTS

ILLUSTRATIONS

Between pages 86 and 87

PREFACE TO THE 1980 REPRINT

IT is more than thirty years since I began work on the first edition (1947) of this book. In the intervening years a great deal has happened in respect of both the subject and the author. In that time musicology has come of age, so that some things that were not known have become known, and some once thought to be fact have been proved fiction. All the same, romantic notions adrift of reality still continue to bemuse the student and defeat the scholar. For instance, in the first edition of this book, having been the first to have been granted access to his bank account by the Bank of England, I was able positively to show that Handel was never bankrupt. But there are those who even now proclaim that he was.

Some errors that had persisted in my text have been corrected and fresh material has been introduced. In conformity with contemporary fashions in planning, the processes of replacement and redevelopment have been as thorough as the limits of a volume in this series allow. The Appendices in general have been brought up to date. In previous editions items in the Catalogue of Works (Appendix B) related to Chrysander's Complete Edition, now being replaced by the Hallische Händel-Ausgabe (Leipzig/Kassel), hereinafter referred to as H.H.-A. Where works are available in the new edition the appropriate references are added. The Catalogue of Works is not entirely comprehensive, mostly omitting items which are duplicates, as well as those of doubtful provenance and those that are incomplete. In the category 'Oratorios and large-scale cantatas' are contained all those works which are of oratorio shape and proportion without distinguishing between sacred and secular.

When I first worked on Handel I did so according to certain environmental conditions. The Handel we were once taught to know was a robust Englishman, emancipated from German and other foreign influences, who composed a great deal of 'religious' music to be sung by god-fearing, working-class and nonconformist provincial choirs in town halls and chapels. I must confess that I still find that image somewhat compelling, and recognize in it aspects of truth that nowadays too often escape notice. To whom, one may still inquire, does the work of a great composer (or any other creative spirit) belong?

Handel, secularized to accommodate present secularities, today perhaps is a little too dandified. At the same time it must be recognized that the perceptive application of scholarship to practice has not only renewed forgotten masterpieces (especially in the field of opera) but also shown those that are familiar in more radiant attire.

For many years now I have been working on Handel at grassroots level. I have been much where he began his career, and have learned to see him, as some others see him, as a great German and (more particularly) as a *caro Sassone*. In this I am in no way wishful of diminishing his Englishness. Indeed, the additional knowledge gained from experiences of different kinds in the place of his origin serves to enhance the concept of him as a European. I promoted this idea in the first form of this book, at a time when only the wildest visionary could have looked forward to any form of European unity. To this fulfilment Handel made his own, unique, contribution.

Being a revision, this book contains thoughts on the subject I had many years ago. While across the years I have accumulated others (which I will hope to display more extensively elsewhere), I do not find them in conflict with my present attitude. That, I suppose, is due to the permanence of the Handelian presence.

P. M. Y.

ACKNOWLEDGMENTS

IN respect of the first edition: the Foreign Office, the Bank of England, the National Library of Ireland; the Duke of Devonshire for permission to quote for the first time the letter on p. 36, Mr T. W. Bourne (portrait by Hogarth), the Director of the Fitzwilliam Museum, Cambridge (portraits by Thornhill and Dandridge, and Hogarth's 'A Musical Party'); Dorothy Lady Brabourne, Lady Hatherton, Mrs Phyllis Brown, Mr Norman Ault, Mr G. J. K. Little, Mr H. Wathall, Canon A. E. Farrow, Mr E. H. Dance, Mr Edmund Blunden, and Mrs A. L. Young.

For the past fifteen years I have been constantly in touch with Handel scholars from many countries through the activities of the Handel Societies in Halle and Göttingen. In those cities not only I but also all others who visit them for Handelian purposes are indebted to

Dr Konrad Sasse, Director of the *Händelhaus,* and Professor Walther Siegmund-Schultze, General Editor of the H.H.-A., the late Walter Meyerhoff, President, and Professor Günther Weissenborn, Musical Director of the Göttingen Handel Festival.

Somewhere along the line Professor O. E. Deutsch helped improve this book. I have been continually grateful to members of the staffs of the British Museum, the Fitzwilliam Museum, the Birmingham Central Reference Library and the Watson Music Library, Manchester.

P. M. Y.

In affectionate memory of
GARETH BERNARD BANTING

'Handel was the Jupiter of music; . . . his hallelujahs open the heavens. He utters the word "Wonderful," as if all their trumpets spoke together. And then, when he comes to earth, to make love amidst nymphs and shepherds (for the beauties of all religions find room in his breast), his strains drop milk and honey, and his love is the youthfulness of the Golden Age.'

LEIGH HUNT (*Table Talk*).

'Whatever good influence we may have had in giving a direction to Handel's genius, however much he may have owed to his long residence among us, Handel was by birth a German, and by education a citizen of the world. Music (let us never forget it) is a universal language, and Handel had the advantage of studying it wherever, for the time being, it was most and best spoken.'

J. P. HULLAH, in a lecture at the Royal Institution of Great Britain, in 1862.

CHAPTER I

BIRTH AND APPRENTICESHIP

IN 1685 Charles II of England died, and with him the prospects of the house of Stuart. In the same year Louis XIV, foreshadowing events to come, revoked the Edict of Nantes and dispersed throughout Europe the skill, intelligence and integrity of unpalatable Huguenotism. In 1685 Handel was born.

An artist may be, and frequently is, oblivious of the vagaries of political machination; but his career, his opportunities and his environment are subject to vicissitudes whose author is the politician. Thus two significant historic events in the year of his birth had some part in the moulding of the future of George Frideric Handel.

The opportunism of Charles II might have staved off the Glorious Revolution, but the stubborn miscalculations of James II, coupled with a respect for the dictatorial technique of the French king, made revolution inevitable. The deposition of James left an ultimate way clear for the Hanoverian succession, the development of modern parliamentarianism, the military achievements of Marlborough, the predominance of Low Church doctrine and such individual qualities *in arte vivendi* as were to excite the later applause of Voltaire and Montesquieu. France, whose habits of depredation stimulated uneasiness throughout Europe in the latter part of the seventeenth century, provoked the enmity not only of princes, but also of peoples by her renewal of religious persecution. England, watchful as ever of the balance of power, viewed with no disfavour the rise of a new, potentially counteractive state: that of Prussia. Under the tutelage of the Hohenzollerns Prussia was beginning to emerge as a unity, and by the time the Great Elector and Frederick I had impressed their personalities on various scattered German domains which had languished in semi-feudal torpor since the Peace of Westphalia she was a great power, with the third army in Europe, an imposing list of achievement in the arts and the sciences, and the competent

I

continental check to future French ambitions in the east. But all this was purchased at a cost. The lives and liberties of her subjects passed from the, sometimes inert or inefficient, control of local princes to that of a centralized and efficient bureaucracy.

It was for the very reason that England provided a tolerable life for a man of independent proclivities that Handel made this country for the greater part of his life his home. It is, however, wrong to consider him an Englishman. It is equally wrong to consider him a German. He was neither, but rather a European, and as such a glory to his own age and an example to others.

The independence to be discerned in Handel's character was (*pace* scientific scepticism) a hereditary endowment. The Händels in general pursued life with a superb faith in their own destinies. And since they were successful they aroused envious respect. Valentin, the first who comes into our field, was born at Breslau in 1583. Thence, having learned his trade as a coppersmith, he migrated to the more prosperous town of Halle, of which he was enrolled as citizen early in 1609. As a tradesman—that is the signification of the family name—Valentin Händel contracted an advantageous marriage with Anna Beichling, daughter of a master coppersmith. Thereafter he prospered, his money went into property, and he nur-tured a large family, whose upbringing was Lutheran, in the fear of God, in bourgeois respectability and in a sound belief in the efficacy of balanced budgets. In 1622 his fifth son, Georg, was born.

As the coppersmith business eventually passed to his elder brothers Georg was constrained to attempt new fields of endeavour. In-fluenced, no doubt, by the prevailing needs of the times and by the contemporary carnage of the Thirty Years War, he chose surgery (with its ancillary craft of barber). Left fatherless at the age of four-teen Georg Händel developed that degree of self-dependence which necessity so often mothers. He was first apprenticed to Andreas Beger, whose wife was the daughter of the English musician William Brade. Next he assisted Christoph Oettinger. After his death, in 1643, Händel acquired both his practice and his widow, who thus became Frau Händel. Of this *mariage de convenance* six children were born, of whom two survived the perilous passage of infancy. With that ambition induced by paternity Händel progressed in dignity to appointment as surgeon to the suburb of Giebichenstein and as surgeon-in-ordinary and *valet de chambre* to the Duke of Sachsen-Weissenfels. Some years later an episode occurred to show that municipal and individual rights had their eighteenth-century champions. Handel purchased a house-cum-wineshop (a commend-able departure in medical practice), the *Zum gelben Hirsch* in Halle, but the civic authority refused to renew the wine-selling licence. Händel referred the matter to the Elector, who referred it back to the city. But the indomitable Händel refused to be reduced by his fellow townsmen and shuttlecocked his grievances back to the Elector, who thereupon, exhausted by the strain of attempting de-cisions of such magnitude, settled the matter in the plaintiff's favour. The town council was promised military occupation and monetary penalties should the matter be raised again. Nor was this the only occasion on which Händel asserted his rights. In 1680, on the death of the Duke and consequent political changes, attempts were made, unsuccessfully, to deprive him of his court appointments. Whether, as a matter of fact, this would have entailed much loss of emolument is doubtful. Princes and dukes were conspicuous for the splendour of their surroundings rather than for their capacity for adequately recompensing their *aides*. However, Händel intended to conserve his personal dignity and in so doing ensured his unborn son's first entry into romantic anecdote.

By the Peace of Westphalia Halle had been assigned to Prussia, but this arrangement became operative only on the death of Duke Augustus in 1680. The local effects of this change were that the court was transferred to Weissenfels—where the new duke, Johann Adolf, appointed Johann Krieger as his director of music—and that Halle resumed its more stolid characteristics, in due course changing the Ritter-Akademie—an establishment exclusively devoted to the propagation and preservation of aristocratic privilege—into a univer-sity. Halle-an-der-Saale was a pleasant town, anciently a member of the Hanseatic League, with a sturdy tradition documented in its principal buildings. These included a medieval Rathaus; the re-mains of the castle of Moritzburg, established in 1479 by the Arch-bishop of Magdeburg and largely destroyed by fire during the Thirty Years War; the Moritzkirche; the Liebfrauenkirche (church of

3

Our Lady), conspicuous by a distinctive twin-spired and bridged façade; and the ancient but altered Dom, Calvinist since 1689. The natural situation of Halle, which was a centre of salt manufacture, gave trading advantages, a certain cultural independence and a dignity which is most distinguished alumnus recollected gracefully in later years.[1] But part of the price paid by the seventeenth and eighteenth centuries for such cultural blessings as excite the envy of later generations was plague, famine and sudden death. Georg Händel himself was given up for dead in 1681. His recovery possessed, so far as his kinsfolk were concerned, elements of the miraculous. His eldest son, Gottfried, perished in a general and alarming epidemic in the following year. His wife died in 1683.

Giebichenstein, where Händel worked, had as its Lutheran pastor Georg Taust, of Bohemian descent. He had two daughters. One, Dorothea, became Händel's second wife a few months after the passing of the first. The other, Anna, followed her to the city when the onset of pregnancy demanded sisterly sympathy and domestic reinforce- ment. In 1684 a son was born to Dorothea. He died almost immediately.

On 23rd February 1685 a second child was born who did survive. He was christened on the following day at the Liebfrauenkirche. The names given to him were Georg Friedrich. Confusion with the old-style calendar (in which the year began on 25th March) im- pelled earlier authorities, including the engravers of the memorial inscription in Westminster Abbey, to place the date of Handel's birth in 1684.[2] A further digression may here be relevant. The family name was susceptible of various orthography: thus we meet Händel, Hendel, Händeler, Hendler, Hendtler, and the charming feminine form of Händelin (to Christiana Susanna Händelin Handel ultimately bequeathed £300). The commonest English usage was, and is, Handel. Hereafter the composer shall be called, as he styled himself in England, George Frideric Handel.

Those who, in the period under review, survived the hazards of infancy were, beyond doubt, hardy. Handel, who inherited a good

[1] *Vide* reference to the coat of arms of the Foundling Hospital on page 83.

[2] The Gregorian or new-style calendar was introduced in England in 1752. It was welcomed with the reserve accorded to all innovations.

deal from his father, received therefrom the benefit of a tough con-
stitution. Old Händel mercifully survived his illness of 1681; at
the same period of his own life his son recovered from a severe and
paralytic disorder. They were, literally, a breed of diehards. In
later years Handel's physique became one source of anecdote. More
important than this is the fact that his bodily powers had particular
reference to his creative activities, his capacity for hard work and his
resilience in the face of misfortune being directly consequential.
The bowed legs of maturity may suggest a vitamin deficiency in
childhood, otherwise the parents may be exonerated from any suspicion of early neglect.

The incidents of youth are germane to the later development of
the biographic subject. Accordingly the Händel household needs
to be set in proper perspective. Episodes imperfectly recollected
from J. C. Smith by the gullible Mainwaring and others have
furnished material for romantic screeds of significance only to the
unmusical.

A not unnatural affection for an estimable mother and a later
aversion from the bonds of holy matrimony have been construed into
psychological jargon as 'mother-fixation,' while a fatherly inclina-
tion to suggest a career other than that of music has had the elder
Händel arraigned for tyranny. Such facts as are available suggest
that Georg Händel had excellent good sense, pride in his son's
potentialities, and a willingness to provide for educational opportunity. His surviving portrait adds to these qualities a grave,
patrician dignity. If the percussion instruments of the nursery really
were incinerated and the clavichord acquired only against interdict
the natural desire of an elderly surgeon for a quiet home may be held
responsible. The lusty presence of George Frideric's younger sisters
provided distraction enough.

Somewhere about his seventh or eighth year George Frideric
accompanied his father to the Schloss at Weissenfels. There, with a
precocity not uncommon to the children of elderly parents, he proposed to the duke his intention of becoming a musician.[1] The duke
sensibly advised that self-expression should find its natural outlet

[1] One connection with music was through Cyriacus Berger (related by
marriage), musician at Zeitz.

under competent guidance. Handel was put, therefore, under that of Zachow, organist of the Liebfrauenkirche. At the same time his general education proceeded classically and conservatively towards some respectable, if humdrum, bourgeois career. An incident of these years which appropriately stuck in the mind was the operation which his father performed in 1692 on Andreas Rudloff, the 'Halle sword-swallower.' The incident may be quoted as demonstrating either the incredible surgical gifts with which Händel was endowed or the mythical propensities of many Handeliana.

Halle had enjoyed that sort of musical reputation which would now promote complacency in a similarly placed English provincial town. Before the reign of Zachow it had possessed two notable organists in Wolff Heintz, a friend of Luther's, and Samuel Scheidt, the son of a salt-works manager and a father of German music.[1] In the palmy days before pietism stepped on such displays Halle had gone some way in the inauguration of the *Singspiel* as opposed to the infiltrating Italian opera. Zachow himself combined competence with sobriety, was painstaking and friendly, and had a good collection of Italian and German music.[2] Young Handel learned the organ, the harpsichord, the violin, the hautboy, composition and common sense. The contemporary attitude to music was utilitarian. Much was required for ceremonies of church and state and, library facilities being non-existent, had to be composed *ad hoc*. The embryonic organist was early initiated into the mysteries of ecclesiastical tradition, and Handel, as a matter of course, wrote a weekly cantata as exercise. But sacred music was hardly his first love. 'I used to write like the devil in those days, but chiefly for the hautbois, which was my favourite instrument,' he is reported to have said. Six sonatas for two oboes and bass in Handel's autograph, bought by an English nobleman were given by him to C. F. Weidemann, who described them as having been composed when Handel was '. . . a School Boy, about Ten Year of Age . . .' (B.M., R.M. 18.b.3). It is regrettable that an exercise book with extracts from Froberger, Krieger, Kerll, Ebner and Strungk is lost. Strungk is worth momentary consideration. He was a conspicuous composer,

[1] For his knowledge of English music see p. 219.

[2] Mainwaring, . . . *Life of Handel*, p. 14.

a member of the German resistance party fighting the cause of native opera (*Singspiel*), who left a large catalogue of works which quickly passed into the limbo of forgotten achievement. Some of his titles have a familiar ring, *Nero* (1693) and *Agrippina* (1699) in particular. Handel no doubt spent the impressionable years of his youth reflecting on the splendour of their associations. His own copies of Strungk were probably made from *Ein hundert auserlesene Arien zweyer Hamburgischen Operen, Semiramis und Esther. Mit beigefügten Ritornellen* (1689).

Three or four years of Zachow's able tuition, absorbed together with the tuition of the civic instrumental players, qualified Handel for inclusion among the ranks of the prodigies. In this capacity he visited Berlin in 1696.[1] There Frederick,[2] later to become by imperial grace King of Prussia, held court. While he continued his father's work of Prussian organization and diplomatic opportunism—he had previously supported the claims of William III to the English throne and was later to aid the allied cause in the War of Spanish Succession —his second wife, Sophie Charlotte, occupied herself with the department of *Kultur*. Lest, however, it should be thought that the Elector himself was a Philistine, it should be recorded that he was responsible for the foundation of the University of Halle and of the Academy of Science in Berlin, that he appreciated French culture despite political antagonism and that he was ready to extend a welcome to Berlin to victims of political and religious discrimination. Across this scene Handel flitted meteorically. He impressed the court, the Electress, herself a practising musician, and the Elector. The latter made an offer not unusual for a period in which crowned heads felt easier with a maximum *entourage* of sycophantic retainers. He suggested a further course in musical education, inevitably in

[1] It was not on this visit that Handel met Ariosti and Buononcini, as neither was in Berlin in 1696. Ariosti arrived in 1697 and Buononcini in 1702. Mainwaring was probably right in recording a meeting between Handel and these musicians, but, as usual, he gets his dates wrong. Mainwaring may be credited with the invention of the bed-time story about the youthful Handel sitting on Ariosti's knee.

[2] As Elector of Brandenburg this ruler was Frederick III, as King of Prussia, Frederick I.

Italy. Old Händel, however, was not enthusiastic. Still supporting the conventional thesis that the precarious possibilities of music offered improbable avenues of worldly success, he emphasized the advantages of a legal career. It may be urged that, as a matter of fact, jurisprudence formed a better training for musicians than music: among German musicians Schütz, Walther, Mattheson, Kuhnau, Telemann, Emanuel Bach, as well as Handel, were 'spoiled' lawyers. Georg Händel died on 11th February 1697. The melancholy event was commemorated by his son in a poetic effusion duly published.

Georg Händel was something of Horace's *justus et tenax vir*, and the value of independence, a quality which dictated his reaction to the Electoral offer, he impressed on his son. The University of Halle, under the progressive leadership of Thomasius, further stimulated intellectual adventure, and the pietistic teaching of Francke, head of the theological faculty, laid stress on the necessity for freedom from sterile orthodoxy. Handel, who had spent two years at the Stadtgymnasium, entered the university in 1702 and, while his academic attainments may have been slight, he could hardly have remained impervious to the new liberalism of thought which characterized the foundation. Music was simultaneously pursued with added zeal. In the same year as entering the university Handel became organist of the Dom, in succession to the unreliable Leporin.

Although the 'Reformed' (that is, Calvinist) liturgy in the cathedral, and the pietism promulgated from the university, were hostile to elaborate church music, Handel, looking forward to the time when he might expect to be freed from Calvinistic restrictions, continued to write works for church performance. Of these there only appears to survive a Latin Psalm, *Laudate pueri*. These Halle activities created a reputation that was not merely local, so that Georg Philipp Telemann, a young man of varied abilities, called on Handel round about the year 1701. Telemann was four years older than Handel, a native of Magdeburg, a nominal student of law and an undergraduate of the University of Leipzig.[1]

A capacity for loyal friendship was a characteristic of Handel, and that with Telemann was lifelong. Forty years on they were still in amicable correspondence with each other. These early days were

[1] Johann Mattheson, *Grundlage einer Ehren-Pforte*, p. 358.

days of serious intent and, whereas the latest letters were devoted to horticulture, between 1701 and 1703 they engaged their pens technic-ally on the 'working-out of melodious compositions.' At that time melody was the *fons et origo* of all music. Personal intercourse also took place, and if this was not at Halle then it was at Weissenfels, for which court Telemann wrote a number of pieces. The recipro-city of musical thought in the eighteenth century is indicated by the extent of Telemann's studies. Being as fluent in literature as in music —and Handel commented that he 'could write a motet for eight voices more quickly than one could write a letter'—Telemann left valuable evidence in this respect. His recorded models were Kuhnau's fugues, the French overtures of Lully and Campra, 'the true and barbaric beauty' of such Polish music as he came across while sojourning in Upper Silesia and the ubiquitous productions of Italy.

But experience of foreign schools could only come to the home-staying student fortuitously. The proper way to learn was to travel, and this, influenced by Telemann's example and irked by the mono-tony of the Calvinist round at the *Dom*. Handel proposed to do. He finished his year's probation as organist in the spring of 1703, leaving his place to Johann Kolhart, disconnected himself from the university, took leave of his family and started on the first stage of his Odyssey.

CHAPTER II

'IL CARO SASSONE'

THE magnetic town of northern Germany was Hamburg, handsomely prosperous and culturally progressive. There would be met travellers from overseas and ample opportunities for intellectual exercise. By 1703 the onslaught of Italy was biting into the inner defences of German opera, despite the vigorous protective measures undertaken in Hamburg's opera house. But this fact was an inducement to the young. Artistic theories worried Handel little. His career, law being now finally rejected, was to be that of a musician, which then implied craftsman. Music was required and therefore must be written, and if a particular style was in vogue then it must be obeyed; although later on Handel sometimes indulged in anti-popular stylistic dictation. The Italian manner was favoured because it exalted melody. Therefore throughout the century we find great stress being laid on 'air.' In view of the later genius of the age it cannot on the whole be complained that public taste miscalculated in its postulations. Handel arrived at Hamburg with a provincial reputation and with provincial deficiencies. From a metropolitan point of view his achievement was thus summarized: 'He was strong in the organ, stronger than Kuhnau in fugue and counterpoint, especially *extempore,* but he knew very little about melody until he came to the Hamburg operas.' [1]

Thus the first stage in Handel's emancipation from German influence opened. Over the period with which this chapter is concerned presides the benign influence of one of the most remarkable of eighteenth-century worthies: the Abbate Steffani. Born in 1654 in obscurity, carried off to the Bavarian court as a promising choir-boy, tutored by Johann Caspar Kerll and Carissimi, Steffani acquired a high musical reputation by his twentieth year. But in addition to music he studied theology, mathematics and philosophy with equal

[1] Mattheson, op. cit., p. 93.

success. He became a priest in 1680, after which he left Munich for Hanover, where an appointment as *Kapellmeister* awaited him. There he wrote operas for Giusti's new and elegant theatre, and in so doing increased the artistic reputation of Hanover. His operas were also performed at Brunswick and Hamburg. For the latter town, significantly, they were translated into German.

But this was only one side of Steffani's life. In 1698 he became the Elector's ambassador at Brussels, and thenceforth his duties as plenipotentiary overshadowed his artistic activity. But not so much as to prevent the continuance of his enthusiasm therein. If there was one figure in Europe whose acquaintance and encouragement were worth a young man's acquisition it was Steffani. Handel was fortunate.

Precisely when he first met the Abbate is doubtful. His own statement, as recorded by Hawkins,[1] reads:

When I first arrived in Hanover as a young man, under twenty, I was acquainted with the merits of Steffani, and he had heard of me. I under-stood something of music, and could play pretty well on the organ; he re-ceived me with great kindness, and took an early opportunity to introduce me to the princess Sophia and the elector's son, giving them to understand that I was what he was pleased to call a virtuoso in music; he obliged me with instructions for my conduct and behaviour during my residence at Hanover; and being called from the city to attend to matters of a public concern, he left me in possession of that favour and patronage which himself had enjoyed for a number of years.

The latter part of this statement applies to 1709, in which year Handel attached himself to the Hanoverians. But the first part refers to an earlier period: prior, in fact, to 1705. Remembering that Handel had left Germany at least thirty years before Hawkins obtained this statement, it is reasonable to assume that what were two separate events had unified in mental coalescence. By emending Hawkins's punctuation[2] the antithesis becomes quite clear. Brenet suggests that when Handel called at Hanover *en route* for Hamburg in 1703 he made the acquaintance of Steffani. Such a meeting, resulting in mutual respect, would have been profitable. Steffani's

[1] Hawkins, *A General History of Music*, v. 267.
[2] e.g. '. . . a virtuoso in music. He obliged me . . .'

good opinion would help to explain the trail of glory which Handel blazed at Hamburg and, to a greater degree, in Italy. And the later offer of the Hanoverian *Kapellmeister* post is more compre‑ hensible if understood as the result of a more or less prolonged interest on the part of Steffani.

Arrived at Hamburg during the summer of 1703 Handel quickly made the acquaintance of Johann Mattheson, an aspiring singer, composer, author and man of the world. In the latter capacity he was serviceable to Handel: as an author to posterity. He left sufficient information in his encyclopaedic *Grundlage einer Ehren‑Pforte* for a full‑size portrait of the young Handel (an individual too seldom considered) to be re‑created.

In this we discern a youth characterized as much by industry as by brilliance. Handel wrote arias, which were apparently inter‑ minable, and cantatas, visited organs, did the round of choirs, operas and concerts, became domesticated 'at a certain house, in which music was practised with the utmost devotion,' absorbed the correct dramatic style from Mattheson, to whom—after sociable meals at the expense of Mattheson's father—in return he gave contrapuntal assistance. 'I learned from him as he learned from me. *Docendo enim discimus.*' [1] In his capacity as second violin (perhaps after this example it will no more be regarded as undignified to sit at a second violin desk) in the theatre orchestra he 'behaved as if he couldn't count five, being naturally inclined to a dry humour.' His manner was engagingly modest, it being only with difficulty that he was induced to substitute for an absent harpsichordist. But life was punctuated by such pleasant trivialities as river excursions. And Mattheson, writing in 1740, looked back wistfully and whimsically on the occasion which brought them together at the Maria Magdalena church, where the organ‑blower was a pastry‑cook's son. 'I know well enough,' he says of Handel, 'that he will laugh heartily when he reads this, though as a rule he laughs but little.' And then there was the August expedition to Lübeck, in a pigeon‑fancier's company. At Lübeck the bait was the prospect of succeeding Buxtehude at the Marienkirche. This was made more attractive by the municipality who, alive as always to the possibility of rate reduction, offered not

[1] Mattheson, op. cit., p. 93.

12

only an organ stool but also a marriage bed to the successful applicant. The intended pensioner was Buxtehude's daughter, whose lack in allurement and relative wealth in years recommended a quick return to Hamburg. What was refused by Handel and Mattheson, and three years later by Sebastian Bach, came eventually to one of Keiser's juniors—Johann Christian Schieferdecker.

The later months of 1703 passed less excitingly but more profitably. Handel became music tutor to the family of the English Resident— John Wich.[1] This dignitary was an amiable soul, whose wine a few months previously had filled Addison with satisfaction and whose swollen legs with concern.[2] In addition to his tutorial activities Handel was composing. As a private music teacher he would naturally have turned to writing chamber music for his pupils. However, from this time none is certainly identifiable.

An anonymous and indifferent setting of Postel's Passion libretto— the music was severely criticised by Mattheson in his *Critica Musica* of 1725—was once assigned to Handel. It is not surprising that such an ascription should have been made, for when Handel came to leave Hamburg he was said by Mainwaring to have left behind 'two chests full' of his works. On 18th March 1704, Mattheson then being in Holland, Handel wrote to his friend, ending his letter: 'I therefore beg you to notify me of your departure so that I may have the opportunity of fulfilling my duty, and come and meet you with Mlle Sbülens.'[3] The lady has this solitary entry in history. Whether she came, as has been suggested, from Halle is a matter for speculation, as is the possibility of her having exercised particular claims on the affections of Handel. It may be suspected that some good reason prompted a joint welcome home for the nomadic Mattheson.

The Handel-Mattheson friendship went through rather rough

---

[1] John Wich continued in office until 1713, in which year he was succeeded by Cyril (afterwards Sir Cyril) Wich.

[2] Letter from Addison to Wich, May 1703.

[3] A Mr. Sbuelen is twice mentioned in letters from Handel to Michaelsen (10th August 1731 and 28th August 1736). On the second occasion we learn that wedding presents to Handel's niece were sent to Sbuelen at Hamburg.

waters in 1714. First Mattheson usurped his friend's place in the Wich household and then brawled with him in the theatre. The circumstances leading to this much publicized incident are peculiar, and one suspects more than meets the eye. On 20th October Mattheson produced his *Cleopatra,* in which he sang the part of Antonius. His custom was, having (dramatically speaking) expired, to descend to the orchestra and to supplant Handel at the harpsichord. The opera ran smoothly, with this curious arrangement not apparently disapproved, until 5th December. On that night Handel suddenly refused to resign his place at the harpsichord, and the irate composer took the opportunity, when outside the theatre, of slapping his colleague on the face. Anticipating Hawkins's bloodthirsty charge[1] at a later date Mattheson archly commented that 'a dry slap on the face was no assassination, but rather a friendly hint, to put him on his guard.' He further described Handel as 'tall, strong, broadshouldered and muscular; consequently well able to defend himself.' The sequel was a Sheridanesque duel in which tradition assigns Handel's deliverance to a fortunately placed button or score[2] which broke Mattheson's sword. The spectators must have repined at so anticlimactic a dénouement. A happy ending was effected by a dinner of reconciliation on 30th December engineered by a pacifically minded town councillor (Schott?) who held shares in the theatre. Brawls, bloodshed and hot emotion were part of the eighteenth-century mode of life, and Handel was not immune from their incidence.

Tranquillity again prevailing, Handel and Mattheson turned to the business of wage-earning. This centred round Handel's first *Singspiel*—the text, by Feustking, in German and Italian—*Almira.* Mattheson was the *primo uomo.* After *Almira,* which ran from 8th January 1705 to 25th February, came *Die durch Blut und Mord erlangte Liebe, oder* [less sensationally] *Nero.* This had a run of three nights, and then came off. But Handel had achieved two things. First the opportunity of demonstrating to himself and to Hamburg in general that he was possessed of an exceptional dramatic flair; secondly and consequently the sour enmity of Keiser. Keiser was much annoyed and began work on new settings of both

[1] Hawkins, op. cit., v. 265.   [2] Mainwaring, op. cit., p. 35.

Nero and *Almira*. Neither was a success but, reading between the lines, Handel came to the conclusion that life would be more tolerable in another place. His mind turned to the prospects of an Italian journey. Steffani would have urged this; Ariosti and Buononcini,[1] whose acquaintance Handel had made in the days of his apprenticeship, would similarly have advised; and a new friend, Prince Giovanni Gastone de' Medici, still more importunately.

Gastone de' Medici was Micawber-like in impecuniosity, in good nature and in constant optimism. He had few grounds for optimism, which, doubtless, is why he was optimistic. His father was the despotic Cosimo III, who handed Tuscany to the bondage of clerical taskmasters; his wife, tied to him by statecraft and not by love, the stout, unrefined Anna Maria of Saxe-Lauenburg; his official home an isolated castle in the hinterland of Bohemia. Not surprisingly Gastone dedicated one half of himself to Venus and the other, less dangerously, to opera-going and flute-playing. It was these latter occupations which brought him into contact with Handel.

Thus encouraged to look south, Handel took practical steps to implement his desires. He set to work on a third *Singspiel*, one of such proportions that for practical purposes it needed dichotomy and became therefore *Florindo* and *Daphne*. Leaving behind him these scores and, according to Mainwaring, a good many other miscellaneous compositions, he packed his bag, counted his savings—200 ducats—and shook the dust of Hamburg off his feet. His travelling companion was an acquaintance named von Binitz who, if Mattheson's testimony is correct, subscribed the travelling expenses.[2]

Italy in the eighteenth century, like Greece at a more remote period of history, was in process of conquering her conquerors. Fragmented—Venice a nominally independent State, of consequence to Europe in general as a pleasure resort, Lombardy and Naples subject to Spanish viceroys, Florence and Tuscany under Austrian rule, Savoy on uneasy terms with France, and the Papal States perpetuating reaction and obscurantism—she left practical affairs to the northern nations, setting herself the task of cultural diffusion. Which, in the realm of music, she did so inexorably that opposition was impossible.

[1] It is probably correct to assume that Handel met Ariosti and Buononcini during his residence at Hamburg.   [2] ibid.

The schools of music were the courts, both lay and ecclesiastical, and the patrons-in-chief were such as Handel encountered.

His career in Italy was so unnaturally successful (for a Saxon to outshine the Italians on their own ground was surely unthinkable) that one is tempted to see behind it influence, then as now a surer guide to popular acclamation than ability. The influence, it might reasonably be surmised, was that of Steffani. First Handel went to Florence, where Gastone's brother Ferdinand, a patron of Alessandro Scarlatti, controlled the culture ignored by his father. This was towards the end of 1706. In the autumn of the next year a new opera, *Rodrigo,* probably begun when Handel first arrived at Florence, was produced at the Florentine court. The reward from Ferdinand, who had come to the recent conclusion that Scarlatti had deteriorated in amusement value, was a hundred sequins and a service of porcelain. Judging by the social assets which stood him in such good stead at this period an amorous interlude, detailed with customary factual inconsistency by Mainwaring, would not be out of place. Mainwaring's heroine—Vittoria Tesi—is ruled out by reason of immaturity: she was born in 1700. Although it may be that Mainwaring's lady was right, but his date wrong. Handel probably met her later, in 1719. Vittoria Tarquini, a celebrated prima donna (an alternative candidate to Tesi), was well ensconced in the good graces of the Prince Ferdinand, and therefore unlikely to have spent her energy in chasing an impecunious composer, however flashing his immediate reputation, all over Italy. Thus in uncertainty dies a promising anecdote.

Early in 1707, having established useful contacts in Florence, Handel went to Rome. Temporarily papal authority was frowning on opera, and inferior princes of the church were compelled to divert their interest to a more godly form of recreation. Cardinal Pietro Ottoboni was the principal connoisseur of the arts and, being also a friend of Ferdinand of Tuscany, he welcomed Handel on his arrival. With the entrée to the cardinal's musical evenings Handel added to his growing list of acquaintances Corelli, in charge of the Ottoboni music, Pasquini and (if he had not previously met him) Alessandro Scarlatti. Handel was not only a musical but a social success. He proceeded from Ottoboni's to the favour of the Prince Ruspoli, prince by papal dispensation, and in the luxury of his palace stayed for the most of March and April 1708.[1]

In the Palazzo Bonelli Handel wrote *La resurrezione*, which was performed in succession to Scarlatti's *Della Santissima Annunziata*. *La resurrezione* was received with satisfaction: the only discord was struck by the Holy Father, who dispatched a pained note to Ruspoli complaining of the employment in the oratorio of a female singer.[2] The next work was contrived with less care. It was a setting of Cardinal Pamphili's *Il trionfo del tempo e del disinganno*, fifty years later to be remodelled into *The Triumph of Time and Truth*. Although *Il trionfo* was a relative failure Handel felt sufficiently sure of his standing in Italy to remonstrate with Corelli for his inability to cope with the overture. 'My dear Saxon,' complained Corelli, 'the music is in the French style, of which I have no knowledge.'[3] Nor was there any reason why he should have had in view of Italy's prerogative of supplying music to the rest of Europe. *Il trionfo*, performed for Ottoboni's Arcadians, was given under the shadow of political discontent and the imminence of yet another of the many sieges of Rome. Therefore Handel went south to compose *Aci, Galatea e Polifemo*, possibly for the marriage of the Duca d'Alvito, solemnized on 19th July at Naples. While in Naples Handel dallied with another lady, of whom no more is known that that her name was Donna Laura.[4] Next year, in Venice, Handel made the pleasant acquaintance of Domenico Scarlatti, who later reappeared in Handel's London life in 1720. An attractive trait was this capacity for remembering old friends with affection, and often with gratitude. Instances occur so frequently that the underlining of their incidence may be forgiven in that thus the conventionally drawn Handel is softened in outline. Handel also met Scarlatti's tutor Gasparini and Antonio Lotti, organist of St. Mark's Cathedral.

[1] The Ruspoli archives are precise regarding hospitality to Handel, even detailing charges for the hire of his bed.

[2] See letter quoted in 'New Sources for Handel—*La Resurrezione*,' Rudolf Ewerbert, in *Music and Letters*, April 1960, p. 128.

[3] At this time Handel composed his *Airs français* (see p. 211).

[4] Mainwaring, op. cit., p. 66.

There was also in Venice the Earl of Manchester.[1] The Earl was an incompetent diplomat—he had failed in previous missions to Paris and Venice—but well-mannered: therefore, after normal convention in these matters, he was given full opportunity to continue in the wrecking of his own professional reputation and his country's interests. At this time he was negotiating the adherence of the Venetians to the Grand Alliance. They for their part were entertaining him with diversionary operations. Thus he came into contact with Handel and commenced an interest in his music which was maintained in later years. One advantage of a Grand Tour, whether for rich or poor, was a healthy diminution in chauvinistic intention. The intelligent were not over-conscious of nationality. The Earl of Manchester loved the Venetians, while deploring their policy of *attentisme,* and approved their opera in which the rising star was the German Handel. English lack of artistic perception, a deficiency more rare than is commonly believed, did not disgrace Her Majesty's representative. His lead was followed by another English resident. Joseph Smith, whose address Handel made use of on a later visit to Italy,[2] was beginning to lay the foundations of his bibliophile reputation in 1707. And a final stimulus came to English affairs in Venice during Handel's visit, through the presence of Ernst of Hanover, brother to the future George I, who was basking in the glory attached to his house by the Act of Settlement (1701) and in the official satisfaction of diplomacy at its loyalty to the allied cause.

At some point during his travels Handel met the Viceroy of Naples, Cardinal Grimani, a friend of Lady Mary Wortley Montagu's, a connection of the family which built the San Giovanni Crisostomo theatre at Venice and a good librettist. Grimani prepared the libretto for Handel's next opera, *Agrippina*. This overshadowed all the other events of the Carnival season which opened at Venice on 26th December 1709, running for twenty-seven nights. Two of the singers later came to London. They were Margherita Durastanti, whose appearance in *Agrippina* at the age of fourteen or fifteen was less remarkable then than it would be now, and Giuseppe Boschi, the

[1] Created duke 1719.

[2] *Vide* letter from Handel to Michaelsen, 11th March 1729.

greatest and most demonstrative bass of the age, renowned for his extensive range.

Agrippina was Handel's greatest achievement to date, and he let it be his valediction to Italy. After the hysteria of 'Viva il caro Sassone!' which punctuated every pause in each performance he determined to try his fortunes elsewhere. Invitations from Hanover were pressing, Prince Ernst had seen the success of *Agrippina,* and Steffani was pleased with the progress of his protégé. He had learned something of the favourable impression Handel had made when in Rome a year earlier. Steffani was too involved by now in affairs of Church and State to continue his *Kapellmeister* office. Therefore he vacated it, applied himself to episcopal duties—he had been consecrated Bishop of Spiga *in partibus infidelium,* and appointed the Pope's representative in Northern Germany—and deposited Handel at Hanover.

The three years in Italy were to Handel as a post-graduate course. He had previously learned the fundamentals of musicianship in good schools, those of Halle and Hamburg, but Italy provided the opportunity of absorbing, at first hand, the principles which were to dominate the eighteenth century. Stylistic considerations will be dealt with at a later juncture, but a sufficient guarantee of the value of this experience is denoted by the manuscripts collected of works by Alessandro Scarlatti, some of which eventually found their way into the library of Charles Jennens. In Italy Handel was reminded of the welcome which would greet him in England, when he cared to make the journey. He left the country having gained in knowledge, in friendship and in reputation. The laity impulsively referred to him as 'L'Orfeo del nostro secolo,' which Germany subsequently thought of as 'a rare honour, for no German is spoken of thus by an Italian or a Frenchman, these gentry being accustomed to scoffing at us'; the clergy with commendable zeal looked on him not only as a great musician, but as a worthy subject for proselytism. Handel reacted to this compliment by resolving 'to die a member of the communion, whether true or false, in which he was born and bred.' At the same time he produced a large number of effectively apposite works, some of which, motets, are preserved in the collection formed by the Abbate Santini (1778–1862) in Rome and now kept in Münster, Westphalia.

CHAPTER III

ENGLISH PATRONAGE

LIKE other employers of labour the eighteenth-century disciples of Maecenas had their faults. But Johnson's letter to the Earl of Chester-field and Mozart's humiliation at the hands of the Archbishop of Salzburg have been allowed to overshadow the positive benefits accorded to numerous artists more fortunate in their selection of patron. The good and bad of the system will be evident from the progress of this book; with Handel's appointment to Hanover we enter upon a period in his life singular for its pleasant association with the great. It was in the middle of June 1710 that he took up his duties in place of Steffani. His emoluments amounted to 1,000 thaler per annum. Within a month or so he was, however, again peripatetic. First a dutiful call at Halle and then a visit to the Electoral court at Düssel-dorf. Here he already had contacts: the Electress Anna Maria was sister to Ferdinand and Gastone de' Medici; Steffani was a regular correspondent of the Elector; and Corelli was *persona grata* there. For a short time the splendour of Düsseldorf, apparent in its opera and its picture galleries, beguiled Handel, but during the autumn he made his way to London. As a cultural demonstration this visit would have met with Hanoverian approval and Handel's success in London been regarded as of slightly more than artistic value. Handel did one important thing. He impressed many people of influence with what to them was a singular fact: that a foreigner, possessed of certain attributes, could override that insular prejudice which insisted that aliens were of necessity comic and/or offensive.

Heidegger, manager of the Opera, was both.[1] A Swiss by birth,

---

[1] Heidegger's appearance can be wondered at in Hogarth's 'Cuzzoni, Farinelli and Heidegger' (1734) or in Pope's succinct

> 'And lo! her bird (a monster of a fowl,
> Something betwixt a Heideggre and owl).'
>
> *Dunciad*, i. 289-90.

he essayed various professions speculatively and graduated to opera by way of a privacy in Queen Anne's Life Guards. This he judiciously relinquished to invest his wits in the new potentialities of Italian opera. Thus he met Handel in 1710 with a view to establishing a fortune out of the latter's high reputation and the whims of the aristocracy. They, indignant at any suggestion that England (particularly after Blenheim and Ramillies) could be bettered in any department of life, but none the less slaves to continental fashion, were sympathetic to the newer form of operatic entertainment. The nearest modern parallel to the influence of Italian opera is that of the American domination of the film industry. If in some measure the reader understands the further implications of this parallel the difficulties of Handel's career will be better appreciated.

Had he lived, Purcell might have prevented the overwhelming success of foreign opera. But in the interregnum between his death in 1695 and Handel's arrival in 1710 developments had taken place which eased the way for Heidegger, Handel and the consequent combined operations of continental singers and composers. That Purcell went so soon was a permanent regret to the discriminating, and Henry Carey, a keen enough Handelian, was to voice the feelings of many who loved opera but had a shrewd idea that England, given a chance, could do it as well as anybody:

> Ev'n heaven-born Purcell now is held in scorn;
> Purcell, who did a brighter age adorn.[1]

It was not only, however, the dearth of composers which was responsible for a changed outlook. It was first such singers as Francesca de l'Épine and Francesco Tosi who demonstrated the histrionic possibilities of the Italian language. Superimposed was snobbery, which assumed that what was presented unintelligibly in a foreign tongue must be a symbol of high cultivation. Italian influence was insidious. *Arsinoe,* produced at Drury Lane in 1705, had English words and Italian music. A year later came Buononcini's *Camilla,* in translation. In 1707 the same work was done macaronically; l'Épine and Valentini sang in Italian, Mrs. Tofts, Mrs. Lindsey, Mrs. Turner, Leveridge and Ramondon in English.

[1] 'The Poet's Resentment,' from *Poems on Several Occasions,* 1729.

Addison's *Rosamund* did nothing to set the clock back. Addison had himself principally to blame. The text of *Rosamund* is a flaccid effort. In Italian the ridiculous would have passed unnoticed, but in English verse Addison descends below banality with such lines as

> Here will I stand
> With hat in hand
> Obsequiously to greet him.

Nor was Thomas Clayton a good enough composer to deal with such infelicities. The only interest of *Rosamund* is in its anticipation of romantic historiography and the revived balladry of Percy. Addison put his defeat down to stupidity on the part of others and upheld his dignity by poking through the chinks in the Italian armour. He had a prejudice, but his remarks on *Rinaldo* are very funny and not pointless. In 1709 Nicolini, 'the first truly great singer who had ever sung in our theatre,'[1] arrived and took London by storm.[2] Early in 1710 the first three operas to be done entirely in Italian were given: *Almahide, L'Idaspe fedele,* in which Nicolini strangled a lion with great gallantry,[3] and *Etearco.* The conductor was Pepusch.

This new form of entertainment won the approval of society as a whole, but the intellectuals were against it from the start. Addison for obvious reasons, Tickell because he was a henchman of Addison. Elijah Fenton gave vent to England's latent Puritanism by recalling nostalgically in 1711 that

> There was an age, (its memory will last!)
> Before Italian Airs debauch'd our taste;[4]

Hogarth came later, and Pope with him, to protest that opera had damaged the true tradition of native drama. English singers ranged themselves, if not against Italian opera as such, at any rate against imported singers. Mrs. Tofts had expressed their point of view with

---

[1] Burney, *History*, iv. 208.

[2] For Nicolini's acting ability, *vide* Steele, *Tatler*, No. 115.

[3] Letter from Lady Mary Wortley Montagu to Mrs. Hewet, 1711.

[4] Elijah Fenton, 'An Epistle to Mr. Southerne, from Kent, January 28, 1710–11.'

some emphasis by employing a domestic to throw oranges at l'Épine during a Drury Lane performance as long ago as 1704.

> Effeminate in dress, in manners grown,
> We now despise whatever is our own.[1]

So Carey put forward the moral issue which was energetically thrashed during the years to come with particular regard to the exotic and repulsive race of *castrati*. All this being taken into consideration, Handel's success in opera is remarkable. But in these circumstances may be discerned the seeds of destruction.

Heidegger acted as Handel's cicerone in 1710. Among the quality to whom Handel was introduced was Sir John Stanley, a minor court official, to be precise a commissioner of customs, whose moderate Jacobitism ensured his subsequent rustication. With him lived his ward—Mary Granville. At this time she was a volatile child of ten, and her first impressions of Handel were later memorialized:

> I was struck with his playing, but struck as a child, not a judge, for the moment he was gone, I seated myself at the instrument, and played the best lesson I had then learnt: my uncle archly asked me whether I thought I should ever play as well as Mr. Handel. 'If I didn't think I should,' cried I, 'I would burn my instrument.' [2]

So began a lifelong friendship.

Handel's first opera in England was *Rinaldo*,[3] commissioned by Aaron Hill for the company which he had a year or two earlier transferred from Drury Lane to Vanbrugh's new theatre in the Haymarket. The libretto was adapted by Giacomo Rossi from Tasso; Handel, with a characteristic burst of energy, wrote his music, much too fast for the unfortunate librettist, in a fortnight. The singers included Boschi, his wife Vanini, and Nicolini. The work was first produced on 24th February 1711. The *éclat* was terrific. For this the singers should claim as much responsibility as the composer: fashionable audiences at all times have a habit of paying devotion not to the quality of music so much as to its extraneous embellishments. It was Nicolini who carried the house away. Addison's

---

[1] *Vide* Carey, 'The Poet's Resentment.'
[2] Mrs. Delany, *Life and Correspondence*, pp. 5 and 6.
[3] *Vide* Addison, *Spectator*, Nos. 5, 29 and 31.

trunk/maker 'upon Nicolini's first appearance was said to have demolished three benches in the fury of his applause.'[1] The absence of Nicolini two years later led to the failure of *Il pastor fido*. But in 1711 Handel could not foresee the possibility of failure.

At that time Thomas Britton's musical evenings in Clerkenwell were one of the wonders of London, demonstrating how common interest could unite in amiability individuals of widely contrasted social status. Courtesy and intelligence intermingled at Britton's to form a pattern of democratic behaviour. Britton himself was a seller of small/coal: outside of business hours a bibliophile, rubbing shoulders at Bateman's bookshop by St. Paul's and at the stalls in Little Britain with earls and dukes. He was also an amateur in chemistry, a Rosicrucian and a musician. 'There goes the famous small/coal man,' they used to cry after him, 'who is a lover of learn/ing, a performer in music, and a companion for gentlemen.' Among his visitors in 1711 was Handel, who must have been surprised at the unconventional music/room over the coal/store, at the numerous quality who used to clamber shin/dangerously up the narrow stair, at the standard of amateur performance and at the sensitive under/standing of contemporary music.

Here Handel met Pepusch, Abiel Whichello and Philip Hart, organists and harpsichord players, and Obadiah Shuttleworth,

> Envy of foreigners, thy country's pride,
> Whose soul is harmony, nor ought beside,
> Oh! could Corelli hear thy charming lays,
> He'd hug thee in his arms, and give thee praise;
> For thou such justice to his works has done,
> He need not blush to call thee son.[2]

Also John Banister, the younger, the leader of the opera orchestra, the little prodigy Dubourg, and the talented young harpsichordist William Babell. Outside the ranks of professional musicians were Wollaston, a portrait painter; John Hughes,[3] poet and dramatist;

[1] Addison, *Spectator*, No. 235.

[2] Henry Carey, *To Mr. Obadiah Shuttleworth. Made and Spoken Extempore, on hearing him perform a Solo of Corelli with great Propriety.*

[3] Hughes's *Venus and Adonis* provided Handel with the first English texts which he set (B.M., Add. MS. 31993, nos. 23 and 24).

and the indefatigable and musicologically inclined Henry Needler, recently appointed accountant for the candle duty at the excise office, who drank and fiddled by turns at the 'Crown' in the Strand and rattled off Corelli to his boon companions at the Academy of Vocal Music. Add the bibulous Ned Ward, the eccentric Duchess of Queensberry and Justice Robe, and the gallery is reasonably complete. Such experience as this taught Handel that below the surface of English society ran an undercurrent of sympathy and understanding, and that between posing nobility and crapulent rabble came a middle class of friendly philosophers with whom he could find much in common. Unless in the Hanseatic towns, which Handel knew well, this section of the community was without parallel in Europe. With such exemplars of independence he felt himself at home.

The passing of the season reminded Handel of his Hanoverian commitments. Therefore he returned, but by way of hospitable Düsseldorf, and with a sufficiently long stay there to concern both himself and the Elector over his reception at Hanover. However, he eased his conscience by writing for the Princess Caroline acceptable duets and for the court chamber music. During the year he was in correspondence with his English friends. This correspondence, couched in the lingua franca of the time, demonstrates Handel's faculty for pertinent expression without too precise attention to ortho-graphical detail. 'Faites bien mes compliments à Mr. Hughes,' he wrote to Andrew Roner in July.

Je prendrai la liberté de lui écrire avec la prémiere occasion. S'il me veut cependant honorer de ses ordres, et d'y ajouter une de ses charmantes poésies en Anglois, il me fera la plus sensible grace. J'ai fait, depuis que je suis parti de vous, quelques progrés dans cette langue.

So another visit to England was in the wind. But before this was undertaken Halle called. Handel's sister Dorothea, married to a rising lawyer,[1] produced a daughter whose christening provided an opportunity for compassionate leave. Another year at Hanover followed, and then came the complete translation.

[1] Dr. Michael Michaelsen, later a member of the Prussian Imperial Service and the War Council. Handel was always on the most cordial terms with him.

In the autumn of 1712 Handel was back in London. On 26th November *Il pastor fido* disappointed him by its failure. Nicolini was away in Italy, and the new *castrato* Pellegrini, on his first visit, was too little known to attract a sufficiency of hero-worship. There was another reason why this opera failed. On 15th November the Duke of Hamilton had been murdered after a duel with Lord Mohun. This was more sensational than a new opera, and the after-gossip precluded other activities. *Teseo*, produced on 10th January, restored Handel's prestige. This was dedicated by its librettist, Haym,[1] to the Earl of Burlington. This was astute, for Burlington, who came of age only in 1715, was about to become a leader in the field of the fine arts. His inherited wealth, his enthusiasm for and skill in architecture, his knowledge of Italian culture, and his great charm were his assets. 'He possessed every quality of a genius and artist except envy,' said Horace Walpole. It was to Burlington that Handel owed the establishment of his reputation during the declining years of Queen Anne. Handel was a close friend of Henry Needler, a familiar drinking-companion, and a frequent caller at Needler's house in Clement's Lane. Needler was a useful friend. He was, as a gentleman—so qualified by his clerkship in excise—and a musician, on terms of friendship with many of the nobility, a frequent performer at the town houses of the Duke of Rutland, Lords Burlington,[2] Essex and Percival. He had probably brought Handel into touch with Burlington. The concerts at which Needler played are worthy of mention as factors of importance in musical education. Uffenbach [3] describes one enthusiastically: 'The famous Pepusch often gets up such a concert at the request of some noble lords. The orchestra was not very strong, consisting of not more than 16 persons [an average-size band in those days], but it was incomparable.' L'Épine sang, but not so well as at the opera because 'she sang whatever was put before her and did not take much trouble.' The instrumental music, however, was very beautiful and the whole concert lasted for two hours. 'I could have listened the whole night with the greatest pleasure.'

[1] Who based his text on one prepared for Lully by Quinault in 1675.
[2] Handel frequently had the direction of these concerts. Hawkins, v. 410.
[3] *London in 1710, from the travels of Zacharias von Uffenbach*, pp. 66–7.

A Pension from the Queen

Handel became a true citizen of London. In these early years of his residence therein we can visualize him as spending his off-duty hours at Britton's, until 1714, when Britton died, at the concerts at the 'Swan' and at the 'Crown,' at Lœillet's séances in Hart Street and with the choirmen from Saint Paul's at the nearby 'Queen's Arms.' He was a frequent visitor to the cathedral, completely finished only in 1710, and pushing past the ballad-singers and vendors of nuts, apples and ginger-bread who shouted their wares at the west door, would go in to hear the organ and the music of Purcell. In Italy Handel showed himself a master of Italian style; in England he paid like tribute to his hosts by taking as model the most brilliant (and how they lamented him at Britton's!) of recent composers. Purcell's *Te Deum* and *Jubilate* of 1694 encouraged the *Te Deum* and *Jubilate* which Handel wrote to celebrate the overdue Peace Treaty of Utrecht.[1] Its performance, however, followed that of another significant work, the *Birthday Ode* for the queen. This was sung on 6th February (a very wet day), and the *Te Deum* at St. Paul's on 7th July. Bernard Gates (see p. 33) was among the singers on both occasions. We may presume friends at court to have engineered these works, for it was unusual for alien musicians to write ceremonial music, and without proper influence being brought to bear we can hardly imagine an obstinate woman like Queen Anne, and no particular lover of the prospective Hanoverian succession, prejudicing herself in Handel's favour, and so far forgetting herself as to settle on him a pension of £200. In the good graces of the English, Handel had no particular desire to return to his duties at Hanover. He did not return.

He was intoxicated by social success and by the free-and-easy life of London. Prospects in the opera were generally good, the nobility was obliging, other people were generous in hospitality—Andrews of Barn Elms had given him house-room for a year—money was flowing in. In 1716 he started his investments by putting £500 into the South Sea Company. And he was living well. He appreciated the gouty results of the Methuen Treaty of 1703, which brought port into the country almost duty free, and respected the

---

[1] Thomas Tudway wrote of Handel's debt to Purcell in respect of this work (B.M., Harl. MS. 3782).

enthusiasm of the English for the pleasures of the table. The times had altered less in some respects than might be imagined since the classic remark of Erasmus: 'Britanni, praeter alia, formam, musicam, et lautas mensas proprie sibi vindicent.'

The death of Queen Anne on 1st August 1714 involved Handel less than other notabilities. Bolingbroke, for instance, having been engaged in dictatorial aspirations and king-making negotiations, was caught most uncomfortably, and so were all the high Tories. The new king had more to do than to contemplate the caprices of an errant *Kapellmeister,* a minor official whose activities could have been of little consequence set against the panorama of politics. In any case, with the Prince and Princess of Wales, he was present at a performance of the Utrecht *Te Deum* on 28th October, as was reported in a Hamburg newspaper on 9th November 1714. The *Water Music* legend, then, goes down the drain. It is true that this was performed for the gratification of George I, that fifty players did add to the delights of a seductive evening spent with the Duchess of Bolton, Lady Godolphin, and Mesdames Kielmansegge and Ware, and that Kielmansegge paid the bill. But that was on 17th July 1717.

The king's accession produced neither ode nor anthem, but Handel was busy concocting with Heidegger another opera for the Haymarket. In the meantime *Rinaldo* was revived as a contribution to the coronation festivities. The king came to *Rinaldo,* with one or other of his mistresses, and to *Amadigi,* the new opera first performed on 25th May, on a number of occasions during 1715.

Handel had written no opera for three years, from *Teseo* to *Amadigi,* except for the miniature *Silla,*[1] which, if performed at all, was done in privacy, possibly for Lord Burlington. This sabbatical period may be accounted for by the anarchic state of affairs, which reigned at the Haymarket after the Irishman MacSwiney, an able producer but, like so many of his countrymen, possessed of no financial acumen, had left his management of the theatre in haste and bankruptcy in the middle of the run of *Teseo.* Poor MacSwiney was more sinned against than sinning. He had left the army in 1705 in the optimistic belief that Rich would live up to his promise to provide '100 Guineas

[1] Librettist unknown; fragments of Handel's autograph, B.M., R.M. 20. c. 8.

per annum Salary, a place at Court, and the Devil and all.' Only the last clause matured, and MacSwiney took his grievances and the contents of the box-office to Italy. After this episode Handel kept off the Haymarket, but occupied his time in consolidating his social bridge-heads.

Amadigi, so Heidegger notes in his dedication, was composed by Handel at Burlington House, which at that time was being prepared for a Palladian face-lift by Colen Campbell. Handel lived there a good deal between 1714 and 1717 and had rooms at the back of the house. A fellow pensioner was the lively architect Kent, who came under the earl's wing in 1716. More distinguished beneficiaries were Pope and Gay. Another intimate was Dr. Arbuthnot, 'the first man among [writers of the day]. He was the most universal genius, being an excellent physician, a man of deep learning, and a man of much humour.' [1] Arbuthnot was one of Handel's greatest friends.

Gay's *Trivia* (1716) has often been quoted for

> There *Hendel* strikes the strings, the melting strain
> Transports the soul, and thrills through ev'ry vein;

but the whole poem should be read for the complete picture it affords of Handel's London. Splendour, squalor, misery, disease, vice and a little virtue all in proportion quietly blended. The *eheu fugaces* romanticists would do well to feel Gay's stabbing couplets on the seamy side. Heroic couplets is a misnomer. And those who over-estimate the comfort of Burlington House might be reminded of Lord Hervey's opinion that it was

> Possessed of one great hall of state,
> Without a room to sleep or eat.

But then Hervey was no lover of Burlington. Pope found Handel's fame and popularity perplexing. With a distaste for music, a heartier distaste for foreign musicians and a complete contempt for opera, he so far lacked confidence in his judgment as to apply to Arbuthnot on the score of Handel's reputation. Was all the rapture displayed by his audiences genuine or was it not? [2] 'Conceive the highest you can

[1] Johnson in 1763, quoted in J. Boswell, *Life of Johnson.*
[2] Warton's *Pope's Works,* v. 235 n.

of his abilities,' said Arbuthnot, 'and they are far beyond anything you can conceive.' However, Pope interested himself in preparing libretti for Handel, and protested when in due course he learned that the composer was being traduced by those who were both fashionable and ignorant.[1] But Arbuthnot's good opinion was worth more than than Pope's. Formerly physician-in-ordinary to Queen Anne, a political pamphleteer, an occasional poet and a shining light in the company of wit or wealth, he was capable of placing opportunities in the way of the young and ambitious.[2] Years later he proved the endurance of his loyalty by whipping Handel's detractors in *Harmony in an Uproar.*

Amadigi brought Nicolini back to London. With him in the cast was Anastasia Robinson. She was driven to a profession by indigence and, having chosen singing, acquired her technique from Croft and Sandoni. At the time of the production of *Amadigi* she was little more than seventeen and at the outset of a career brief, glorious and not unprofitable. Gay rallied round with a somewhat commonplace compliment:

> When *Anastasia's* voice commands the strain,
> The melting warble thrills through ev'ry vein;
> Thought stands suspense, and silence pleas'd attends,
> While in her notes the heav'nly Choir descends.[3]

Success on the stage and a modest behaviour recommended Anastasia to the gallant and erratic Earl of Peterborough, Swift's hang-dog whom he loved dearly. Peterborough married Anastasia in 1722, but disallowed her the title of countess until 1735, when he assembled his friends, informed them of the lady's merits and announced his thirteen-year-old marriage. So ended with universal satisfaction the mystery of the virtuous lady who had apparently permitted herself the licence of noble concubinage.

By 1715 Handel was regarded as a great composer, but also as a

[1] W. Coxe, *Anecdotes of Handel*, 1799, p. 40.
[2] 'The doctor has great power with the queen.'—Swift, op. cit., Letter XXXI.
[3] 'To the Right Honourable William Pulteney Esq.' (*Epistles on Several Occasions, 1720*).

great performer. As the best available harpsichord player he re-
entered the immediate entourage of the king. Geminiani, an old
client of George I, brought himself to the notice of Kielmansegge
and, having insinuated himself into that gentleman's graces and been
invited to play at St. James's, insisted that he would play to no other
accompaniment than Handel's. As a result of his renewed association with royalty Handel was granted a further £200 a year (titles
and emoluments fell thick on German subjects in the king's English
service), and this sum was added to, in like measure, by the Princess
Caroline, who put the musical education of her daughters in his
hands.

On 9th July 1716 George retired to his electorate as a respite
from the responsibilities of constitutional monarchy imposed on him
by an English parliament. Handel went with him. Here was an
opportunity for him to air his English accent, a vile one according to
his biographers but apparently effective enough for general purposes
at Halle. For a visit to Halle formed part of this itinerary. Mother
and aunt must have found it difficult to apportion their pride as
between a relatively prodigal but clearly distinguished son and a
wholly prosperous and respectable son-in-law. Old Zachow was
dead, but Handel, with characteristic generosity, went out of his way
to relieve the widow's straitened circumstances.

Correspondence was going on at this time between Mattheson and
Handel, and Handel was apparently composing a setting of Brockes's
Passion for the Hamburg church musicians. Mattheson avers
that this was written in London 'and was sent by the post in a score
written very minutely.' Later writers cast doubts on this statement
and preferred to have the Passion written in Germany during this tour.[1]
In default of positive evidence it is uncharitable to question Mattheson's veracity on this point. In any case Handel was clearly travelling
a good deal during this vacation.

He was, among other places, at Ansbach, on some mission contrived by the Princess Caroline. Here he met an old associate in
Johann Christoph Schmidt. Schmidt was impecunious, and Handel
recommended London as a city in which broken fortunes might be

[1] The first documented Hamburg performance was on 3rd April, 1719.

mended. Schmidt accordingly went to London, shortly afterwards sending for his family to join him. Thus Handel combined self-interest (he needed a secretary) and charity.

Handel's Passion was performed at Hamburg after he left Germany. Its later history is not without interest. Bach came across it and, with the help of Anna Magdalena, made a copy for use at Leipzig.

In January 1717 King George, refreshed by beer and oysters, solaced by Mesdames Schulenburg and Kielmansegge, and rested from the unconscionable English, who disapproved paraded paramours who were fat and foreign, returned to London. Back went Handel, to take up residence with a new Maecenas, the Duke of Chandos, who wrote to Arbuthnot in the autumn that Handel was now in his establishment.

It is important to remember that Handel's activities continued to be noticed in Germany although he was an expatriate. Because of his Wich friends in Hamburg (Cyril, his former pupil, was Britain's diplomatic representative there until 1742) and his reputation among the musicians of the city, his works were performed there with some frequency. The Passion, in particular, was highly esteemed. So much so that Telemann withheld his own setting from performance by the Collegium Musicum in its favour in 1722. J. S. Bach came across the work and, with the help of his wife, made a copy for use in Leipzig.

CHAPTER IV

'AN ACT FOR NATURALISATING . . .'

THE principal profiteer out of the War of Spanish Succession was James Brydges, who, as Paymaster-General to the Forces, had paid the accounts of Marlborough's overseas armies and kept a good deal of the change. In 1711 the disappearance of £35,000,000 caused a parliamentary stir, and Brydges, though defended with warmth by Mr. Secretary,[1] was named as partly responsible. Nevertheless, the fuss died down, and like many military heroes whose duties keep them at a safe distance from the firing-line, Brydges won the customary rewards of successful peculation. In 1714 he became Viscount Wilton and Earl of Carnarvon, and five years later Marquis of Carnarvon and Duke of Chandos. In the middle of this prosperity (retribution later overtook him in ill-judged speculation in the South Sea Bubble and lost him £300,000) he built a palace at Canons, by Edgware, and as a necessary adjunct a chapel.

The Chapel is a singularity not only in its building and the beauty of its workmanship, but in this also, that the Duke maintains there a full Choir and has the Worship performed there with the best musick, after the manner of the Chapel Royal.[2]

Not only was the music after the manner of the Chapel Royal, but some singers came from the Chapel Royal. Certain of them—Hughes, Elford, Weely, Gates—became life-long associates of Handel and principals in the development of oratorio. The duke's director of music was Pepusch, but when Handel's star rose in the sky he was taken on in the role of 'composer in residence'. His royal associations—he still continued in his capacity as music-master to the king's grandchildren—and his virtuosity in performance and composition fitted him well for the atmosphere of Canons and complemented Pepusch's learning. From Handel's point of view this appointment was a welcome addition to his emoluments, there being a lull in

[1] Swift, op. cit., Letter XXI.   [2] Defoe, *Tour in England*, 1725.

operatic interest in town. He celebrated the grand duke worthily in the Chandos anthems as well as in the *Te Deum*. In the early days at Canons he collected a number of harpsichord pieces, those which perplexed royal fingers, and other pieces with which he had been accustomed to impress his select audiences; these he published in 1720 with Cluer. 'I have,' wrote Handel in an introductory note necessitated by the recent issue of *Pièces à un et deux Clavecin* by Roger of Amsterdam,

been obliged to publish some of the following lessons, because surrepticious and incorrect copies of them had got abroad. I have added several new ones to make the work more useful, which if it meets with a favourable reception, I will still proceed to publish more, reckoning it my duty, with my small talent [tongue well in cheek here!], to serve a nation from which I have received so generous a protection.

Two works of larger stature were produced under the ducal aegis; these were *Acis and Galatea* and *Haman and Mordecai*. The charming libretto of the first was done by Gay, though assisted by Hughes and Pope,[1] and was prompted by Handel's previous affection for this Sicilian fable. That of the second work (later known as *Esther*), which was said to have brought from the duke a gift of £1,000, was prepared by Pope (in 1732 it was added to by Humphreys) from Racine. These two works, privately rehearsed, indicated new direction: towards landscape and towards oratorio. But in 1720 their significance was not apparent to their author. He was by now newly involved in an ill-fated operatic adventure.

The Hanoverian dynasty securely fixed, Jacobitism gone underground or to Saint-Germain since the miscarriage of 1715, the Tories suffering political exclusion and no greater excitement to hand than could be provided by the Mohocks, aristocracy turned its head towards culture. Therefore a Royal Academy of Music was launched. This, in 1719–20, appeared a no less profitable speculation than anything else. In fact, more than in the case of most newly formed companies of that time, there was a definite chance of the thing working. There were composers, librettists and managers available and there was a probable market. A capital of £50,000 was raised

[1] Passages from Pope's *Autumn* (ll. 43–6) and *Iliad* (xiii, ll. 17–33) appear almost unaltered in *Acis and Galatea*.

n £100 shares, and the king was induced to contribute £1,000 to he scheme.

Under the governorship of the Duke of Newcastle, and with Lord Bingley as his second-in-command, twenty directors were elected. These included the Dukes of Portland and Queensberry, the Earls of Burlington (who apparently didn't mind Handel's working at Canons), Stair and Waldegrave, Lords Chetwynd and Stanhope, a collection of military gentlemen, including the celebrated road-maker General Wade and Scarlatti's pupil Colonel Blathwayt, Sir John Vanbrugh and William Pulteney. Burlington, whose voice was raised authoritatively on artistic matters, had the bright idea of inviting Buononcini to come from Rome; somebody else suggested Attilio Ariosti. By 1720 they were banded with Handel in brief amiability. The next development was the engagement of singers. To effect this Handel was dispatched abroad.

A new lease of life to opera was a congenial prospect to Handel. He undertook his responsibilities in connection therewith with high seriousness. He complains in letters to Mattheson, whose request for a biographical entry for the *Ehren-Pforte* he disappointingly refused and whose questions on Greek modes receive a pragmatic answer,[1] and to his brother-in-law, of pressure of work.

Do not [he writes to Michaelsen,[2]] judge of my desire to see you by the delay connected with my departure; for, to my great regret, I find myself detained here by indispensible business, on which it is not too much to say that my whole fortune depends, and which lasts much longer than I expected.

Handel's sister Dorothea had lately died of consumption, so that personal grief overshadowed the excitement of the inception of the Royal Academy. However, shortly after writing Handel was *en route* for the Continent.

[1] Letter from Handel to Mattheson, 24th February 1719: 'As to the Greek Modes, Sir, I find that you have said all that can be said upon the subject. It is no doubt necessary that those who wish to practise and execute Music composed in those Modes should study them: but, since we have escaped from the narrow bounds of antient Music, I cannot see in what way the Greek Modes can be useful in connection with the Music of modern times. This, Sir, is my opinion: . . .'

[2] 20th February 1719.

Business took him to Düsseldorf and Dresden, and painful pleasure to Halle. Here he stayed for too short a period to allow of a meeting with Bach who, hearing of his presence there, undertook a fruitless ride from Anhalt-Cöthen. At Düsseldorf Handel impressed Baldassari, at Dresden Durastanti. In the middle of his Dresden negotiations Handel wrote to the Earl of Burlington. Because the letter has not previously been published it is given in full:

My Lord

C'est toujours autant par une vive reconnoissance, que par devoir, que je me donne l'honneur de Vous dire le zele et l'attachement que j'ay pour Vôtre personne. Je Vous dois de plus un conte exact de ce que j'ay entrepris, et de la reussite du sujet de mon long voyage.

Je suis icy à attendre que les engagements de Sinesino, Berselli, et Guizzardi, soyent finis, et que ces Messieurs d'ailleurs bien disposés, s'engagent avec moy pour la Grande Bretagne. tout sera decidé en quelques jours; j'ay des bonnes esperances, et dès que j'auray conclû quelque chose de réel, je Vous l'ecrirai My Lord comme a mon bienfaiteur, à mon Protecteur. Conservez moy, My Lord, Vos graces, elles me seront pretieuses, et ce sera toujours avec ardeur et fidelité que je suivray Vôtre service, et Vos nobles volontés. C'est avec une soumission egalement sincere et profonde que je serai à jamais

à Dresde	My Lord
ce 26/15 de Juillet	Vôtre
1719	tres humble tres obeissant, et tres devoue
	Serviteur
	GEORGE FRIDERIC HANDEL [1]

The negotiations with Senesino and Berselli went satisfactorily, but not with Guizzardi, who never came to England. However, Salvai and Boschi made up for that deficiency. In addition to contriving these arrangements Handel was playing the harpsichord at the Dresden court. For this the elector, with generosity under the circumstances, made him a present of 100 ducats. As for German noblemen, Handel found them inferior to the English variety, and the Count von Flemming, Commandant of Dresden, displeased with Handel's manners, wrote to Melusine von Schulenburg [2] in London,

---

[1] Devonshire MSS., 1st Series, 150, 0.
[2] Daughter of the Duchess of Kendal, formerly Madame von Schulenburg, a pupil of Handel's, and in 1733 married the Earl of Chesterfield.

that he was a little mad. That was on 6th October, so Handel had been a long time at Dresden. His newly engaged singers relieved themselves quickly of electoral responsibility by displaying such bouts of temperament that the Elector of Saxony was glad to terminate their contract.

Back in London Handel began *Radamisto*, his first contribution to the repertory of the Royal Academy. His librettist was Haym and the story from Tacitus. Handel's optimism for the new scheme led him to take the house in Lower Brook Street, No. 57,[1] which was his home for the rest of his life.

The opera season opened on 2nd April 1720 with Porta's *Numitor,* which gave way after half a dozen performances to *Radamisto*. This attracted a seething firstnight audience: the royal family was there, and so great was the crush that free fights ensued in the admission queues with damage to persons and property: women fainted, and of those who didn't many had their dresses torn off their backs. In view of impending developments and disappointment it should be mentioned that this opera season came, with more than a fair share of publicity, after a fallow period in the entertainment world. *Radamisto* is notable among Handelian operas, but fine craftsmanship was beside the point to the majority of those whose lives were governed by a sequence of events whose primary purpose was to relieve boredom. Handel took himself seriously: only a few other people of discernment did. When William Stukeley told Isaac Newton that he had attended a rehearsal of *Radamisto*, Newton expressed a distaste for the subject.[2] As for Handel's playing, Newton was reported to have found 'nothing worthy to remark but the elasticity of his fingers.'[3] But that Newton got so far as to comment on Handel is symptomatic of the pressure of the Handel cult. Nothing, however, is more delusive than to be the temporary hero of fashion.

Radamisto came and went, to be followed by Domenico Scarlatti's *Narciso,* conducted by that unhappy genius Thomas Roseingrave. The chief singers during the season were Baldassari, Durastanti,

---

[1] As renumbered, No. 25 Brook Street.
[2] William Stukeley, *Family Memoirs,* i. 59.
[3] Hawkins, *Life of Johnson,* iii. 176 n.

Anastasia Robinson, Mrs. Turner Robinson (wife of the Westminster Abbey organist) and Alexander Gordon. The last-named, a Master of Arts of Aberdeen University, was a man of wide interests and wide experience. It was just when he joined the Handel company that Alexander Malcolm's *A Treatise of Musick* was published in Edinburgh, with an introductory ode by one Mitchell, who wrote

> Could I live o'er my Youth again . . .
> With *Gordon's* brave Ambition fir'd,
> Beyond the tow'ring *Alps*, untir'd,
> To tune my Voice to his sweet Notes, I'd roam . . .

In March the singers from Dresden arrived, among whom was Senesino, to fill Nicolini's place. Castrati were not approved by virile Englishmen, but they were a box-office draw, since women readily fell for their Mediterranean manners and as readily excused such idiosyncrasies as they would not tolerate in their husbands. *Radamisto* in the meantime was published with Meares and sold by Christopher Smith (formerly Schmidt) and *Esther* got ready for Canons.

The next opera to be performed at the Haymarket was Buononcini's *Astarto*, one of the Earl of Burlington's favourite works. The combination of Buononcini and Senesino was irresistible. In the patchwork operas of Queen Anne's day Buononcini's arias had been highly popular. He was a good composer, an elegant melodist, a competent judge of the requirements of public opinion and an astute courtier. His style, says Hawkins, 'was tender, elegant, and pathetic. Handel's had all these qualities, and numberless others, and his invention was inexhaustible.' [1] Unfortunately Handel had a superfluity of excellence, so that vociferous and ignorant critics were always able to find something to displease them in the differences which separated Handel from Buononcini. *Radamisto* was again revived after *Astarto*, but Buononcini's opera, which had run for ten nights before and ten after Christmas, put him in the ascendant. The season closed with him well pleased, and he disappeared to Twickenham in an aura of self-satisfaction to idle the summer away with Senesino and Mrs. Robinson. He cultivated the quality and supped occasionally with Lady Mary Wortley Montagu (letter to Countess of Mar, 6th September 1721).

[1] Hawkins, *General History*, v. 276.

The Buononcini faction was largely Whig, chief support coming from the disgruntled Marlboroughs with the Duke of Newcastle furnishing a good second string. Handel's associates were of the discredited Tory school and, while his political ideas were necessarily not particularly bound, the fact that he had been among the Arbuth-not, Swift (although there is no direct evidence of a meeting between Handel and Swift it is inconceivable that they were not acquainted),[1] Pope, Gay and Parnell circle would not have gone unnoticed. Moreover, he was a king's man, and that was not conducive to popu-larity; nor was his character pliable to condescension. The letter to Burlington may appear deferential, but in private conversation Handel spoke to all and sundry as man to man.

In the spring of 1721 *Muzio Scevola,* of which the acts were com-posed in turn by 'Filippo Mattei' (F. Amadei, a cellist?), Buononcini and Handel, afforded an opportunity to view the protagonists in close juxtaposition. Handel's *Floridante,* later in the season, was a failure, and Buononcini was able to establish a commanding lead by the popularity of his *Crispo* and *Griselda.*

At this juncture Handel fell back on the expedient of introducing a new singer. This was Francesca Cuzzoni, an ugly little Venetian virago with a dominating personality, a flair for self-advertisement, an obedient husband (Sandoni her accompanist, whom she married on landing in England) and 'a nest of nightingales in her belly.' This pregnant remark was bawled from the gallery by a groom privileged to hear Handel's *Ottone,* which at the beginning of 1723 introduced Cuzzoni to an enraptured public. *Ottone* undermined Buonon-cini's operatic future, which had already suffered from his arrogant demands on the directorate of the Royal Academy. He retreated to enjoy a handsome pension from the Duchess of Marlborough. Cuzzoni drove from the stage Anastasia Robinson, whose voice had been reduced by illness and her interest in the theatre by the importunities of the Earl of Peterborough. Handel thus survived his first depression and celebrated it by a fit of choler at the expense of his new prima donna.

Having refused to sing the first air in *Ottone* in rehearsal, Cuzzoni

[1] Swift was a particular friend of Mrs. Pendarves's uncle, Sir John Stanley, to whom frequent reference is made in the *Journal to Stella.*

suffered: 'Madame, je sais que vous êtes une véritable diablesse, mais je vous ferai savoir, moi, que je suis Béelzebub, le chef des diables.' This was followed up by an intention to throw her through a conveniently open window. But at that point she capitulated.

Next came *Flavio*, in which Gordon's reported threat to jump on the harpsichord is said to have provoked Handel to comment that that would be better entertainment than his singing. And after *Flavio* came *Giulio Cesare*. Cuzzoni and Senesino were carrying all before them; but the latter suffered some diminution in fame by his abjection at the disturbance caused by a falling piece of scenery in *Giulio Cesare* and by his recent horse-whipping at the hands of Peterborough. On 25th May 1724 Ambrose Philips let Cuzzoni know that her tenure of popularity was not eternal:

> Little *Siren* of the stage
> Charmer of an idle age,
> Empty warbler, breathing lyre,
> Wanton gale of fond desire,
> Bane of every heavenly art,
> Sweet enfeebler of the breast,
> O, too pleasing is thy strain,
> Hence to southern climes again;
> Tuneful mischief, vocal spell,
> To this island bid farewell;
> Leave us as we ought to be,
> Leave the *Britons* rough and free.[1]

A year earlier Philips had put a straw in the wind by his publication of *A Collection of Old Ballads*, including *Robin Hood* and *The Children in the Wood*. There were others. Hogarth,[2] at the outset of his career, was, in 'Masquerades and Operas,' displaying a righteous indignation at the sympathies of high society. His butts were Burlington, whom he regarded as an effete play-boy, and Heidegger, who was promoting *ridotti* and masquerades of lewd distinction. Easeful life and the Walpolian policy of a peaceful England were reducing morality to shreds. Heidegger was doing his best to complete the

---

[1] 'To Signora Cuzzoni May 25, 1724,' *Pastorals, Epistles, Odes*, 1765.
[2] Hogarth joined the Academy of Vocal Music in 1729.

process. 'The rules that are observed by this new society,' says Addison acidly, 'are wonderfully contrived for the advancement of cuckoldom.'[1] Handel looked on at the attacks on the opera and considered *Esther* an insurance against the religious revival which Heidegger would undoubtedly stimulate. Already the Bishop of London was inveighing against him and Fielding was coming in to the attack.

Tamerlano, Rodelinda and *Scipione* kept the Academy precariously afloat until 1726. *Rodelinda* was sensational for no other reason than that in it Cuzzoni scored a sartorial triumph by appearing in a brown and silver dress which set the pace for ladies' fashions for a long time. Handel found refuge from such irrelevancies in a nostalgic letter,[2] the first for some time as he ruefully admits, to his brother-in-law. Michaelsen was acting *in loco filii,* but Handel was anxious to revisit Halle. He was feeling somewhat homesick. This is the impression given by his letter.

The affairs of the Academy languishing, the directors committed themselves to the further extravagance of engaging a new singer, at £2,000 a year, in the person of Faustina Bordoni. Considering the eminence in military circles of so many of the directors, it can only be regarded as providential that their inane tactical behaviour was confined to the realm of artistic operations. 'The umbrage given to Cuzzoni by her [Faustina's] coming hither, proves that as Turkish monarchs can bear no brother near the throne, an aspiring sister is as obnoxious to a theatrical Queen.'[3] The degree of enmity engendered between these two was worse 'than even the theological and political parties of high church and low, or Whig and Tory, which then raged in this country.'[4] The main supporters of Cuzzoni were the Countess of Pembroke, Sir Wilfred Lawson, Sir William Gage and Mr. Simon Smith; of Faustina, more impressively, Sir Robert Walpole, the Countess of Burlington, Lady Delawar and Lady Cowper.

They were jointly featured by Handel in *Alessandro,* which ran from 5th May until the end of the season on 7th June. Not un-

---

[1] *Spectator*, No. 8.   [2] 11th/22nd June 1725.
[3] Burney, *History*, iv. 306.   [4] Ibid., iv. 309.

naturally there were good houses. Handel's preoccupation on this score was to effect such division of virtuosity that neither of his ladies felt affronted. The only casualty was Senesino, who, forgotten in this welter of new adulation, advertised his chagrin in the conventional way by falling ill and retiring to Italy for a rest cure.

During the season Quantz was in London. He observed the battle of the singers, but was on the whole more interested in the orchestra which, led by Castrucci and directed by Handel, impressed him. Handel played the harpsichord and the organ; other players were

Geminiani, a great master on the violin; Dubourg, his scholar, an Englishman, who was a pleasing performer on that instrument; the two Castrucci's, who were brothers, and tolerable solo players; Weidemann, a German, and Festing, an Englishman, on the German flute, with Mauro d'Alaia, who came to England with Faustina; he was an excellent performer on the violin, and an excellent leader; his manner of playing was clear and distinct, but he never ventured at great difficulties.[1]

Quantz had an idea of staying in London and received encouragement from Handel, but—and we may hope that Handel appreciated this—'as he was still a servant of the King of Poland [and Elector of Saxony], he did not chuse to perform in public, thinking it a duty to his prince to offer him the first fruits of his travels.'[2]

Senesino returned from Italy in time for Ariosti's *Lucio Vero* on 7th January 1727. In succession to it came Handel's *Admeto,* which kept the flames of Cuzzoni-Faustina animosity well ablaze until Buononcini's *Astyanax* provided the grand conflagration. Polly Peachum and Lucy Lockit behaved as ladies in comparison with the rival singers, who delighted a vast audience with a hair-tearing display which stimulated not only Gay but also Arbuthnot, who celebrated it in *The Devil to pay at St. James's,* and Cibber, who produced honorifically *The Rival Queens.*

During this period Handel's music was by no means ignored in Germany. In Hamburg (where the Passion music was established) Cyril Wich and his lively and gossipy secretary Thomas Lediard, who were very influential in the affairs of the opera, saw to it that Handel's music was used on ceremonial occasions. Thus there was

[1] Burney, *Travels,* ii. 191 et seq. [2] Ibid.

a special performance of *Julius Caesar* (translated by Lediard and 'edited' by J. G. Linicke) in honour of the birthday of George I on 21st November 1725. Between 1715 and 1723 a dozen Handel operas were staged in Hamburg—all respiced and warmed up for local consumption by local musicians.

Handel had been a Composer to the Chapel Royal since 25th February 1723 when he was appointed in support of Croft and Weldon. Early in 1727 he perceived that his position in respect of official music would be strengthened were he to become a British subject. Therefore he submitted a petition to the House of Lords in the following terms:

> To the Right Honourable The Lords Spiritual and Temporal in Parliament assembled. The Humble Petition of George Frideric Handel sheweth That your Petitioner was born at Halle, in Saxony, out of His Majesty's Allegiance, but hath constantly professed the Protestant Religion, and hath given Testimony of his Loyalty and Fidelity to His Majesty and the Good of this Kingdom.
>
> Therefore the Petitioner humbly prays That he may be added to the Bill now pending entitled 'An Act for Naturalisating Louis Sechehaye.' And the petitioner will ever pray, etc.
>
> George Frederic Handel.

Almost immediately after the passage of that private Bill Handel had opportunity to express himself in his new-found condition.

On 11th June 1727 George I died—of apoplexy, in Osnabrück. On the 15th, the news having tardily reached England, George II was proclaimed. For the coronation in October Handel wrote what must be the paragon of all ceremonial music, in his four great anthems. This was a busy period. Music for the court balls was also requisitioned, and *Admeto* was put on at the Haymarket on 3rd October. On 11th November a *pièce d'occasion* was presented in the shape of *Riccardo primo, re d'Inghilterra*.

Mary Pendarves (*née* Granville) wrote to her sister-in-law that she had enjoyed the dress rehearsal of this work. But masquerades were to take place, and people of quality as well as people of no quality were intent on patronizing these. With such a counter-attraction it is small wonder that Handel's opera ran for only eleven nights.

CHAPTER V

ENGLISH OR ITALIAN?

There's Madam Faustina, Catso
And eek Madam Cuzzoni;
Likewise Signor Senesino
Are *tutti Abbandonni*:
Ha, Ha, Ha, Ha, Do, Re, Mi, Fa,
Are now but farce and folly;
We're ravish'd all with Toll, Loll, Loll,
And pretty, pretty Polly.[1]

THUS cheerfully Harry Carey epitomized the state of affairs at the beginning of 1728. *The Beggar's Opera* had its *première* on 29th January. To his title-page Gay added, over-modestly, from Martial: 'Nos haec novimus esse nihil.' The influence of this work, undertaken at the suggestion of Swift, was tremendous. Italian opera, the philandering Walpole, corrupt politicians and lascivious courtiers all came under the lash, and English drama was enriched. In the rumbustiousness of the text Ben Jonson was recalled, in the sharp-edged satire Dryden, in the songs the open-air artlessness of the natural pastoralist. Of all poetry English is, according to Voltaire, the most moral: *The Beggar's Opera* is the prime example. The music was not of less consequence than the libretto. Herein lies Gay's genius. Only a musician could have contrived it. Pepusch scored the work, but the tunes were those to which Gay had been brought up. Handel must often have heard the same tunes, which ravished the general ear when Gay fluted privately at Burlington House. Moreover, Gay knew the ways of opera. Prison scenes were commonplace. Handel provided them in *Tamerlano, Radamisto, Floridante* and, most movingly, *Rodelinda,* while in *Floridante* an excellent farewell scene between Elmira and Floridante suggested that between Polly and Macheath.

[1] 'Polly Peachum,' Carey, op. cit.

44

But of malice towards Handel Gay must be acquitted, nor was Handel the sort of person to have suggested it. At Burlington House they had got on excellently well together and later Handel subscribed to his two volumes of *Poems on Several Occasions*.[1] Further, they were linked by a mutual friendship for Aaron Hill, a fellow Devonian with Gay. That *The Beggar's Opera* ran for sixty-three nights was a surprise to everybody: in advance Rich, who produced it at Lincoln's Inn Fields, had been very dubious, so had Bolingbroke when acquainted with the project, so had Gay's patron the Duke of Queens-berry, and so had Jimmy Quin, who refused Macheath. However, in the curious fashion of literary-dramatic affairs it defied the previous dismalling and exceeded its author's most sanguine expectations.

Handel's *Siroe,* produced in February, containing nothing more extraordinary than Signora Mignotti trousered, lasted nineteen per-formances, and its successor *Tolomeo* only seven. And that was the end of £50,000, the Royal Academy and apparently of Faustina, Cuzzoni, Senesino and Handel. Faustina, fortified by the energy of London life, went off to Venice. There she disappeared into respectability and matrimony. She married Hasse in 1730. Sene-sino also went to Venice, where for a time he sang with Faustina. At another Venetian theatre at the same time could have been found Cuzzoni, Boschi, Nicolini and Farinelli.

Carey solemnized the departure of Senesino in *A Sorrowful Lamentation for the Loss of a Man and No Man*.[2] Handel settled down with customary determination to revive the faded glories by proposing partnership with Heidegger and by taking the King's Theatre for a five-year period. The first step was to replace the vanished singers, and this necessitated another Italian visit. In Italy he signed on—the whole business seems to foreshadow latter-day commercial sport technique—Bernacchi, a *castrato*; Fabri, a tenor (tenor singers had not yet arrived at idolization); Signora Fabri; Merighi and Bertolli, *contralti*; and Strada, to whom the English with their usual flair for graceless observation promptly attached the loveless sobriquet of 'The Pig.'

[1] Pub. Tonson and Lintot, 1720.
[2] Carey, op. cit.

In Italy Handel was in contact with Canaletto's patron, Joseph Smith [1] and exhibited a nice tact in declining an invitation from Colonna [2] at Rome because the Pretender was holding court there. From Italy to Germany. At Hamburg Gottfried Riemschneider was persuaded to come to England to take the place of Boschi. At Halle Handel saw his mother for the last time, blind and paralysed. Again he received overtures from Bach, who wished Handel to visit him at Leipzig; but there was no opportunity for a *rencontre*. To be truthful, it looks as though Handel was lacking in enthusiasm. He was a busy man, he probably reasoned, and provincial cantors had a habit of tedious severity in conversation unpalatable to the travelled and worldly-wise.

Handel went before and the singers followed after, arriving in London in time for *Lotario,* which was to open the 1729–30 season on 16th November. 'Being thus embarqued on his own bottom,' [3] as Mainwaring picturesquely puts it, Handel proceeded to forget the misdemeanours of the former Academy directorate in the enthusiasm of his new scheme. Not that affairs were, at the outset, particularly propitious. *Lotario* and *Partenope* were indifferently received despite the splendid songs written for Fabri. The moderate capacity for stimulation possessed by the singers is instructively indicated by Mrs. Pendarves:

Bernacchi has a vast compass, his voice mellow and clear, but not so sweet as Senesino, his manner better; his person not so good, for he is as big as a Spanish friar. Fabri has a tenor voice, sweet, clear, and firm, but not strong enough, I doubt, for the stage: he sings like a gentleman, without making faces, and his manner is particularly agreeable; he is the greatest master of musick that ever sung upon the stage. The third is the bass, a very good distinct voice, without any harshness. La Strada is the first woman; her voice is without exception fine, her manner near perfection, but her person is *very bad,* and she makes *frightful mouths.* La Merighi is the next to her; her voice is not so extraordinarily good or bad, she is tall

---

[1] Letter from Handel to Michaelsen, 11th March 1729. 'You have only to address your letters to Mr. Joseph Smith, Banker, at Venice (as I have already explained), and he will forward them to me, in whatever part of Italy I may be staying.'

[2] Mainwaring, p. 113.   [3] Ibid.

and has a very graceful person, with a tolerable face: she seems to be a woman about forty, she sings easily and agreeably. The last is Bertoli, she has neither voice, ear, nor manner to recommend her; but she is a perfect beauty, quite a Cleopatra, that sort of complexion with regular features, fine teeth, and when she sings has a smile about her mouth which is extreme pretty, and I believe has practised to sing before a glass, for she has never any distortion of her face.[1]

Bernacchi was dismissed and Senesino re-engaged, through the intermediary offices of His Majesty's Envoy Extraordinary at Florence, Francis Colman,[2] at a fee of 1,400 guineas for the season. The amount is large in view of the fact that Handel had no directors behind him: but his financial transactions were conducted on a large scale,[3] and what he earned by music was increased by judicious investment. The re-engagement of Senesino worked, despite the rumblings of abuse which came from those who subscribed to Carey's

> Curse on this damn'd Italian pathic mode,
> To Sodom and to Hell the ready road,[4]

and trundled off to take pugilistic advice from Figg, to enjoy manly sports at Hockley-in-the-Hole, and to demonstrate Macheath-like the benefits to be conferred on a virile nation by the pursuit of strumpets. Senesino brought large audiences to the Haymarket during the 1730–1 season who were regaled with revivals of *Scipione,* the evergreen *Rinaldo,* whose name *The Beggar's Opera* had done much to make familiar, *Rodelinda* and the new *Poro.* The second act of this opera was composed in a week, and if any reason is required to explain the speed of Handel's execution none other is necessary than his busyness. When he wasn't discussing his finances with his City friends, or struggling with the vagaries of singers (in general

[1] Mrs. Pendarves to Anne Granville, 1728.

[2] Letters from Handel to Colman, 19th/30th June 1730 and 7th/16th October 1730.

[3] A summary of Handel's financial transactions is given in Appendix E.

[4] 'A Satire on the Luxury and Effeminacy of the Age,' Carey, op. cit. Carey, like Addison, writes his prejudices with magnificent anger. The reason therefor is contained in a couplet of universal application:

> But such is the good-nature of the town,
> 'Tis now the mode to cry the English down.

'he resolved to subdue these Italian humours, not by lenitives, but sharp corrosives'[1]), or teaching, or performing at private concerts, he was engaged in the normal pleasures of a normal person.

From here and there fragments may be pieced together to form a composite picture of the man. He had no great library,[2] but he was a subscriber to various works, including John Pine's edition of Horace (1733–7), and his views on literature were put to shrewd use in his later dealings with oratorio librettists. Pictures were a source of considerable pleasure, and two Rembrandts eventually found their way into the hands of Bernard Granville (who had given them to Handel in the first place), while Jennens received his Denners. Among the fleshly pleasures eating and drinking were conspicuous. Many anecdotes abounded concerning his intemperance in these respects, and Goupy perpetuated it by a malicious cartoon. It may be that Goupy had a private score to settle, for he had had dealings with Handel years before 1730, when his cartoon appeared, when he was employed as a scenepainter for the Royal Academy.[3] Mainwaring parsonically proclaims that 'he paid more attention to it [food] than is becoming in any man.'[4] Which, if true, suggests that the capacity of the eighteenthcentury stomach was less than the general evidence leads us to suppose.[5] In most respects Handel was a typical Georgian, and such exaggeration as finds its way into fable is that which inevitably follows the name of a conspicuous member of society. And by this period of his life Handel was conspicuous. The roughness of his manners was limited to

---

[1] Mainwaring, p. 108.

[2] Hawkins, v. 410. 'His attainments in literature cannot be supposed to have been very great . . . but . . . Of the English also he had such a degree of knowledge, as to be susceptible of the beauties of our best poets. . . .'

[3] Goupy must have been forgiven (what a capacity for this virtue Handel must have possessed!), as Hawkins (v. 412) mentions him as one of Handel's intimates.

[4] Mainwaring, p. 140.

[5] Ned Ward and his friends (*London Spy,* Chapter III) could manage two calves' heads and a couple of geese as a *first course,* and then, without notifiable discomfort, follow it up with a 'stately Cheshire cheese, of a groaning size.'

professional points of exasperation; otherwise his relationship with friends and acquaintances is marked by amiability. So he frequented country houses (Handel's rural painting, such as shown in *L'Allegro*, was based on ample experience of the English countryside): he used to stay at Salisbury with the Harris family,[1] at Ashford, in Kent, with Sir Wyndham Knatchbull,[2] with Jennens in Leicestershire and, perhaps, even at Calwich,[3] in Staffordshire, with Bernard Granville or at Teddesley Hall in the same country with Fisher Littleton.[4] His favourite house, however, was that of Mrs. Pendarves. Mrs. Pendarves, whose first marriage was turbulently miserable and whose second was quietly uneventful, had a wealth of sympathy, wit, literary and artistic sensibility and musical knowledge. She could also achieve the conquests of flippant flirtation. All these things attracted Handel and, while we have no reason to doubt that the friendship was of other than the platonic order, he would call frequently to play over new works, to interrupt Mrs. Pendarves in her correspondence or *desipere in loco*. The parties which Mrs. Pendarves gave had that blend of entertaining refreshment and refreshing entertainment to which we may glance nostalgically:

I must tell you of a little entertainment I had last week; I never wished more heartily for you and my mother than on that occasion. I had Lady

---

[1] Streatfeild, pp. 185–6 n.

[2] At the end of August 1734 Handel had to decline a week-end at Mersham-le-Hatch, near Ashford; but the friendship was a durable one in that we find Handel sending his respectful compliments to Sir William (Wyndham) Knatchbull via Jennens in 1741. Lady Knatchbull was a daughter of James Harris, of Salisbury, and was married in 1730. Knatchbull, like Harris, was a Subscriber to the Op. 6 Concertos.

[3] *History of Ashbourne,* 1839, and Lady Mary Fortescue, *History of Calwich Abbey.*

[4] It was believed by the Littletons, and so related to me by the last Lady Hatherton to live in the Hall, that Handel was accustomed to play with Fisher Littleton's amateur band at concerts at Teddesley. An interesting and detailed account of a visit by Handel to Lord Gainsborough's country seat at Exton, Rutland, is given in a letter from James Noel (23rd January 1745) quoted in 'Unpublished Letters concerning Handel,' Betty Matthews, *Music and Letters,* July 1959, pp. 264–5.

Rich and her daughter; Lady Cath. Hanmer and her husband, Mr. and Mrs. Percival, Sir John Stanley and my brother, Mrs. Donellan, Strada and Mr. Coot. Lord Shaftesbury begged of Mr. Percival to bring him, and being a *profess'd friend* of Mr. Handel (who was here also) was admitted: I never was *so well* entertained at *an opera*! Mr. Handel was in the best humour in the world, and played lessons and accompanied Strada and all the ladies that sung from seven o' the clock till eleven. I gave them tea and coffee, and about half an hour after nine had a salver brought in of chocolate, mulled white wine and biscuits. Everybody was easy and seemed pleased, Bunny [Bernard Granville] staid with me after the company was gone, eat a cold chick with me, and we chatted till one o' the clock.[1]

The curious conclusion has frequently been drawn that Handel's sole mistress was Art (always with a capital A). Handel was a bachelor, but that condition did not preclude the eighteenth-century gentleman from becoming acquainted with the delectable possibilities of female companionship. Pope, Gay, Congreve, Prior, Atterbury and Savage were all bachelors: it was not unfashionable to avoid the rigours of matrimony. Regarding Handel an anonymous commentator, said to have been George III, observed that he 'scorned the advice of any but the Woman he loved, but his Amours were rather of short duration, always within the pale of his own profession . . . .'[2] Rolli, in a scurrilous outburst, made rude insinuations concerning Handel and Strada.[3] It may be remarked, as a matter of fact, that the only creditor who pressed hardly on Handel in a period of financial instability was Strada's husband.

But this is to anticipate. Returning to the opera, we find the 1731–2 season less successful than its predecessor despite the début of yet another remarkable bass in the person of Antonio Montagnana, who graced the first performances of *Ezio* and *Sosarme*.

In 1732 a fortuitous set of circumstances diverted Handel from a

[1] Letter from Mrs. Pendarves to Anne Granville, 1734.

[2] *Vide* Newman Flower, p. 188 n. Is Mrs. Pendarves indicated?

[3] Letter to *The Craftsman*, 7th April 1733. '. . . *Strada del Pò*, who is much in his favour. . . .' In *Anecdotes of Handel* (p. 28) two anonymous ladies are mentioned who would have married Handel had he been willing to eschew his undignified profession of musician. They were of rank and fortune.

too rueful contemplation of his operatic disappointments. Bernard Gates, who had been one of those who had sung for Handel at Canons, was now Master of the Chapel Royal. Remembering Handel's earlier works, he gladly revived *Esther* (formerly *Haman and Mordecai*) at the 'Crown and Anchor' on 23rd February. He was allowed by the Dean of the Chapel Royal (Bishop of London) to use his choirboys. (The debt owed by English music to generations of choir-boys is incalculable.) There were additional performances at the 'Crown and Anchor'—meeting-place of the Academy of Ancient Music—on 1st and 3rd March. Next the *Daily Journal* advertised at the beginning of April as follows:

Never performed in public, at the great room in Villar's Street, York-buildings, by the best vocal and instrumental Musick, Esther an Oratorio, or sacred drama, will be performed, on Thursday, April 20th., as it was composed for the most noble James Duke of Chandos, by George Frederick Handel. Each ticket five shillings.

The evening before this event a further advertisement appeared to the effect that

By his Majesty's command, at the King's Theatre in the Haymarket, on Tuesday the 2nd. day of May, will be performed the sacred story of Esther; an oratorio in English, formerly composed by Mr. Handel, and now revised by him with several additions, and to be performed by a great number of voices and instruments. N.B. There will be no acting on the stage, but the house will be fitted up in a decent manner, for the audience. The Musick to be disposed after the manner of the coronation service. Tickets to be delivered at the usual prices.

That the oratorio was performed in static undress was due to the Bishop of London, who, fearful lest true religion should founder on the rocks of histrionic excess, forbade a production after the operatic manner. It is unjust to cavil at the bishop's veto. He, not unaware of the reputation of the Haymarket, must have been much exercised in mind at the projected liaison between the Word of God and the music of the theatre. The wonder is that the performance ever took place. However, it did and was approved by king and court.

On 17th May a pirated version of *Acis and Galatea* was done at the Little Theatre in Lincoln's Inn Fields, under the management of Rich, at the instigation of the eccentric Arne—father of Thomas and

Susanna and, according to Addison, an arm-chair politician [1] who made his own arm-chairs—who saw money in the new-style Handel and an opportunity of starting his daughter on her career. Handel retaliated against this exploitation of his labour and promptly put on at his own theatre a refurbished *Acis*.

by a great number of the best voices and instruments. There will be *no action* on the stage [did Handel mistake his hero and heroine for *St. Acis* and *St. Galatea*?], but the scene will represent, in a picturesque manner, a rural prospect, with rocks, groves, fountains, and grottos, among which will be dispersed a chorus of nymphs and shepherds, the habits and every other decoration suited to the subject.

The singers were Strada, Senesino, Montagnana, a choir-boy for the part of Damon, Mrs. Davis, Miss Robinson (? Anastasia's sister). An enlarged cast was necessary, for Handel, forced to expand his original score by Arne's thunder-stealing, had incorporated part of his Italian *Aci, Galatea e Polifemo*. Thus the audiences who pat-ronized the King's Theatre enjoyed macaronically the best of both works. Susanna Arne's appearance had given a fillip to the growing school of English protagonists, and Handel might have done well at this juncture to jettison Italian libretti altogether. Aaron Hill thought so, and later in the year proposed

that you would be resolute enough to deliver us from an Italian bondage, and demonstrate that English is soft enough for opera, when composed by poets who know how to distinguish the sweetness of our tongue from the strength of it, when the last is less necessary.[2]

Hill had in mind, no doubt, the skill of the lately deceased Gay, whose opera *Achilles* was still awaiting performance and whose heroic theme was ill suited to the pleasant jingle of ballad tunes suggested by the author. But English opera had taken a side turning in 1728 and Handel was reluctant to bring it back to the main road. Italian opera had its vicissitudes, but at best it was extremely remunerative, and at worst no more disastrous than unsuccessful English opera. Besides which oratorio was the new delight. Its record in 1732 was propitious: on 2nd August Handel paid £2,300 into his account at the Bank of England.

[1] Addison, *Tatler*, Nos. 155 and 160.
[2] Letter from Aaron Hill, 5th December 1732.

Orlando was completed on 20th November and produced on 27th January 1733; it was followed by a revival of *Floridante*. In Lent *Deborah*, the text being by Samuel Humphreys, who had had a hand in the 1732 version of *Esther*, came next in the oratorio succession. The royal family was in attendance, which at this juncture was unfortunate. Handel, as has previously been noticed, was often the victim of circumstances over which he could have had no direct control. That Walpole was proposing the introduction of an Excise Bill, and that the Prince of Wales, in the best tradition of his family, was in opposition to his father and therefore to his father's prime minister, were factors for which Handel could hardly be held responsible. But Handel's loyalty to the Crown, combined with the increased price of admission to the oratorios, necessary, so Handel and Heidegger protested, to meet increased expenses due to inflation, were enough to call forth Rolli's letter in the *Craftsman* of 7th April, concluding:

> Quoth W——e to H——l, shall We Two agree,
> And *excise* the whole Nation?
> > H. *Si, Caro, Si*.
> Of what use are *Sheep* if the Shepherd can't shear them
> At the *Hay-market* I, you at *Westminster*.
> > W. Hear him!
> Call'd to order, their *Seconds* appear in their place;
> One fam'd for his *Morals,* and one for his *Face*.
> In half they succeeded, in half they were crost:
> The EXCISE was obtained, but poor DEBORAH lost.

This crude attack, supervening on a house of no more than 260 persons, and a growing deterioration in health worried Handel.

In June the nobility under the direction of Frederick, Prince of Wales, and Marlborough[1] set up a rival opera to Handel's, substituting Porpora for their former champion Buononcini, now in some disgrace for seeming to palm off a madrigal by Lotti as his own. Singers were seduced from Handel's service, first Senesino, then Cuzzoni and then Montagnana: only Strada remained faithful. In this wretched year two gestures relieved the gloom. The first

---

[1] Charles Spencer succeeded to the title on the death, in 1733, of his maternal aunt Henrietta, who had been duchess in her own right since the death of her father, the first duke, in 1722.

was a vigorous polemic by Arbuthnot in defence of Handel and entitled *Harmony in an Uproar*; the second an invitation from the University of Oxford which, in honouring Handel, was paying lip-service to the house of Hanover and thereby giving the lie to its alleged Jacobitism. If Handel was offered a degree he refused it, possibly because tact forbade receiving the honour from a politically suspect institution or possibly because so many people of whom he disapproved, including Maurice Greene, were doctors. Handel preferred the less honorific Mr. to being associated with Greene.[1]

On the whole Oxford greeted Handel with warmth, and what he made out of a series of concerts there amply compensated for the lean period in the earlier part of the year. On 5th July *Esther* was given, on the 7th it was repeated, on the 8th the *Utrecht Te Deum* at St. Mary's, on the 10th 'a spick and span new oratorio, called *Athaliah*,' on the 11th *Athalia* again, and on the 12th, to conclude the festival, *Deborah*. Earless dons, purse-empty undergraduates and recalcitrant Jacobites might carp at the attention paid to 'Handell and (his lousy crew) a great number of foreign fiddlers,'[2] but the *Gentleman's Magazine* reported that *Athalia* was greeted 'with vast applause, before an audience [this must have been the sum of the two audiences] of 3,700 persons.'

But after this interlude the ugly business of fighting the operatic opposition had to be faced. The nobility put in Porpora to bat first. *Ariadne* filled Lincoln's Inn Fields from 29th December. Handel responded with a similarly titled opera (*Arianna*) of his own on 26th January. In this he featured a new *castrato*—Carestini, who had been engaged during a continental tour undertaken after Oxford with this end in view. Lady Bristol described Carestini as 'an extream good singer. The rest are all scrubbs, except old Durastanti, that sings as well as ever she did.' Nor was Lady Bristol far wrong.

---

[1] *Vide Harmony in an Uproar*: 'Why Dr. Pushpin [Pepusch] and Dr. Blue [Greene] laugh at you, and scorn to keep you company; and they have vowed to me, that it is scarcely possible to imagine how much better they composed after the commencement gown was thrown over their shoulders than before; it was as if a musical —— had laid hands upon them, and inspired them with the enthusiasm of harmony.'

[2] Hearne, *Reliquiae Hearnianae*.

Handel faced the nobility with an inferior team, and he had played into their hands by preferring Carestini to the much more famous Farinelli.

Meanwhile opera in English was improving in popularity if not always in quality. In the tradition of ballad opera came Charles Johnson's *Village Opera* and Bickerstaff's *Love in a Village*. In direct competition with Handel, in 1732 Carey produced *Amelia* and *Teraminta*, the first to music by Lampe and the second by John Christopher Smith. *Amelia* gave Susanna Arne her first opportunity, and not only encouraged her father in Handelian depredation, but also put ideas into her brilliant brother's head. He proceeded to take the threadbare script of Addison's *Rosamund* and to give it another trial. With no more famous singers than old Leveridge, a relic of the Purcellian era, one of Rich's pantomimers, a reliable drinker and a massive *basso* who lived ripely on to the age of eighty-eight; Mrs. Barbier, celebrated as the heroine of an elopement escapade; Corfe, of the Chapel Royal; Miss Chambers; Mrs Jones; Miss Arne; and a younger brother, Master Arne, *Rosamund* achieved ten performances and a benefit night for the composer. Carey with his genius for lampoon was at the same time handling the grandiose and the exotic very roughly in *Chrononhotonthologos* which, with its nomenclature (Aldiborontiphoscophornio, Rigdum-Funnidos, the Queen of Queerum-mania), its rude allusions to

A sudden diarrhoea's rapid force

which stimulated disastrously the peristaltic motion of the queen, and with its 'Rough Music of Salt-boxes and Rolling-pins, Grid-irons and Tongs, Sow-gelders Horns, Marrow-bones and Cleavers' (an orchestration later adopted by Burney) sent gusts of ribald laughter round London at the expense of more serious entertainment.

Nor was oratorio left as a Handelian monopoly. Defesch, a Fleming and leader of the band at Marylebone, composed a work in this *genre* to a text by Huggins. The work is known to posterity through Hogarth's castigation in caricature. Maurice Greene, to whom, as has been noted, Handel was particularly allergic, tried his hand at part of *The Song of Deborah*. And Porpora was in the same occupation as a relief from opera.

Yesterday [wrote Mrs. Pendarves] in the afternoon Phil and I went to the oratorio at Lincoln's Inn, composed by Porpora, an Italian, famous for church music, who is now in England: it is a fine solemn piece of music, but I confess I think the subject too solemn for a theatre. To have words of piety made use of *only* to introduce good music, is *reversing* what it ought to be, and most of the people that hear the oratorio make no reflection on the meaning of the words, though God is addressed in the most solemn manner; some of the choruses and recitatives are extremely fine and touching, but they say it is not equal to Mr. Handel's oratorio of *Esther* or *Deborah*.[1]

Mrs. Pendarves was a fair critic and Handel would not have had it otherwise.

In the spring of 1734 Handel fulfilled an occasional engagement by compiling out of *Athalia* a *Parnasso in festa* and by writing an anthem to celebrate the marriage of the Princess Royal with the Prince of Orange. Maurice Greene composed an anthem, *Blessed are all they* (B.M., Add. MS. 17859), for the same occasion. A magnificent example of the English verse anthem form, this work clearly left ideas in Handel's head, for the alto recitative 'The virgins that be her fellows' is identical at the outset—in respect of melodic initiative, harmony, and instrumentation—to 'A virgin shall conceive' in *Messiah*.

At the end of the season Handel's agreement with Heidegger was terminated, and before he had had time to readjust his affairs the nobility rushed into the Haymarket. There was in their party sound business direction. They took the best theatre and then produced a sensational addition to their company—Farinelli. With Farinelli, Montagnana, Cuzzoni and Senesino the directorate could confront Handel with the ace, king, queen and knave of hearts.

---

[1] Letter to Anne Granville, 28th March 1734. Porpora's oratorio was *Davide & Bersabea*, which was also performed during the next season (see p. 59).

CHAPTER VI

THE TRANSITION

On his [Farinelli's] arrival here, at the first private rehearsal at Cuzzoni's apartments, Lord Cowper, then principal manager of the opera under Porpora, observing that the band did not follow him, but were all gaping with wonder, as if thunder-struck, desired them to be attentive; when they all confessed, that they were unable to keep pace with him: having not only been disabled by astonishment, but overpowered by his talents. This band was small, consisting only of Carbonelli, Mich. Christ. Festing, Valentine Snow, afterwards sergeant-trumpeter, and Mr. Vezan, a dancing-master, who was likewise a steady and excellent player on the violin, and constantly employed whenever Carbonelli or Festing was the leader: it was from this worthy that I had this anecdote.[1]

The prince of *castrati* stayed in London for three years, sufficiently long to be in at the kill of Italian opera, to see Handel reduced to financial disorder, and society to a state of emotional exhaustion. The incredible furore his presence created is still without parallel in the long history of stage idolatry. He doubtless was the best singer of his kind in Europe, but this was not entirely relevant. His acclamation came because he was the Farinelli. Towards the end of his sojourn he had the mortification of playing to near-empty houses, but his fortune was made and he could retire to Spain to endorse the truth of Mattheson's remark that 'he who in the present time wants to make a profit out of music betakes himself to England.' Handsome fees were dispensed by private purses when the presence of Farinelli was indicative of social standing. Among his patrons were the Spanish ambassador, the Portuguese chaplain for whom Farinelli sang 'on the occasion of the Princess of Brazil's being brought to bed of a daughter,' the Duke of Leeds and the Prince of Wales.

His Royal Highness the Prince of Wales was pleased to make a present of a fine wrought snuff-box, richly set with diamonds and rubies, in which was inclosed a pair of brilliant diamond knee-buckles, as also a purse of one hundred guineas, to the famous Signor Farinelli, who had constantly attended all his Royal Highness's concerts since he came from Italy.[2]

---

[1] Burney, *History*, iv. 380. [2] Ibid., iv. 384.

'One God, one Farinelli!' shouted Lady Bingley with accurate impiety at the opera, thus achieving immortality in Hogarth's denunciation of the whole disgusting orgy of *castrato* worship in the fourth scene of 'Marriage à la Mode.' In 'The Rake's Progress' (Scene ii) the gifts enumerated above are listed, with T. Rakewell both pertinently and impertinently named as donor, as the eleemosynary outcome of *Artaserse,* Farinelli's first opera at the Haymarket. This scene of Hogarth's illuminates distressingly the degeneracy of fashionable artistic proclivities. There are Figg, the instructor in quarterstaff, Dubois the fencing-master, Essex the professor of dancing, hatters, tailors and other miscellaneous clients, a horn-player blowing indiscriminate noises and Handel (the wig is of the ripe variety favoured by him, although the figure is less massive than we have been accustomed to imagine). The latter rehearses with blissful unconcern the score of *The Rape of the Sabines* at the harpsichord. The repulsiveness of Farinelli exercised a particular fascination on Hogarth, who lashed the idol again in his 'Farinelli, Cuzzoni and Senesino' of 1734.

Handel, excluded from the King's Theatre, took the smaller house, under Rich's management, in Lincoln's Inn Fields. It is suggested by Streatfeild [1] that this theatre was temporarily taken for the benefit of the newly wed Princess Anne, who wanted to hear some music before leaving for Holland. He stayed at Lincoln's Inn Fields until 18th December with *Arianna* and *Il pastor fido,* the latter being rearranged to include dances for the Parisian ballerina (if the term is not too euphemistic) Sallé, who had been used for her talents of dubious propriety in earlier pantomime. After 18th December Handel moved to Covent Garden.

For the new year his singers were Carestini, Beard, Waltz, Stoppelaer, Strada, Negri and Cecilia Young. John Beard was a former chorister of the Chapel Royal under Gates. He was a singer of charm and intelligence, but of limited technique. Cecilia Young was one of three sisters, all of whom sang themselves into marriage: Cecilia with Arne, Isabella with Lampe, and Esther with Charles Charles Jones, of the Royal Band. Waltz, the other singer who calls for comment, was reputedly Handel's cook,[2] and had certainly sung in

[1] Streatfeild, p. 134.

[2] See 'Gustavus Waltz: was he Handel's cook?' in *Concerning Handel,* W. C. Smith, 1948.

the Oxford celebrations in place of the miscreant Montagnana. Previously Waltz had put himself in temporary disgrace by taking part
in Arne's *Acis and Galatea* production.

Against *Artaserse* and *Polifemo* at the Haymarket Handel set
Ariodante at Covent Garden. The king generously, and with a
deprecatory sigh at those of the nobility who made such sacrifice
necessary by attempting 'the ruin of one poor fellow,' contributed
£1,000 towards the running expenses. For Lent, Handel, 'as his
capital singers were inferior in number and renown to those of his
rival . . . very wisely discontinued the performance of operas for a
considerable time, and rested his fame and fortune on his choral
strength in the composition of oratorios.'[1] Burney felt strongly here:
after all as a young man he had had the honour of playing for
Handel, and as a schoolboy he had experienced the greater thrill of
witnessing the great man so ordinarily engaged as in drinking a cup
of coffee and smoking a pipe. He continued his communiqué with
gallant satisfaction at Porpora's discomfiture after sending a *David*
into the oratorio sector of the battle. 'In this attack he seems to have
sunk under his antagonist's superior force and fire. For this oratorio
was executed but three times. . . .' *Esther* was given six times, *Athalia*
five and *Deborah* three. Between the acts of *Esther* Handel 'performs a
part in two concertos, that are the finest things I ever heard in my life.'

In introducing organ concertos Handel was wise. Many would
come to hear him play who found less to interest them in the singing
of indifferent singers. Handel was a great organ-lover with modern
tendencies and was apparently helpful in inducing the Germans
to adopt the English-invented swell-box. As far back as 1722 his
playing stimulated the Rev. Daniel Prat, M.A., to Browningesque
enthusiasm:

> Yet as thy volant touch pursues
> Though all proportions low and high
> The wondrous fugue, it peace renews
> Serene as the unsullied sky.[2]

The concertos indicate that the touch was still volant [3] in 1735.

[1] Burney, *History*, iv. 383.

[2] 'Ode to Mr. Handel, on his Playing on the Organ, 1722' in Nichols's
Select Collection of Poems, 1781, vii. 150–6.

[3] *Vide* Hawkins, v. 413.

On 16th April *Alcina,* with a preliminary puff in the *London Daily Post* stating that 'the new opera will exceed any composition of Mr. Handel's hitherto performed,' completed the season. In the other house, during the performance of *Polifemo,* unnecessary notoriety was gained by a show of anarchy on the part of the footmen who terrified the ladies 'by crowding into the lobby with lighted flambeaux, and refusing to retire when ordered by the gentlemen.' The assistance of the guards was called for and 'the Marquis of Tweedale's servant received a wound of which he died a few days after.'[1] An episode such as this often enlivened the theatre of the heroic age. With Handel's triumph in *Alcina,* a lightweight among his operas designed more than was usual with Handel to suit popular taste, and including more dances for the disreputable Sallé, was mingled the by now familiar touch of disillusionment. Carestini, affronted by his director's corrosive treatment (the old story of the singer refusing to sing an aria and being subjected to a salutary course of brow-beating repeats itself), affirmed his intention of leaving the cast. Handel thereupon took £300 from the bank and left town for the summer. Some time during the recess he had another of Mattheson's periodic requests for autobiographical matter. To this Handel returned his customary polite refusal: 'It would be impossible for me to recall the events of my past life, since continued application to the service of this Court and Nobility prevents me from giving my attention to any other matters.'[2] Which wasn't quite true, as a letter written to Jennens at the same time shows:

I received your very agreeable letter with the inclosed oratorio. I am just going to Tunbridge; yet what I could read of it in haste, gave me a great deal of satisfaction. I shall have more leisure time there to read it with all the attention it deserves. There is no certainty of any scheme for next season, but it is probable that something or other may be done, of which I shall take the liberty to give you notice, being extremely obliged to you for the generous concern you show upon this account. . . .[3]

In 1736, after diplomatic disappointment over the miscarried 'double marriage project,' designed to detach Prussia from Austria, the Prince of Wales was married to the Princess of Sachsen-Gotha on 27th April. Handel carried out his proper duties with another

[1] Burney, *History,* iv. 384.   [2] 29th July 1735.   [3] 28th July 1735.

wedding anthem to add to his royal offerings. *Sing unto God* was about the only token of piety in a sordid affair. The prince, indifferent to considerations other than those of unpleasant consequence to his father and to women who were honest, seized the opportunity to make the occasion a parliamentary issue in which his financial position gave the Opposition a stick with which to beat the Government. The debate was notable for the appearance on the floor of the House of Cornet Pitt, who was, for his championship of the prince, deprived of his rank. Occasional music was in these conditions a minor issue. Nevertheless Porpora put on *The Feast of Hymen* to keep the scores even, anticipating that Handel would cap his wedding anthem with a piece of secular *réjouissance*.

At the beginning of this year Handel, embarrassed by the late secession of Carestini, had turned Purcellian in a setting of one of Dryden's odes for St. Cecilia. *Alexander's Feast,* the text arranged by Newburgh Hamilton, was very successful, if for no other reason because it was in English. In May the opera, in the form of *Atalanta,* returned under princely protection, for it was a *Festgesang*. The details of presentation recall the Jonsonian masque but also the public relations productions under Wich's aegis in Hamburg—in particular the Birthday performance of *Der Britten Freude und Glückseligkeit* of 1727. For *Atalanta,* according to the *Daily Post,* there was

an avenue to the temple of Hymen, adorned with statues of heathen deities. Next was a triumphal arch, on the summit of which were the arms of their Royal Highnesses. Under the arch was the figure of Fame on a cloud sounding the praises of the happy pair. The names Fredericus and Augusta appeared above, in transparent characters. The opera concluded with a grand chorus, during which several beautiful illuminations were displayed.

The prince and princess from now on were staunch Handelians, to the temporary annoyance of the king, who felt, as a matter of principle, obliged to withdraw his support.

In the summer and autumn Handel took comfort from the obviously declining fortunes of the opera of the nobility. Senesino had already gone and Farinelli was on the point of departure. Handel himself had lately engaged new singers—Gioacchino Conti (alias Gizziello), a soprano who had appeared in *Atalanta* and possessed, according to Burney, delicacy and tenderness; and Domenico Annibali, a contralto from Dresden. The scores of the operas for the coming season were prepared and as completed were taken round for Mrs. Pendarves's approval.[1]

By November the scene was set for the final show-down between the rival schools: Handel in good heart, although his health was a source of anxiety; the nobility banking on their new arrivals— Merighi, Chimenti and Francesina. The new singers on both sides were paraded before the queen and the princesses at Kensington and impartially approved. Strada, back from a vacation in Holland, acclimatized herself by singing at the Swan Tavern in Cornhill.

Handel got off this season to a flying start with revivals of *Atalanta* (with 'several fine devices in fireworks' in honour of the Princess of Wales's birthday) and *Poro,* whose production was somewhat delayed by Strada's sore throat, under royal patronage. In the new year came *Arminio* (12th January), *Giustino* (16th February) and *Berenice* (18th May). But little success attended these works, and Handel's health was no longer proof against rapid deterioration. He survived the oratorio performances during Lent—the days were Wednesdays, Fridays and the first four days of Holy Week—but on 30th April the *London Daily Post* referred to Mr. Handel's indisposition with rheumatism and his hopes of being sufficiently recovered to accompany *Giustino* on 4th May. During his illness his cast staged Vinci's *La Didone abbandonata,* of which J. C. Smith's copy (B.M. Add. 31607) carries alterations by Handel. The last opera of the season was *Berenice* and the theatre closed on 1st June.

At the Haymarket affairs were in no better state. Operas failed with monotonous regularity, operas with intermezzi (*Il Giocatore,* introduced between the acts of Hasse's *Siroe,* was the first ever seen on the stage in England) failed, Hasse, Porpora, Pescetti failed, and Farinelli, perturbed by houses worth no more than £35, developed a cold, thus preventing further performances of the concluding *Sabrina,* and cleared out of the country having completely knocked the bottom out of the aspirations of the nobility.

Giustino had featured a sea monster. Harry Carey grinned broadly, picked up his ready pen, scribbled a farce, dragged in the agreeable Lampe and threw into London the pleasant ribaldries of *The Dragon of Wantley*. To visualize Handel enjoying this burlesque[1] is to recognize the greatness of his heart and the instinct for chivalry which prompted him to approve Carey's opportunism. The Dragon was killed by a kick on the backside. This (sixty-three performances during the season) was also the death-blow of Italian opera. Carey refreshed his audiences by action and words which were intelligible, by a Yorkshire accent and by slapstick comedy. His final chorus mocked at the noise of Italian vowels, and winked wickedly at the new Lenten occupation of oratorio. Thus was morale restored:

> Sing, sing, and rorio
> An Oratorio
> To gallant Morio,
>   Of More-Hall.
> To Margereenia
> Of Roth'ram Greenia,
> Beauty's bright Queenia
>   Bellow and bawl.

Upon which supervened a concluding salvo of loud huzzas.

Handel's illness has previously been referred to as rheumatism. In the summer it culminated in a paralytic disorder which affected his right side and, more disastrously, the state of his mind. For cure he was recommended to the waters of Aix-la-Chapelle. Having been soused with (sulphurous) holy water by attendant nuns, he returned to England much restored, miraculously so they said, in health early in November. It is worth remarking that those who refer to Handel as bankrupt at this period do him an injustice. He had lost pretty heavily by operatic misadventure, but in 1737 his banking account was in credit, and neither then nor at any other time did his name appear in the published lists of bankrupts.[2]

He returned to London in time to furnish the obsequies of Queen

[1] *Wentworth Papers*, p. 539.

[2] 'Bankruptcy is the status of a debtor who has been declared by judicial process to be unable to pay his debts.' *Ency. Brit.*, iii. 56.

Caroline with *The Ways of Zion do mourn*. 'This fine anthem of Mr. Handel's', says the *Daily Post* in reference to the melancholy events of 17th December,

was performed about nine; the vocal parts were performed by the several choirs of the Chapel Royal, Westminster Abbey, St. Paul, and Windsor, and the boys of the Chapel Royal and Westminster Abbey; and several musical gentlemen of distinction attended in surplices, and sung in the burial service. There were near 80 *vocal* performers and 100 *instrumental,* from His majesty's band and from the Opera, etc. [1]

The queen's death sent the town into mourning, and Handel's *Faramondo*, which had been begun early in November, was set aside until the new year. Neither this nor the patchwork *Alessandro Severo* nor *Serse* (*Xerxes*) materially improved Handel's fortunes; but a benefit concert, given in March, did. More than this (and more than the fact that its receipts enabled Strada to be paid and her husband quieted), the concert, consisting of oratorio excerpts and organ concertos, renewed Handel's confidence in his friends. A further demonstration in his favour occurred when, a little later in the year, Tyers, the prosperous proprietor of Vauxhall Gardens, spent £300 on the erection of that Roubiliac statue which is now in the Victoria and Albert Museum. Tyers's gesture was prompted by the use he had made of Handel's music in enhancing the pleasures of his playground. According to the Russian Nkarinstev Handel was a 'people's composer.' If so, no better evidence can be afforded than by the amount of his music presented to the citizens and citizenesses who nightly flocked to Vauxhall for a variety of diversions, some innocent, others not. There, said a gentleman of Oxford,

> ... plac'd marmoric in the vocal grove
> He guides the measures listening throngs approve.

In view of the major events of biography which are chronicled in headlines it may tend to be assumed that in between opera and oratorio production Handel was lacking in occupation. The present period is a case in point. Nothing of great significance appears, but all the time Handel is engaged fully: preparing material for

[1] Details of this and of performances of 5th and 7th January 1738 were given in the Hamburg *Relations-Courier* (7th Jan.).

publication (Handel was the most frequently published of all eighteenth-century composers), interviewing Heidegger as to the prospects of renewed partnership, exercising his charitable instincts, as in the foundation, in 1738, of the Society of Musicians, or essaying collaboration with Jennens.

To refer to the century under review as the Age of Reason, or as the Classical Era, is to obscure its principal attributes. It was the age of high romance, of glorious irrationality, of the novel. Above all, it was the age of the individual. The life of London (population in 1750 was 676,250[1]) was still sufficiently compact for people to be known, and the precision of classical education, which impinged even on the relatively illiterate, combined with a native genius for idiosyncratic observation enlarged names into characters. And conversation, not then a lost art, took leisurely opportunity at coffee-house, tavern or pleasure garden to embellish familiar characters with picturesque anecdote. When the royal linen, that perennial source of indignant amusement, had been disposed of, conversation turned to this and that. Handel stories were frequent. Sometimes his appetite set the inventive going. One day Handel ordered dinner for three and, on being asked whether he would wait for the company, replied pontifically: 'Bring up the dinner *prestissimo*. I am the company.' Stories like this were improved by being put into the pidgin-English which Handel was reputed to have spoken. (So far as can be judged from quoted examples of Handel's speech it would seem that he changed his consonants as in the Halle dialect of boyhood German.) In 1738 the clubbable were diverted to hear that Handel and Jennens were on agreeable terms.

Charles Jennens, of Gopsall in Leicestershire, was a notable conversation piece. He was rich, his fortune coming from the industries of Birmingham, and lived well. In town Jennens graced Great Ormond Street and impressed the impressionable by the ostentation of his wealth on the one hand (he used to drive the distance of a few hundred yards with four footmen in attendance, one deputed on descent to clear the footpath of garbage) and his patronage of the polite arts on the other. He understood, although Steevens and

---

[1] M. Dorothy George, *London Life in the XVIIIth Century*, p. 329.

Johnson held a different opinion, literature, music and painting. And in time they called him 'Solyman the Magnificent.'

Jennens met Handel and projected ideas for oratorios. He sent a libretto, which may well have been that of *Saul,* to Handel in 1735. (*Saul* was in other people's minds as a possible subject, and one act of a dramatic work thereon, by Aaron Hill, appeared in the *Gentleman's Magazine* for February 1736.) A good deal of the autumn of 1738 was spent in fruitful collaboration, the outcome being *Saul* and *Israel in Egypt.* The important partner, according to Jennens, was Jennens. While we may sympathize with Handel for having to work with an opinionated poetaster we should not overlook the fact that in matters of art he was not slow in expressing himself with rough dogmatism. And the aftermath of his illness was often disturbing in social reper, cussions. However, Jennens had the grace to keep his opinions private and to circulate them only in family correspondence. A letter to the Earl of Guernsey, written by Jennens on 19th September 1738, hints at domestic disorder:

Mr. Handel's head is more full of maggots than ever. I found yesterday in his room a very queer instrument which he calls carillon (Anglice, a bell) and says some call it a Tubalcain, I suppose because it is both in the make and tone like a set of Hammers striking upon anvils. 'Tis played upon with keys like a Harpischord and with this Cyclopean instrument he designs to make poor Saul mad. His second maggot is an organ of £500 price which (because he is overstocked with money) he has bespoke of one Moss of Barnet. This organ, he says, is so constructed that as he sits at it he has a better command of his performers than he used to have, and he is highly delighted to think with what exactness his Oratorio will be per, formed by the help of this organ; so that for the future instead of beating time at his oratorios, he is to sit at the organ all the time with his back to the Audience. His third maggot is a Hallelujah which he has trump'd up at the end of his oratorio since I went into the Country, because he thought the conclusion of the oratorio not Grand enough; tho' if that were the case 'twas his own fault, for the words would have bore as Grand Musick as he could have set 'em to: but this Hallelujah, Grand as it is, comes in very nonsensically, having no manner of relation to what goes before. And this is the more extraordinary, because he refused to set a Hallelujah at the end of the first Chorus in the Oratorio, where I had placed one and where it was to be introduced with the utmost propriety, upon a pretence that it would make the entertainment too long. I could tell you more of his maggots: but it grows late and I must defer the rest till I write next, by which time, I doubt not, more new ones will breed in his Brain.

The maggots came from mental derangement on the one hand and flooding inspiration on the other. So that any host was likely to have had his patience stretched. The Tubalcain (the name was surely a joke at Jennens's expense) is indicative of Handel's Straussian out/ look on orchestral colour and is a warning to extreme purism. Through mention of the organ a glimpse can be obtained of the anarchic conditions which obtained in choral singing, and which justified Carey's 'roratorios.' Moreover Mr. Moss's new organ ex/ plains the prominence given to the instrument in the score of *Saul,* where there are two more or less complete organ concertos.[1] Both *Saul,* finished on 27th September, and *Israel in Egypt,* finished on 1st November, are impressive in their intensity. Handel fought the nightmare of mental disturbance with deep concentration.

The completion of these works was therefore the triumph which their author desired. That neither succeeded worried him little. Some of his critics complained of the noise, a perennial annoyance to the witless who regarded any instruments which overpowered conversation as supernumerary. The kettledrums borrowed from the Tower would have effectively put an end to gossip. Then some of the singers were castigated. But the truth was that the psychological insight of *Saul* and the *Lear/*like vasture of *Israel in Egypt,* at first pre/ faced by the *Funeral Anthem,* were out of time and out of place. John Beard's participation in the latter work reminded some people of other matters, for he had stimulated drawing/room tittle/tattle by marrying, above his station, Lady Harriet Herbert in the previous year. Lady Mary Wortley Montagu was much distressed. The failure of his two oratorios drove Handel to his side line of pasticcio: *Jupiter in Argos,* based on the libretto of Lotti's opera of that name, which Handel had seen twenty years before at Dresden, was given a single performance on 1st May.

The year 1739 was a bad one altogether. No one was in the mood

[1] See *Saul,* H.H.A. edition (Bärenreiter, 1962).

for music. As Jenkins was bringing his ear out of pickle, and opinion was hardening against foreigners in general and Spaniards in particular, opera and oratorio became insignificant against the necessity for moving the stubbornly pacific Walpole to declare war.

In October the king moved to St. James's from Kensington and on the night of the 27th went to the Playhouse with the duke and the princesses, 'where the Tune of Britons Strike Home, etc. being played for a Dance the House seconded it with a loud and long Huzza.'[1] That was the feeling of the times. In Lincoln's Inn Fields on 22nd November 'it being St. Cecilia's day [Handel] first performed *Dryden's Second Ode,*[2] with two concertos for several instruments, preceded by *Alexander's Feast,* and a concerto on the organ, at opera prices.' A month later *Acis and Galatea* was again revived and two more *Concerti grossi* (all twelve were written this year) appeared.

In the winter the roasting of oxen on the frozen Thames was a familiar sight, but the elements responsible for so elevating and so olfactory a spectacle put the draughtriddled seats of Lincoln's Inn Fields out of bounds. Handel was a notable curser: his vocabulary was fully exercised at this time. Nevertheless he picked up Jennens's 'improvements' to Milton and turned out the enchanting music of *L'Allegro*. In September 1740, according to the Hamburg newspaper, Handel played the great organ in Haarlem on his way to Berlin, where, it was thought possible, he was investigating an offer to join the staff of the new King of Prussia. However, he returned to London and in October and November wrote his last opera, *Deidamia*. It was performed three times in January and February 1741. In March there was a special performance of *Parnasso in festa* in aid of the new 'fund for the support of decayed musicians and their families', and on 8th April Handel performed *L'Allegro* and the *Ode for St. Cecilia's Day* in what was described as a 'Farewell' concert.

---

[1] *Gentleman's Magazine,* October 1739.

[2] i.e. The *Ode* (Dryden's *Song*) *for St. Cecilia's Day*; cf. pp. 61 and 71.

CHAPTER VII

'SACRED GRAND ORATORIO'

DUBLIN in 1741 had not yet reached its peak in architectural achieve‑ment: Gandon's crowning glories were still to come. But among European capitals Dublin held high place, despite the Liberties, for elegance in town‑planning and for beauty in situation. Trinity College focused attention in the city centre; medieval Dublin spoke proudly through the typical Irish crenellations of her parish churches; Christ Church sat in grave ruination on its own eminence overlooking the changing colours of the Liffey; not far away St. Patrick's nursed a sick dean and entertained the lords of state. The bay of Dublin, flanked by its headlands, welcomed the English visitor and the quiet serenity of the Wicklow mountains hinted at not‑too‑distant rural enchantment. Society in Dublin was feverishly gay. For many years appointment to the Irish service had been a pleasant insult to those who had failed, or proved disagreeable in other ways, in English government or diplomacy. The rusticated, therefore, concentrated on the pleasantest way of killing time. Posterity should be grateful that this took the form of building houses, making libraries, beautifying a city, engaging in that brilliance of conversation which was the foundation of the great Anglo‑Irish literary tradition, patronizing the fine arts in general with taste and understanding and in reading nostalgically the news from England.

The great name in English music was that of Handel. Handel's fortunes were declining. What better opportunity could there be, then, argued Castle circles, for Dublin to restore his fame by fêting him in Ireland? Dr. Delany, who, when he wasn't in London dancing attendance on Mrs. Pendarves, was in Dublin, knew all about Handel. He approved him as a friend of Mrs. Pendarves and reflected that a course in oratorio would help to spread godliness among a society not conspicuous for its cult. The lord lieutenant, William Cavendish, fourth Duke of Devonshire, was impressed by what he heard and issued an invitation which Handel gratefully accepted.

Between 22nd August and 14th September Handel, again with the collaboration of Jennens, had written a new oratorio: *Messiah*. By 11th October he had done the most of *Samson*, the text ably extracted from Milton by Newburgh Hamilton. After this furious burst of energy Handel went north. For some days he waited at Chester for the contrary winds to subside before hazarding the notorious waters of St. George's Channel. Young Burney saw Handel at the 'Falcon' in Lower Bridge Street and got all the details of the *Messiah* rehearsal, at which the sight reading errors and smugness of a Welsh lay clerk attracted Handelian sarcasm, from Baker, the cathedral organist and Burney's music master. And so to Ireland.

Among old friends there were Dubourg, leader of the viceroy's band, and Mrs. Cibber (*née* Susanna Arne), whose exquisite Polly Peachum excused those moral lapses which had driven her to Ireland out of the range of the anger of Theophilus and the scandals of litigation. Other performers went with Handel. A new concert hall had lately been built not far from Christ Church: Neal's Music Hall in Fishamble Street. The architect was a German immigrant— Richard Cassels—who had already designed Leinster House, the Rotunda, the dining hall of Trinity and a series of mansions for the wealthy. He was, as the examples quoted still show, a good architect, and in his concert hall he triumphed, where most architects fail, in producing good acoustics. This pleased Handel. Indeed, everything pleased Handel (except when they miscalled him doctor), and he wrote with old time enthusiasm to Jennens on 29th December:

The Nobility did me the honour to make among themselves a Subscription for 6 Nights, which did fill a Room of 600 Persons, so that I needed not to sell one single ticket at the Door, and without Vanity the Performance was received with a general Approbation. Sig^{ra.} Avolio, which I brought with me from London, pleases extraordinary. I have found another Tenor Voice which gives great Satisfaction, the Basses and Counter Tenors are very good, and the rest of the Chorus Singers (by my Direction) do exceedingly well. As for the Instruments they are really excellent, Mr. Dubourgh being at the Head of them, and the Musick sounds delightfully in this charming room, which puts me in good Spirits (and my Health being so good) that I exert myself on my Organ with more than usual success.

I open'd with the *Allegro, Penseroso, and Moderato,* and I assure you that the words of the *Moderato* are vastly admired. The Audience being composed (besides the Flower of Ladies of Distinction and other People of the greatest Quality) of so many Bishops, Deans, heads of the Colledge, the most eminent People in the Law, as the Chancellor, Auditor General, etc. etc., all of which are very much taken with the Poetry, so that I am desired to perform it again the next time. I cannot sufficiently express the kind treatment I receive here, but the Politeness of this generous Nation cannot be unknown to you, so I let you judge of the satisfaction I enjoy, passing my time with honour, profit, and pleasure.

These six subscription concerts were followed by six more. And Dublin, which had previously welcomed [1] such of Handel's music as had come its way, rallied round a god's-plenty of *Alexander's Feast*, the *St. Cecilia Ode, Esther*, a revision of *Imeneo*, renamed *Hymen*, and unspecified orchestral works. In one of these latter occurred Dubourg's celebrated cadenza which, having returned from labyrinthine modulation to the safe haven of the tonic, provoked Handel's 'You are welcome home, Mr. Dubourg.' That was the sort of comment which went (and still goes) down well in Dublin. Handel's rooms in Abbey Street, near a later centre of laudable artistic achievement, were a hive of activity in February and March. *Messiah* was coming. On 8th March a crowded rehearsal greeted it with acclamation. The first performance was given, and to increase the accommodation ladies were requested to attend hoopless,[2] on 13th April.

On Tuesday last Mr. Handel's Sacred Grand Oratorio, *The Messiah* [*sic*] was performed in the New Musick Hall in Fishamble Street; the best judges allowed it to be the most finished piece of Musick. Words are wanting to express the exquisite Delight it afforded to the admiring crowded Audience. The Sublime, the Grand, and the Tender, adapted to the most elevated, majestick and moving Words, conspired to transport and charm the ravished Heart and Ear. It is but Justice to Mr. Handel that the World should know he generously gave the Money arising from this

---

[1] *Vide Pue's Occurrences*, 1st April 1736, and *Dublin News-Letter*, 12th–16th January 1741.

[2] The wording of the 'hoopless' advertisement in *Faulkner's Journal* (6th–10th April 1742) suggests that *Messiah* was a commissioned work: 'Many Ladies and Gentlemen who are well-wishers to this Noble and Grand Charity *for which this Oratorio was composed* . . .' (my italics—P. M. Y.).

Grand Performance, to be equally shared by the Society for relieving Prisoners, the Charitable Infirmary, and Mercer's Hospital, for which they will ever gratefully remember his Name; and that the Gentlemen of the Two Choirs [Christ Church and St. Patrick's], Mr. Duburg, Mrs. Avolio, and Mrs. Cibber, who all performed their Parts to Admiration acted also on the same disinterested Principle, satisfied with the deserved Applause of the Publick, and the conscious Pleasure of promoting such useful and extensive Charity. There were above 700 People in the Room, and the Sum collected amounted to about £400, out of which £127 goes to each of the three great and pious Charities.

What the self-conscious correspondent of *Faulkner's Journal* fails to note is the Christian charity which Dr. Delany was impelled to display at Mrs. Cibber's 'He was despised.' His reputed comment was: 'Woman, for this thy sins be forgiven thee.'

Messiah was performed again on 3rd June, and other summer activities were *Saul* (25th May), Avolio's benefit on 16th July and Mrs. Arne's benefit on 21st July. In between whiles Handel told funny stories to Dr. Quin and Mrs. Vernon and exercised their understanding in Italian, French, German and English, all of which languages he used indiscriminately. He also composed *Forest Music* —the last two movements being arrangements from *Forest Harmony* (Walsh, 1733)—for some Irish lady whose guest he had been.

Back in London early in September Handel was at something of a loose end. A report that he was to take over the opera again was without foundation in fact. He had left opera for good and had arrived at the stage when he could laugh at its absurdities.[1] The ageing Handel—he was by now fifty-seven—looked at life more gravely. Added piety came resultant on recovery from illness, and a new evangelical spirit infused his outlook on his work. 'My Lord,' he is reported to have said to Lord Kinnoul after the London production of *Messiah*, 'I should be sorry if I only entertained them; I wished to make them better.'

Samson was quickly finished on returning home and with *Messiah*

[1] Letters to Jennens, 29th December 1741: 'The first Opera [*Alessandro in Persia*] I heard myself before I left London, and it made me very merry all along my journey. . . .'

formed the mainstay of the 1743 season. *Samson* went down well, *Messiah* badly. *Samson* was sufficiently pagan to avoid damaging the susceptibilities of piety, induced by William Law and John Wesley, whereas *Messiah* had a blasphemous look in the title which was accordingly disallowed on the play-bills. None the less, *Messiah* impressed the eclectic and at its first performance—it had three this season as against eight of *Samson*—George II set the fashion (which persisted all over Britain for two hundred years) of standing during the 'Hallelujah' chorus.

In 1743 the king was a man of war and distinguished himself by being the last reigning monarch in England to appear at the head of his troops in the field. In the war, which had been greeted so ecstatically four years before, things were going badly, but at Dettingen, de Noaille's pincers movement going wrong, a surprising and unwarranted victory was snatched from defeat. Hence the *Dettingen Te Deum,* which enraptured all who heard it and which was pronounced by Mrs. Pendarves 'heavenly.' During the year Handel had another bout of illness. 'Handel has had a palsy and can't compose,' noted Horace Walpole.

At this period Mrs. Delany (on 9th June 1743 the *Gentleman's Magazine* advised the world of the marriage of the Rev. Dr. Delany 'to the Relict of Alex. Pendarvis Esq.') was very busy. Marrying a clergyman, seconding his efforts to gain preferment, cutting down unbecoming flirtation and writing for and about Handel took the best part of her time. In May 1744 she was pleased for her husband's sake that he was elected to the vacant deanery of Downpatrick, but her pleasure was permanently tempered with anxiety for Handel. She records a row, of short duration, between Handel and the Prince of Wales—it was at Carlton House, where rehearsals frequently used to take place—and praises *Semele*. 'But it being a profane story D.D. [Dr. Delany] does not think it proper for him to go.' *Semele,* a reversion to the masque form of *Acis and Galatea,* suffered, like all Handel's music, opposition—from 'the fine ladies, petit [*sic*] maitres, and *ignoramus's*. All the opera people are enraged at Handel, but Lady Cobham, Lady Westmoreland, and Lady Chesterfield never fail it.'[1]

---

[1] Letter to Mrs. Dewes (*née* Anne Granville), 21st February 1744.

On 10th March Mrs. Delany wrote to her sister a letter which has greater interest:

The oratorios fill very well, notwithstanding the spite of the opera party; nine of the twelve are over. Joseph is to be performed (I hope) once more, then Saul, and the Messiah finishes; as they have taken very well, I fancy Handel will have a second subscription; and how do you think *I have lately been employed*? Why, I have made a drama for an oratorio, out of Milton's *Paradise Lost,* to give Mr. Handel to compose to; it has cost me a great deal of thought and contrivance; D.D. approves of my performance, and that gives me some reason to think it is not bad, though all I have had to do has been collecting and making the connection between the fine parts. I begin with Satan's threatenings to seduce the woman, her being seduced follows, and it ends with the man's yielding to the temptation; I would not have a word or a thought of Milton's altered [a rare act of eighteenth-century self-denial]: and I hope to prevail with Handel to set it *without* having *any of the lines put into verse,* for that will take from its dignity.'[1]

Handel, however, avoided the task set for him. The story was hardly in his line: not sufficiently strong in that clash of heroic personality which was his especial province. What happened to Mrs. Delaney's text is not known, but Edward Dent tentatively suggested that it furnished the original of Haydn's *Creation*, and that Lidley was the nearest that German scholarship could approximate to Delany.

From Covent Garden Handel returned to the Haymarket in November 1744. The theatre had again become available through the inability of Lord Middlesex, whose efforts at opera management had amused Handel previously, to succeed where better than he had failed. Subscription concerts, *Hercules* and *Belshazzar* were ill received, to Handel's 'great loss, and the nation's disgrace,' and once again he was taken ill.

Lady Shaftesbury went to *Alexander's Feast,*

but it was such a melancholy pleasure as drew tears of sorrow to see the great though unhappy Handel, dejected wan and dark, sitting by, not playing on the harpsichord, and to think how his light had been spent by being overplied in music's cause. I was sorry, too, to find the audience so insipid and tasteless (I may add unkind) not to give the poor man the benefit of applause; but affectation and conceit cannot discern or attend to merit.[2]

---

[1] Letter to Mrs. Dewes, 10th March 1744.   [2] *Malmesbury Papers,* i. 2.

Society wanted amusement and novelty. Handel to the generality was too familiar, too severe and too incomprehensible. In his youth he had provided gay fantasy; in his old age, so it seemed, his line was moral philosophy. Lord —— saw in the oratorio an opportunity to attack the outworks of Amelia's virtue.[1] The bucks at the masquerade gave their opinion of oratorio when they discovered Dr. Harrison's philippic against adultery:

'Tom,' says one of them, 'let us set the ditty to music; let us subscribe to have it set by Handel; it will make an excellent oratorio.'
'D——n me, Jack,' says another, 'we'll have it set to a psalm-tune, and we'll sing it next Sunday at St. James's Church, and I'll bear a bob, d——n me.'[2]

In the summer of 1745 Charles Edward Stuart landed at Moidart. For six months he kept England in agitated suspense. He 'liberated' Scotland, passed through Carlisle and Manchester, and reached as far south as Derby. At Ashbourne he was proclaimed king in the market-place. For Handel this was an uncomfortable thought. He knew Ashbourne, for Calwich Abbey near by, in what is now known as the George Eliot country, was the seat of Bernard Granville. Handel was a frequent visitor. The local tradition that *Messiah* was written at Calwich is improbable in view of the fact that Granville's new house was not yet ready in 1741. However, it may be reasonably assumed that Handel's fullest inspiration did not always come in London. Between Prince Charlie and London, as he had by-passed Wade's forces, lay only the indomitable volunteers. In them only insobriety would have reposed confidence. They had changed little since the early days of the century when they were affectionately designated 'The Cuckolds-all-in-a-row' and thus pleasantly delineated by the effervescent Ned Ward:

I could not forbear laughing to see so many greasy cooks, tun-bellied lick-spiggots, and fat wheezing butchers, sweating in their buff doublets, under the command of some pig-faced brewer, whose belly was hooped in with a golden sash, which the clod-skulled hero became as well as one of his dray-horses would an embroidered saddle.[3]

---

[1] Henry Fielding, *Amelia,* iv, Chapter IX.
[2] Ibid., x, Chapter II. [3] Ned Ward, *London Spy.*

But the train-bands, despite Handel's exhortation in a 'Song made for the Gentlemen Volunteers of the City of London,' were not called on. Charles Edward misjudged his strategy, retreated from Derby to have his forces finally routed by the bloody Duke of Cumberland at Culloden, on 16th April 1746. In 1745 Handel had been unable to complete his series of subscription concerts. The disappointment of his patrons he mitigated by giving them the *Occasional Oratorio*. This successfully celebrated the duke, who

> allur'd by glory's charms
> Flew with a lover's haste to arms [1]

and gave disappointed ticket-holders their money's worth. Thus honourably did Handel always keep to the spirit of his commitments.

The year 1745 is significant in Handel's life. It divides the old unhappiness and disappointment from an autumnal season of mellowed brilliance and general esteem. The *Occasional Oratorio* preluded a period of *ad hoc* composition. Its successor was *Judas Maccabaeus*. The librettist was the Rev. Dr. Thomas Morell. A neighbour of James Thomson, Hogarth and Garrick at Turnham Green, Morell was a scholar of standing, and the editor of a number of classical texts. He was also a knowledgeable musician, who played the organ and urged the need for choral services in parish church worship. In 1747 he preached at the Three Choirs Festival on the 'Use and Importance of Music in the Sacrifice of Thanksgiving.' He left some notes on collaborating with Handel:

. . . As to myself, great lover as I am of music, I should never have thought of such an undertaking (in which, for the reasons above, little or no credit is to be gained) had not Mr. Handel applied to me when at Kew in 1746, and added to his request the honour of a recommendation from Prince Frederick. Upon this I thought I could do as well as some who had gone before me, and within two or three days carried him the first act of *Judas Maccabaeus*, which he approved of. 'Well,' says he, 'and how are you to go on?' 'Why, we are to suppose an engagement, and that the Israelites have conquered, and so begin with a chorus as "Fallen is the foe," or something like it.' 'No, I will have this,' and began working it, as it is, upon the harpsichord. 'Well, go on.' 'I will bring you more

---

[1] *Gentleman's Magazine*, May 1746.

to-morrow.' 'No, something now.' 'So fall thy foes, O Lord——'. 'That will do,' and immediately carried on the composition as we have it in that most admirable chorus. That incomparable air, 'Wise men, flattering, may deceive us' (which was his last chorus) was designed for *Belshazzar*, but that not being performed, he happily flung it into *Judas Maccabaeus*. N.B.—The plan of *Judas Maccabaeus* was designed as a compliment to the Duke of Cumberland, upon his returning victorious from Scotland. I had introduced several incidents more apropos, but it was thought they would make it too long, and they were therefore omitted. The Duke, however, made me a handsome present by the hands of Mr. Poyntz. The success of the oratorio was very great, and I have often wished that at first I had asked in jest for the benefit of the 30th night instead of a 3rd. I am sure he would have given it to me; on which night there was above £400 in the house. He left me a legacy, however, of £200.[1]

Judas was produced on 1st April 1747 at Covent Garden. Sensitive to the feeling of the English that they had lately been delivered out of a great danger, and ignoring the brutal process of repressing the Scottish nation, Handel had aimed at producing a *Triumphlied*. He succeeded brilliantly. *Judas Maccabaeus* has remained a favourite among the oratorios in England. When it was first performed it also gave pleasure to the Jewish community in London. There were in England at that time probably 5,000 Jews: their chief synagogue had been established in Duke's Place, Aldgate, in 1722.[2] Persecution had brought them or their forbears to England, and Handel's flamboyant glorification of the Maccabees filled them with pride and gratitude. It would appear that George Amyand, Handel's friend and executor, had Jewish blood,[1] so that an interest in Jewry was of

[1] Historical MSS. Commission, Report XV, Appendix, Pt. 2. Stephen Poyntz (1665–1750) had been a member of the Duke's household.

[2] M. Dorothy George, op. cit., p. 126.

[3] George Amyand, after Handel's death M.P. for Barnstaple and created baronet in 1764, was the second son of Claudius Amyand and his wife Mary Tabache, and grandson of Issac Amyand and Anne Hottot, refugees from Mornac, Saintonge. He was a 'Hamburg merchant' and married in April 1746 the daughter of the 'late John Abraham Korten.' Handel met Amyand at court, where Claudius was principal surgeon to George II from 1729–40.—*Gentleman's Magazine* and Daphne Drake, *Members of Parliament for Barnstaple.*

personal origin. Morell, therefore, was instructed to choose another Jewish subject. The result was *Alexander Balus*.

Burney saw a good deal of Handel domestically at this time. He had lately come to London and was preparing his own literary career by noting the characteristics of the great whom it was his privilege to meet.

Handel's general look was somewhat heavy and sour; but when he did smile, it was his sire the sun, bursting out of a black cloud. There was a sudden flash of intelligence, wit, and good humour, beaming in his countenance, which I hardly ever saw in any other.[1]

Thus we can picture Handel. At Carlton House in rehearsal, severe and concentrated; tempestuous at the prince's late arrival; swearing at undertones of maid-of-honour conversation ('Hush! hush! Handel's in a passion,' urged the Princess of Wales); wig vibrating in moments of satisfaction, discarded as a sign of dissatisfaction. In the afternoons walking in the park, talking to himself. 'The devil! the father was deceived; the mother was deceived —but I was not deceived; he is a damned scoundrel—and good for nothing,' he was once heard to mutter after a charity boy entrusted to his care had betrayed his testimonials and absconded. In the evenings, and particularly on Sundays, occupied in amiable conversation at Mrs. Cibber's or Frasi's. If he was a little in love with Mrs. Cibber his taste was commendable. She was a lovely woman, honest—hence she cast off the odious Theophilus, intelligent, full enough of conviction to defy convention in more ways than one. She was a Catholic. She was also a great actress with an unrivalled career as Juliet to her credit and a singer of attractive accomplishment.

No person of sensibility, who has had the good fortune to hear Mrs. Cibber sing in the oratorio of *The Messiah*, will find it very difficult to give credit to accounts of the most wonderful effects of music produced from so powerful a union. And yet it was not to any extraordinary powers of voice (whereof she has but a moderate share), nor to a greater degree of skill in music (wherein many of the Italians must be allowed to exceed her) that she owed her excellence, but to expression only, her acknowledged superiority in which could proceed from nothing but skill in her profession. [2]

---

[1] Burney, *Commem.*, p. 53.
[2] Sheridan, *British Education*, p. 369.

With Mrs. Cibber should be mentioned Jimmy Quin, a staunch friend of Handel's since the day on which he walked out of *The Beggar's Opera* to devote his Hibernian affection to the destruction of the anti-Handelians. He too was a great actor: a notable Othello, Falstaff and Lear. Handel went to the theatre sometimes, and in addition to his two particular friends would have seen David Garrick.

Occasionally Handel still went for recreation to the opera, more often to St. Martin's-in-the-Fields to hear Kelway play the organ. Kelway was a great player, possessed of 'a masterly wildness' and a highly individual style, 'bold, rapid, and fanciful.'[1] He was also a devotee of Domenico Scarlatti. But Handel went to church not only for the purpose of listening to the organ. His piety was not inconsiderable. It was reported that he prayed twice a day. He certainly exhibited his faith beneficially through works. He was rarely absent from the charity concerts for the benefit of decayed musicians and their families and was a great supporter of Captain Coram's new foundation, the Foundling Hospital.

Handel still worked in terrific bursts, spasmodically. A libretto was ready. He put everything on one side and wrote his music in a fortnight or three weeks. He was no believer in cold iron. *Alexander Balus* took from 1st June to 4th July 1747; *Joshua* from the end of July to 19th August; *Solomon* from 5th May to 13th June 1748; *Susanna* from 11th July to 24th August. The precision with which Handel's works can thus be dated is due to his methodical habits of annotation. *Susanna* bears the following inscriptions:

Ouverture Sussana Oratorio angefangen 11 July ·) 17. . . . .
Fine della parte prima geendiget July 21 ♃ 1748
Fine della parte 2da | völlig Agost 21 —
Fine dell Atto 3^{zo} | S.D.G. G. F. Handel Agost 9 ♂ 1748
aetatis 63 völlig geendiget | Agost 24 ☿ 1748 [2]

The five languages here employed give some hint of Handel's linguistic capacity which, in conversation (plus a wealth of broad oaths), must have been impressive.

[1] Burney, *History*, iv. 665.
[2] The astrological signs for the days of the week were consistently used by Handel after 1737.

In October 1748 the Peace of Aix-la-Chapelle was signed. So ended another war. No doubt on the conclusion of this egregious campaign Handel reflected on Jonathan's air:

> From cities storm'd, and battles won,
> What glory can accrue;
> By this the hero best is known,
> He can himself subdue.

But dutifully he turned his attention to a royal command for fitting music.

CHAPTER VIII

TELLUS SUPERATA

Country Tradesman

When will Profusion leave a Bankrupt realm?
When Folly cease? and Prudence guide the helm?

Court Politician

O! When will dull mechanics cease to prate,
With blind presumption, on affairs of state!
To break a glorious peace lest *France* should dare,
'Tis right to shew, We 've powder still to spare.[1]

To celebrate the return of peace with a royal salute of 101 brass ordnance (viz. 71 six-pounders, 20 twelve-pounders and 10 twenty-pounders), with a near-lethal display of fireworks, and with music arranged for warlike instruments obviously was not everybody's idea of propriety. But it was that of George II and his masters of ceremonies. Handel, who wrote music with godlike detachment for any occasion attractive to puny mortality, flung all the wind and percussion he could lay hands on into the April celebrations of 1749. Twenty-four hautboys, twelve bassoons, nine trumpets, nine horns, three pairs of kettledrums, a serpent (although this is crossed out) and a double bass are all listed in the score of the *Fireworks Music*.

The wonder is that this virtuous age, which has brought to bear all the resources of musicology on Tchaikovsky's *1812 Overture,* has been able to resist a proper-scale, near-original performance of the *Fireworks Music* in Hyde Park (the Albert Hall if wet). Judging by what happened on 21st April 1749 the result would be highly diverting. On that day a rehearsal at Vauxhall drew 12,000 people, stopped the traffic over London Bridge for three hours, and led to disorderly queues in which heads were duly broken. This rehearsal was one sensation in a bout of glorious licentiousness. Another was the masquerade at Ranelagh. There George II, disguised in an old English habit, viewed with lewd satisfaction the classical

[1] *Gentleman's Magazine*, January 1749.

nudity (emphasized by a modest covering of flimsy gauze) of Elizabeth Chudleigh arrayed as 'Iphigenia for the sacrifice but so naked,
the high priest might easily inspect the entrails of the victim. The
Maids-of-Honour (not of maids the strictest) were so offended they
would not speak to her.' The Princess of Wales threw a shawl over
the lady and a veil over the proceedings.

On 27th April Peace came into her own with impressive salvos
from the aforementioned guns (a bombardier lost his life in preparing
them[1]), with Handel's music, with fireworks which would not at
first function and which, when they did, set ablaze the great temple
erected *ad hoc* by the Chevalier Servandoni.

A few days later Handel turned his thoughts to the Foundling
Hospital, of which his publisher John Walsh had just become a
Governor. On 4th May Handel was at a committee and offered a
performance of the *Fireworks Music* in aid of the foundation, as well
as of the Peace anthem; pieces from *Solomon* relating to the dedication
of the temple; and several pieces composed for the occasion. With
this began a long-standing association which continued after Handel's
death. Continuity was ensured through the appointment of J. C.
Smith (jr.) as organist and later as governor. The foundation was
due to two widely contrasted facets of eighteenth-century life: on the
one hand gin,[2] which reduced women to depravity and their un-
wanted offspring to the dubious hospitality of the pavement; on the
other to the crescent power of middle-class initiative. Captain
Coram urged that something must be done (the wheels of government
eventually turned, but not before amateur organization had achieved a
monument of empirical piety), and something was done. This independence of action was after Handel's own heart. He did not place
much trust in governments, as his anger at the hospital's intention to
have its interest in *Messiah* safeguarded by Act of Parliament shows.
'Mine musick shall not go to the Parliament.' But added to an
appreciation of Coram's gesture was lonely bachelordom and growing

[1] *Gentleman's Magazine*, April 1749.

[2] Because of the prevalence of gin-drinking children were 'starved and
naked at home' and 'either become a burthen to their parishes or . . . are
forced to beg . . .' *Order Book*, Middlesex Sessions, January 1735-6.

age, both of which helped to turn the full magnificence of a broad sympathy to the fatherless and destitute. In 1750 he presented an organ to the hospital and opened it himself with *Messiah*.[1] Thereafter he presided annually at a Foundling Hospital *Messiah* and was instru-mental thereby in enriching the hospital to the extent of nearly £7,000. A fair copy and parts of the oratorio were bequeathed to the foundation in his will. The suggestion sometimes made that Handel was segregated from intellectual activities outside of music is not borne out by his connection with the Foundling Hospital. On 9th May 1750 he was elected a governor. In this capacity he was called into consultation, not only on musical matters, but 'also in affairs connected with the interior ornamentation of the Chapel.'[2] And an interest in heraldry, attached to a nostalgia which naturaliza-tion and long residence never entirely removed, is romantically signified in the coat of arms granted to the hospital in 1749. This contains a 'Crescent Argent between two Mullets of six points Or': a part also of the arms of the town of Halle.[3]

In 1749 Handel mourned the death of his old friend Sir Wyndham Knatchbull, who died on 23rd July. But being given to sublimating his private griefs in assistance for the living he busied himself with the composition of *Theodora,* in the consideration of music for Smollett's *Alceste* (which was never performed but which was rehashed in *The Choice of Hercules*) and in advising Jennens on the subject of organ specification. The clergy, who are frequently anxious for informa-tion on this head, are recommended to Handel's good sense and austerity. He wrote to Jennens on 30th September:

Yesterday I received Your letter to which I hereunder specify my Opinion of an Organ which I think will answer the Ends you propose, being every-thing that is necessary for a good and grand Organ, without reed Stops, which I have omitted, because they are continually wanting to be tuned, which in the Country is very inconvenient, and should it remain useless on that account, it would still be very expensive althou' that may not be

---

[1] The first performance on 1st May attracted an audience of 600; a second was called for and given a fortnight later.

[2] Nichols and Wray, *The History of the Foundling Hospital,* pp. 204, 250.

[3] Ibid., p. 250.

your consideration [herein out-peers German frugality]. I very well approve of Mr. Bridge who without any objection is a very good Organ builder, and I shall willingly (when he has finished it) give you my Opinion of it. I have referr'd you to the Flute Stop in Mr. Freeman's Organ being excellent in this kind, but as I do not referr you in that Organ.

The System of the Organ I advise is. Vizt.

> The Compass to be up to D and down to Gamut,
>   full Octave, Church Work,
> One Row of Keys, whole Stops and none in halves.

STOPS

An Open Diapason —	of Metal throughout to be in Front
A Stopt Diapason —	the Treble Metal and the Bass Wood
A Principal —	of Metal throughout
A Twelfth —	of Metal throughout
A Fifteenth —	of Metal throughout
A Great Tierce —	of Metal throughout
A Flute Stop —	such a one is in Freeman's [1] Organ.

Theodora came off with indifferent success in March 1750. Handel was annoyed. Among his oratorios the work was his favourite. But he chose the wrong year for its production. It was the year of the great earthquake, and superstition having been so little eradicated by the rationalism of the age people began to set their affairs in order against the apparent imminence of the last trumpet. Handel was angry or amusing. It depended on his gout. 'Oh, your servant, mine Herren!' he said to two gentlemen who applied for 'orders of admission' to the May performance of *Messiah*, 'you are damnable dainty! You would not go to *Theodora*—there was room enough to dance there, when that was perform.' To another who remarked on the exiguity of audience: 'Never mind; the music will sound the better.'

In this year's *Messiah* Cuzzoni, old and voiceless, was charitably given an engagement. But she was a shadow from another world. She sang for Handel and for the newly arrived Giardini at the Little Theatre in the Haymarket and 'returned to the continent, more miser-able than she came,' to die in a short time in the pauper's ward of a

[1] William Freeman, to whom the libretto of *Alexander Balus* is inscribed, donor of the Oxford Music Room organ, 1748.

HANDEL THE FASHIONABLE OPERA COMPOSER
From a portrait by Bartholomew Dandridge (d. 1751?)

HANDEL THE PERFORMER

From a portrait by Sir James Thornhill (1676 – 1734)

HANDEL

From a portrait by Hogarth

E. H. Gooch

'THE RAKE'S PROGRESS' (SCENE II)

By Hogarth

A MUSIC PARTY
By Hogarth

HANDEL
Pottery bust ascribed to Enoch Wood (1759 – 1840)

HANDEL IN MIDDLE AGE
From a portrait by Giuseppe Grisoni

VAUXHALL, WHERE HANDEL WAS A POPULAR COMPOSER

Bolognese hospital.[1] Other ancient history was revived by the de-
falcations of Dr. Croza, the latest in the tribe of opera managers.
On 15th May Handel would have smiled sardonically at a newspaper advertisement, signed by Henry Gibbs, a tea-merchant of
Covent Garden, offering £30 for the production of the person of
the said Croza.[2]

During the summer Handel left England for a holiday in Germany.
A coach accident between The Hague and Haarlem nearly achieved
a second remarkable coincidence of history. Bach, born within a
month of Handel, died in that year. But on 21st August the *General
Advertiser* announced that Handel was out of danger.

At the beginning of 1751 *Jephtha* was written. As he wrote
Handel had some idea that this might be his last major work. On
13th February he had to stop work because of his failing sight. Ten
days later he felt better and resumed his score with a determination
that this should be a fitting close to a career which he knew to be
not without distinction. *Jephtha* is (in one opinion at all events) the
most magnificent of all the oratorios. On 18th April and 16th May
there were *Messiah* performances at the Foundling Hospital, and afterwards an unavailing effort to recapture elusive health by a month in
Cheltenham. By the end of the year sight was so far gone as to admit
of none but drastic treatment. Handel resigned himself to the hands
of Samuel Sharp.

Sharp, lest all medicine and surgery of the eighteenth century
should be regarded as a compound of old wives' tale and elemental
butchery, was an influential figure in medical history. He was the
first great surgeon of Guy's, to which he was elected in 1733, a
lecturer to naval surgeons and the author of learned works which
proved him to be an innovator in surgical technique. As a traveller,
a *littérateur* and the husband of a wealthy wife he anticipated later
consultative practice.[3] But he was unable to cure Handel. The best
he could do after operating unsuccessfully was to suggest that Handel
should go into partnership with John Stanley. 'If the blind lead

---

[1] Burney, *History*, iv. 460.

[2] Ibid.

[3] Wilks and Bettany, *Biographical History of Guy's Hospital*, p. 120, et seq.,
and *Gentleman's Magazine*.

the blind, shall they not both fall into the ditch?' was the observation of Handel's grim humour.

By 1753, despite the further attentions of William Bramfield and the Chevalier Taylor, blindness was complete. Indeed reports got about that Handel was preparing for death by composing his own funeral anthem to be sung in the chapel of the Foundling Hospital. This rumour distressed the governors of the hospital so that they issued a statement saying:

the said Paragraph has given this Committee great concern they being highly sensible that all well-wishers to this Charity must be desirous for the continuance of his life, who has been and is so great and generous a benefactor thereto.

> Total eclipse! No sun, no moon!
> All dark amid the blaze of noon.

When Beard sang those words a great wave of sympathy swept over his audience and many were seen in tears. But Handel was courageous as ever. He carried on, calling in Christopher Smith to manage his affairs, to act as amanuensis and to control the rough edge of his tongue,[1] playing at the oratorio, writing letters and composing.

Habit rather than inspiration kept the latter faculty in operation, and nothing of greater moment than a duet and chorus for *Judas Maccabaeus* ('Zion now her head shall raise') and a revision of the *Trionfo del Tempo (The Triumph of Time and Truth)* appeared. In 1753 it was a nice thought on the part of Thomas Linley—who took part in Handel performances in Bath—to have his first-born son named after his hero, George Frederick. Alas! the child did not survive infancy.

In 1754 we are reintroduced to Telemann.[2] He had been reported as dead, so that, on confirmation of the falseness of this report, Handel wrote to him with relief and promising to send some flowers which Telemann had requested.

The last years of Handel's life were uneventful. He rested in the satisfaction that his music was the most durable of all that was written in England during his lifetime. He heard with pleasure of the

[1] Particularly when Handel had a sudden quarrel with old Smith, which led to the (temporary) withdrawal of Smith's name from his will.

[2] Letter from Handel, 20th September.

popularity of his oratorios in the west country where the Three Choirs Festival was emerging to occupy its particular niche in the history of English music. In 1757 *Messiah* was first performed at this festival. With the faithful Beard new singers appeared, and among them a high preponderance of English: there were Mence and Wass, Baildon and Denham, Miss Turner and Frasi; among the players Adcock, Millar, Vincent, Malchair, Richards and Storace.[1] Mention of the last-named, father of Ann and Stephen, indicates the passing of the years. A new era was opening, that of Haydn and Mozart. In the world too events were inexorably pressing forward. The Great Commoner was in power at the close of Handel's life, the Seven Years War was bringing new distresses to his native city, and Josiah Wedgwood was prefacing the Industrial Revolution with rural spoliation and exquisite craft. Of all these things Handel was perhaps aware, but he really lived with his music and his friends.[2]

On 30th March and 6th April 1759 *Messiah* was, as usual, performed for the Foundling Hospital. Handel was present on the first occasion, and this was his last appearance in public. He was taken home unwell. On 11th April he added a third codicil to his will. On 14th April, being the Saturday before Easter Day, he died.

According to your request to me when you left London [wrote James Smyth to Bernard Granville], that I would let you know when our good friend departed this life—on Saturday last, at eight o'clock in the morn, died the great and good Mr. Handel. He was sensible to the last moment; made a codicil to his will on Tuesday; ordered to be buried privately in Westminster Abbey, and a monument not to exceed £600 for him. I had the pleasure to reconcile him to his old friends[3]: he saw them and forgave them, and let all their legacies stand! In the codicil he left many legacies to his friends; and among the rest he left me £600, and has left to you the two pictures you formerly gave him. He took leave of all his friends on

---

[1] Lysons, *Origin and Progress of the Meeting of the Three Choirs* (1895 edition), p. 36. Portions of *Messiah* had been performed in Salisbury Cathedral in 1752.

[2] To those already mentioned should be added 'one Hunter, a scarlet-dyer at Old Ford' and Gael Morris, 'a broker of the first eminence.'—Hawkins, v. 410–11.

[3] Including old Smith, presumably.

Friday morning, and desired to see nobody but the doctor, and apothecary, and myself. At seven o'clock in the evening he took leave of me, and told me we 'should meet again.' As soon as I was gone, he told his servant not to let me come to him any more, for that he had now done with the world. He died as he lived, a good Christian, with true sense of his duty to GOD and man, and in perfect charity with all the world. If there is anything that I can be of farther service to you, please let me know. I was to have set out for Bath to-morrow, but must attend the funeral, and shall then go next week.

London made amends for earlier lapses in its behaviour by sending 3,000 of its citizens to the obsequies. These took place with due solemnity in Westminster Abbey on the evening of 20th April. The music, including Dr. Croft's *Burial Service*,[1] was sung by the Gentlemen of His Majesty's Chapels Royal, the choirs of St. Paul's and the Abbey. The sermon was preached by Dr. Zachary Pearce, Dean of the Abbey and Bishop of Rochester. The grave was placed in the Poets' Corner and now has as near neighbour that of Charles Dickens. The proximity of their ashes may, perhaps, be symbolic of the similar massive influence which each has exercised on the hearts and minds of generations they never knew. The fitting epitaph for Handel (Roubiliac added none to his monument) was written over a thousand years before his time by another musician—Boethius:

Tellus superata
Sidera donat.

[1] The *Public Advertiser* for 20th April mentioned Croft's *Funeral Service*.

CHAPTER IX

STYLE

THERE exists a popular fallacy that all music of the first half of the eighteenth century not written by Bach was written by Handel. Thus a song cast in this mould:

being not obviously Bach-like, would provoke the averagely well-read to father it on Handel. In fact, the responsible composer was James Oswald,[1] a relatively obscure figure in musical history whose misfortune it is, alongside Greene, Arne, Boyce, Carey and many other English musicians of the period, to be counted out as insignificant because imitators of Handel.[2] *The Moderate Wish* is chosen, more or less at random, to illustrate particular qualities characteristic of the eighteenth century. Balance, proportion, mellifluence, lyrical aptness and harmonic insouciance are combined so as to satisfy the hedonistic ear. And, peeping through, comes the amiable modesty of urban pastoralization. Now to dismiss so charming a by-product as merely *ersatz* Handel is to misunderstand the basis of eighteenth-century

[1] A Scotsman, an assiduous editor, a music-seller and publisher in St' Martin's Lane, and founder of the Society of the Temple of Apollo. The above quotation comes from *Ten Favourite Songs sung by Miss Formantel at Ranelagh* (1747).

[2] Handel, however, from time to time did not disdain to imitate some of them!

89

style and to allow the romantic picture of the great Cham of music to obscure that clarity of intellectual vision which the age consciously invites.

That a family likeness is apparent between the works of Handel and any contemporary of his is due not to the fact that Handel was the prime source of formal inspiration, but that homogeneity of thought prevailed with regard to the purpose of music in the community and the style in which it should generally be cast. That music should convey more or less specific ideas was the keystone of musical philosophy and that lucidity of expression should prevail was regarded as a necessary symbol of good breeding. In emphasizing the necessity for clear communication the eighteenth century was doing service to art if disservice to itself. It rendered music generally intelligible, but invited the later charge of uninspired uniformity. At this point Dryden's apophthegm that 'a great thought comes dressed in words so commonly received, that it is understood by the meanest apprehensions, as the best meat is the most easily digested' may be introduced to indicate the deeper significance of the classical outlook. Style may remain constant, but the underlying ethos can still preserve independence and individuality. Thus it is that in Handel we meet the paradox of an individualist without ostentatious individuality.

A common mode of speech is the ideal towards which art perpetually aspires, and at certain stages in history the ideal has not been far from realization. Dante's master, Brunetto Latini, writing in the days when the romance-poem carried itself to universal comprehension through the medium of French, commented that 'la parleuse en est plus délitable et plus commune à toutes gens.' A similar community of expression led the medieval pilgrim to find in the ubiquity of Gothic architecture a genius making every foreign city a home from home. After the Renaissance a particular set of circumstances developed a mode of musical address more than at any other period in the history of music *plus commune à toutes gens*. Under those conditions which obtain when a style is generally accepted and approved a major artist tends to be accepted as representative of his age. Chaucer, Leonardo, Goethe are cases in point. Each is more than himself, confluential. All the tributaries of the eighteenth century flow into Handel and so he stands apotheosized.

A robust and generative period concerns itself more with the summarization of anterior effort than with the novelty of experiment. Therefore most of what appears characteristically eighteenth-century is in fact discoverable in the seventeenth. The simple mechanics of both centuries involved melody, counterpoint, the harmonic basis of triadic repose interspersed with regulated discord and utilitarian rhythm controlled by dance and poetry. In the later period emphasis was laid on certain points so that retrospectively we recognize inevitable mannerisms. It may, however, be considered that superior observation on the presence of such mannerisms is the result of mental restlessness rather than of objective criticism. The perfect cadence and the easeful modulation, to take two obvious and easily recognized habits, were to the style of Handel as the pointed arch to Gothic architecture, essential to large-scale and monumental planning.

The tripartite aria, regularized by Alessandro Scarlatti, the forms of recitative peculiar to seventeenth-century dramatic music, the conventions of suite, sonata, fugue, overture, ground-bass were all ready for Handel's employment, but on whatever form he used he impressed a sense of fluency only comparable to that of Mozart. Fluency, however, is not *per se* a complete virtue: Handel achieved fluency, but he did more. Matthew Arnold added to Chaucer's other qualities a 'large, free, simple, clear yet kindly view of human life—so unlike the total want, in the romance-poets, of all intelligent command of it.' The observation fits Handel and should be borne in mind throughout any attempt to estimate his significance.

The language of Handel was that of his contemporaries, but often they were lacking in the capacity for deep penetration. In so familiar an example as the 'Dead March' from *Saul* Handel's profundity of sympathy extends itself through nothing more complex than a four-bar sequence of tonic and dominant harmony. Placing this movement by the side of a not dissimilar passage from the overture to Clayton's ill-fated *Rosamund* music, we shall see that what Clayton achieved is negative:

This is merely not unpleasant and has no particular dramatic sense.

Handel was pre-eminently a dramatic writer, and in the simplest passages he demonstrates the two essentials of dramatic intention: timing and placing. Among the moving passages in Handel one of the most intense occurs in *Hercules* where Iole laments her dead father in the strangely Schubertian 'Peaceful Rest.' With grave memory Iole reflects:

The extension of thought engendered by the orchestral repetition of the operative phrase is miraculous. Nothing could be simpler nor more obvious, yet placed in its setting of poignant pulsation the spacious crotchet movement is entirely fitting. Inspired simplicity of this order recalls the emotional finality of Lear's 'I am a very foolish fond old man.' Within this aria Handel reserves one more telling blow until the end:

dear par-ent shade,   In thy daugh-ter's pi-ous_ mind   All thy vir-tues live en-shrin'd.

This aptitude for realizing unerringly the point of climax was partly the gift of the gods and partly—industry is rarely neglected by the great—the result of extensive experience, wide reading and absorbent memory. It has already been stated that the eighteenth century was a recapitulatory epoch, and the scholar will not be slow to point out that Handel was so typical in this respect that he reiterated often the spirit and sometimes the substance of other men's music. And yet the unassailable fact remains that what he wrote was so dramatically synthesized that it never leaves the impression of being the music of any one but Handel. At this point we may tread lightly round the plagiaristic slough which has led so many 'sapient trouble-tombs' from the contemplation of music to the anatomy of morals and merely comment that the two common and alternative theses, (1) that it was a great blemish to copy out Muffat, Erba, Kerll, Stradella, Urio or Habermann, (2) that since Handel turned mediocrity into perfection it was satisfactory behaviour (although not too prominently so), ignore the major issues of musical philosophy.[1]

In the eighteenth as in the thirteenth and the sixteenth century there was, despite such contrary appearances as are indicated by

[1] This matter is treated more fully in Appendix F, pp. 229–31.

political rivalries, a reciprocity which viewed artistic achievement with massive impartiality. The achievement was the thing, and whether Pope employed agents to translate his Homer or Handel represented an incorporated society mattered as little to their audiences as did the fact that Shakespeare looked over Marlowe's shoulder and quarried in Holinshed to his. Epochal literature came because it outcropped from the seams of lively conversation. Music of comparable quality also grew from the fecundity of commonplace phraseology. The desiccation of both music and literature by the academies leads sometimes to the suppression of this vital point, but without its absorption the rapidity of Handel's creation and the normality of his clichés become of inflated significance. The speed in execution was inevitable when mastery of language was so complete, and the continual appearance of particular idioms equally inevitable when each was universally regarded as a useful vehicle of competent ex⁄ pression. Triteness develops not when clichés are used, but when they are used in the wrong place. There is a resemblance in method and achievement between Handel and Virgil. Virgil was dependent on what earlier poets had said: words, stories, technical devices came from everywhere; complete lines from Homer and Ennius.

The impulse to say the verse or tell the story over and over again [came], partly because there was a mysterious, self-sufficient delight in the poetry, and partly because it fitted Virgil's own feelings, expressed them, clarified them, and made them acceptable and friendly to himself. . . . Everything went into the dream world . . . the 'hooked atoms' parted and recombined.[1]

So in Handel's case the 'esemplastic' imagination worked in fertility to produce new combinations of integrative miracle.

The places of Handel's residence explain his technical antecedents in the main. The influence of Italy, however, is proportionately more significant than his brief sojourn there would suggest, the reason being that from the beginning of the seventeenth century all music was tending towards the Italianate. Italy was the first home of madrigal, opera, oratorio and the major instrumental forms of sonata, concerto and suite: these and their virtuosic exponents were nurtured under the shadow of Renaissance humanism and at the expense of princely

[1] *The Times Literary Supplement,* 1st April 1944.

patrons whose interest came not entirely from ostentation. Under enlightened patronage circumstances were helpful and music was subjected to a degree of refinement unknown since the monastic organization of polyphony. The tendency of the age was away from the austerity of the ancient *a cappella* style (which was as out‚ moded then as Stainer is now) towards virtuosic display, an obvious adjunct of specialization, and towards that expressiveness perceived through the medium of musico‚dramatic performance. Reacting against the inherent moralization of old counterpoint, Galuppi, Vivaldi, Corelli and the Scarlattis evolved a new melodic sensibility in long, sensuous melismatic lines, pointed with wit, grace, fire or whatever dramatic quality was considered proper, and supported by slender pillars of conventional chording. The revolution was noteworthy in the same way as that which produced walls of painted glass in late Perpendicular. The insistence on melodic integrity which culminated in the Scarlatti‚Handel aria was an unconscious reversion to the self‚sufficiency of Gregorian chant, to the popular approach of troubadour art and to the simpler urge of folksong. Once again the nature of the melody in Handel depends on environ‚ ment, and on further examination the range suggested will not seem extravagant. The outlook of the age was summed up by Telemann thus: 'Singen is das Fundament zur Music in allen Dingen.'[1]

Although aristocratic in setting, seventeenth‚ and eighteenth‚century music aimed at popular understanding in that its basic concern was with that interplay of tonal nuance such as can hardly leave un‚ affected even the confessedly unmusical. Handel learned more than formality from Italy: he learned the theory that what is to be quickly influential must be effective in immediate application. Thus his melodies are ever warmed with the rich voluptuousness of the south and are readily apprehensible. The danger in Italian teaching lay in the facility it promoted, and on occasion Handel fell victim to that 'Deluge of unbounded *Extravaganzi,* which the unskillful call Invention, and which are merely calculated to shew an Execution, without either Propriety or Grace.'[2] Hence the fluent emptiness of

[1] 'Singing is the foundation of music in all things.'—Romain Rolland, op. cit., p. 73.
[2] Avison, *An Essay on Musical Expression*, 1752, p. 35.

the following in *Hercules,* where for a moment the customary irradiation of personality is lacking:

That Handel so seldom pursued fluency for its own sake was due to influences other than that of Italy. He had early been nourished on the strong meat of Teutonic severity. Rugged Lutheranism turned the attention of art to the power of personal experience and to the continual wrestling of contrary mental forces: thus *Sturm und Drang* imbue religious music from Schütz to Bach. Handel betrays his German origin when he leads us into agony with Iole:

or when he sacrifices dramatic logic to massive counterpoint as in the stupendous 'Wretched lovers' of *Acis and Galatea*. Elsewhere, chorale influence [1] serves to make direct reference to Germany, and dramatic recitatives recall the forgotten talent of Keiser.

Between the extremes of German intensity and Italian virtuosity English style characteristically steers a middle course. And it is the influence of England which acts catalytically for Handel. The particular may be taken first. Purcell was not forgotten when Handel first arrived in London. His music could be still heard in the cathedrals, at Britton's, where also scores were available for reference, [2] and elsewhere domestically. From Purcell Handel learned the possibilities of rhythmic extension along the lines of resilient syncopation. The lesson was well learned for it was Handel who wrote:

in *Theodora*, and casual listening will reveal that Handel uses this turn of rhythm with continual enthusiasm. [3]

[1] Passion music and Funeral Anthem. The fact that Handel used a motet of Jacob Handl (Gallus) in the Funeral Anthem, that was well-known in Saxony, was noticed by J. A. Hiller in his edition of Handl's *Ecce quomodo* (1791).

[2] Britton's well-stocked library included the music for *Dioclesian, Ode for St. Cecilia's Day, Te Deum and Jubilate*, two volumes of *Harmonia Sacra*, airs from the operas, catches and miscellaneous music, all by Purcell.

[3] This is of French origin. Handel's intimate knowledge of French musical manners, and mannerisms, is displayed in his youthful French cantata.

In 1745 Gluck visited England and Handel, but was discouraged by the latter in a moment of disillusionment from extending his visit. He did, however, discover that England had some contribu' tion to make to the development of musical thought.

He then studied the English taste; remarked particularly what audience seemed most to feel; and finding that plainness and simplicity had the greatest effect upon them he has endeavoured to write for the voice, more in the natural tones of the human affections and passions, than to flatter the lovers of deep science or difficult execution . . .'[1]

Handel detected and admired the simplicities of English style. He was a subscriber to the *Two Concertos and Six Songs* (1736) of Barnabas Gunn, of Gloucester, and to the settings of Shakespeare by Thomas Chilcot, of Bath, published in 1745. Chilcot's songs, rivalling those of T. A. Arne—which Handel must have known—and like them with orchestral accompaniment, are of the highest quality, and 'Hark, hark the lark' in particular is a masterpiece in the art of illustrating little and pretty things with delicacy and without sentimentality. On the other hand larger works of Purcell and Croft, as Tudway suggests, influenced Handel. From them there are echoes in the primeval strokes of triadic majesty in the Jews' chorus 'Recall, O King' in *Belshazzar,* in 'Make them to be numbered with Thy saints' in the *Dettingen Te Deum,* in 'Moses and the Children of Israel' in *Israel in Egypt* and in the superlative 'But their name liveth evermore' in the *Funeral Anthem* for Queen Caroline.[2] This last chorus, with its cross' rhythms (throughout Handel conductors may be urged to treat bar' lines without exaggerated respect) consciously renews the glories

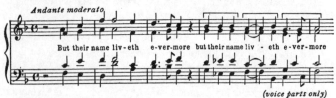

(voice parts only)

[1] Burney, *Travels,* I. 268–9.

[2] See Burney, *Commem.,* 'First Performance', 37 n (a). In general terms there can be no doubt that the anthems of (among others) Croft, Greene, and Boyce also influenced Handel's choral thinking.

of Renaissance polyphony. Here it may be interjected that with rare exceptions, one of which is the clumsy handling of

The dou-ble, dou-ble, dou-ble beat of the thun-d'ring drum

in the *Ode for St. Cecilia,* Handel's treatment of the English language is, from an accentual point of view, so meticulous as to suggest that he not only understood it as well as most Englishmen but that he loved it. Could otherwise

which with its succeeding chorus recalls the first scene of *The Fairy Queen,* have been penned? This leads to the observation that the English outlook on music is largely literary, with the result that songs from Dowland to Britten have a studied lyricism based on the dictation of melodic and rhythmic contour by the shape and situation of individual words. Handel's extension of the Purcellian technique in this respect softens the Italian-inspired roulades and divisions so beloved by contemporary singers, so indifferently mastered by those of later generations, and gives point to virtuosic embellishment. Frequently Handel allowed the delicacy of verbal rhythm to catch his imagination and proceeded to eliminate bar-line tyranny. One instance, from *Jephtha,* will serve representatively in this respect:

Laud her, all ye— vir-gin train,— In glad songs of— choicest strain:

Charles Lamb and Handel are odd bedfellows, but in one respect they are well matched—in a philosophic realization that the surface of life runs at every turn over the main springs of human emotion. Eclecticism belonged to Italy, large-eyed wonder to Germany; to England an eccentricity that saw silk purses in every sow's ear. 'I have sat through an Italian Opera,' says the unrepentant and unmusical Elia,

till, for sheer pain, and inexplicable anguish, I have rushed out into the noisiest places of the crowded streets, to solace myself with sounds which I was not obliged to follow, and get rid of the distracting torment of endless, fruitless, barren attention! I take refuge in the unpretending assemblage of honest common-life sounds; and the purgatory of the Enraged Musician becomes my paradise.[1]

Handel took inspiration from, rather than refuge in, honest common-life sounds. Therefore he rushes to meet Hercules with the noise of bucolic bagpipery:

David, in *Saul*, with the cheering glitter of Flemish carillon; the infant Jesus with the recollected naïveté of the *pifa*. A Roman holiday in *Theodora* is celebrated with a ripe tavern song—hiccups in the rhythm and the tessitura indicate that tenors should hesitate to essay 'Venus laughing from the skies' when sober—whose fitting place is in those collections of catches and glees, catholicly embracing almost every composer from Morley to Harrington, which when pleasure was taken gladly used to keep the tap-room alive with harmonious gurgitation. That Handel recognized degrees in intoxication may be gathered from a comparison of this plebeian revelry with the dignified Commemoration Dinner merriment of Belshazzar's court: his nobles invoke their tutelar gods with well-trained octave passages and the king sings the praise of wine in the sort of

[1] *A Chapter on Ears.*

rum-tum-tum measure one might have expected from an eighteenth-century don. It may be suspected that the picture was truer of London than of Babylon.

Handel himself confessed that street cries fascinated and inspired him:[1] the direct evidence is in *Serse*, and the flower-seller's song, honoured frequently enough by reference but never by quotation, may be found below on page 138. The quality of rusticity achieved in *L'Allegro* and *Susanna* suggests that Handel was susceptible to the influence of folksong.[2] The sunny charm of

When first I saw my love-ly maid, be-neath the cit-ron's shade

and the Helston Furry excitement of

Come, Come, thou god-dess fair and free, fair and free, In
Heav'n y-clep'd Eu phro-sy-ne

summarize this aspect of Handelian universality. The merry bells of *Saul* have already been heard: in later contrast come the thunderous peals of ominous profundity which darken the canvas in 'Envy, eldest born of Hell' and threaten the wicked with a horrific *Dies irae* prospect. *L'Allegro* places all sorts of bells in happy neighbourhood: there are the pleasant Sunday morning chimes of 'Or let the merry bells,' the rich urban ring of 'Populous cities,' the distant enchantment of the faintly heard curfew and the domestic jangle of the bellman's instrument of office. Clearly one might say *nullum tetigit quod non ornavit*.

The synoptic outlook of Handel, which is his most distinctive

---

[1] Lady Luxborough to Shenstone: 'The great Handel has told me that the hints of his very best songs have several of them been owing to the sounds in his ears of cries in the streets' (*Luxborough Correspondence*, 1775, p. 58).

[2] An Irish folksong, 'The poor Irish Boy,' appears in Handel's Fitzwilliam MSS.

quality, recalls Waller's epitaph on Ben Jonson: 'Mirror of poets! mirror of our age!' Therein we may leave the comprehensiveness of Handel temporarily suspended.

In a period so prolific as the eighteenth century supply and demand were particularly interdependent. The consideration of what Handel, or anybody else for that matter, wrote cannot be fully undertaken without some conception of the obligations laid upon them by society. When art functions actively in a community which regards some degree of artistic endeavour as normal rather than abnormal it is not unhealthy that those who pay the piper should take some responsibility for calling the tune. Frequently Handel outdistanced his patrons in imaginative exploration, but from time to time he called himself back to the standards required. What these standards were is defined by Burney at the outset of his *History*. His definitions may help us to discover to what extent Handel was representative of his age and to what extent he outgrew its limitations.

MUSIC is an innocent luxury, unnecessary, indeed, to our existence, but a great improvement and gratification of the sense of hearing. It consists, at present, of MELODY, TIME, CONSONANCE, and DISSONANCE.

By MELODY is implied a series of sounds more fixed, and generally more lengthened, than those of common speech; arranged with grace, and, with respect to TIME, of proportional lengths, such as the mind can easily measure, and the voice express. These sounds are regulated by a scale, consisting of tones and semitones; but admit a variety of arrangement as unbounded as imagination.

CONSONANCE is derived from a coincidence of two or more sounds, which being heard together, by their agreement and union, afford to ears capable of judging and feeling, a delight of a most grateful kind. The combination and succession of CONCORDS or SOUNDS in Consonance, constitute HARMONY; as the selection and texture of Single Sounds produce MELODY.

DISSONANCE is the want of that agreeable union between two or more sounds, which constitutes Consonance: in musical composition it is occasioned by the suspension or anticipation of some sound before, or after, it becomes a Concord. It is the DOLCE PICCANTE of Music, and operates on the ear as a poignant sauce on the palate: it is a zest, without which the auditory sense would be as much cloyed as the appetite, if it had nothing to feed on but sweets.

Of MUSICAL TONES the most grateful to the ear are such as are produced by the vocal organ. And, next to singing, the most pleasing kinds are those which approach the nearest to vocal; such as can be sustained, swelled, and diminished, at pleasure. Of these, the first in rank are such as the most excellent performers produce from the Violin, Flute, and Haut-bois. If it were to be asked what instrument is capable of affording the GREATEST EFFECTS? I should answer, the Organ; which can not only imitate a number of other instruments, but is so comprehensive as to possess the power of a numerous orchestra. It is, however, very remote from per-fection, as it wants expression, and a more perfect intonation.

With respect to EXCELLENCE OF STYLE AND COMPOSITION, it may perhaps be said that to practised ears the most pleasing Music is such as has the merit of novelty, added to refinement, and ingenious contrivance; and to the ignorant, such as is most familiar and common.

There, in a fair-sized nutshell, is a monument to the rational hedonism which Handel sought to serve.

It may be complained that morality, such as should surely fit a composer of oratorio, is ignored. Avison does something to fill this gap when he speaks of 'the peculiar Quality of Music to raise the *sociable* and *happy Passions,* and to *subdue* the *contrary ones.*' But a musician's first duty was to please: after that he could take a risk and, like Dr. Johnson and the B.B.C., try his hand at instruction through pleasure. The glory of Handel is that he worked through all these stages until he arrived by intelligible steps at the *ne plus ultra* of musical expression. This was because he worked in a style which had, so far as music ever can have, utilitarian significance. A utilitarian style, approved and generally understood by an intelligent and not insensitive community, is indivisible. Therefore opera and oratorio use the same language. A comparison may not be inapt with the architectural style of the Tudors wherein both God and man were served in the same homely, well-bred idiom.

CHAPTER X

At the beginning of the eighteenth century there was, as we under-stand it, no orchestra: there were instrumentalists who on occasion played together. Their function, both individually and collectively, was a subordinate one; to assist prandial conversation, to enliven the pageantry of city streets, to serve the gaiety of the dance, to enwrap the amorous excursions of royalty, to furnish pompous atmosphere for military display, to support ecclesiastical ceremony, to add zest to holiday and to sauce the conceit of operatic heroes and heroines. For each of these purposes music was necessary, and what in the way of players happened to be available was united in relative concord. This relativity varied from place to place, but a general deduction is that those were congenial days for players to whom faulty tonality came naturally. Cacophonous memories are contained in Avison's remark about 'the irremediable Disagreement of their [wind instru-ments] rising in their Pitch, while the others are probably falling.' [1] That strings had their limitations too is indicated by Corelli's protest against Handel's impatience. This episode immediately suggests that Handel had orchestral vision beyond what was then considered normal. But whatever his aspirations, he was constrained always to make the best use of the material to hand.

It is always the privilege of one generation to regard previous generations as barbaric. It happened in the eighteenth century, it happens to-day, and in no respect more markedly than when ears accustomed to the variegated effects of the modern orchestra meet that of Handel's day. To put that orchestra in perspective one must consider it from an eighteenth-century angle.

The first factor for realization is that then music possessed a unique sense of homogeneity. Sophistication had not so far progressed as to remove music from the focal position it should occupy in life in general. There was still apparent an Elizabethan or Jacobean

[1] Avison, op. cit., p. 114.

influence which contained music, despite the forward-looking aspiration of the virtuosic, within almost universal limits of comprehension. Airs from opera and oratorio with movements from concertos kept in agreeable spirits the patrons of Vauxhall, Ranelagh or Marylebone: the same works, together with divers suites, sonatas and lessons, found their way into the editions of Walsh, Arnold or Cluer, or else less expensively through supplements to the *Lady's* or the *Gentleman's Magazine,* to the hands of the Sophia Westerns of the countryside. Amateur music-making flourished so extensively that it was possible for teachers of instrumental music to make fortunes from their teaching, the flautist John Festing, for instance, leaving the sum of £8,000 as a monument to his industry.[1] It was also not regarded as improper by professional players that the quality should associate with them on equal terms. In country houses music was indulged in with such frequency that, were we to fall victim to jingoism, we should protest that English music in a practical way had a spirited reply to make to the Continent. James Harris at Salisbury and Fisher Littleton at Teddesley each had bands in which it is recorded that Handel used to play. Court Dewes, who married Mrs. Delany's sister and lived at Wellesbourne in Warwickshire, had a concert daily at which the vicar, presumably as a necessary part of his pastoral function, played the bass viol. Hogarth's 'Music Party' mixes tea-drinking, conversation, the cat's milk and music in the proportions which might have been expected at Mrs. Delany's. A later picture by Zoffany shows the Sharp family making water music. In the eighteenth century it was difficult to escape the sound of music, and so much energy being apparent in its culture compels the opinion that it was then more likely to be understood than when, as in the succeeding century, musicians were regarded as 'ingenious puppets, sir, who live in a box and look out on the world only when it is gaping for amusement.'

The variety of instruments used by Handel in combination related to the improvisatory character of performances of the time. Whether in private house or theatre, there were always differences in the number and quality of instruments available; but this factor of uncertainty partly led to the mastery achieved by Handel over the

[1] Every English town had its concert society at this period.

orchestral forces at his disposal. The variety met with in his scores may be gathered from a survey of selected works. In the autograph copy of *Messiah* strings, trumpets and drums are employed (a harpsi/ chord should be taken as constant in every score, whether expressly indicated or not); in 1759 the Foundling Hospital noted with un/ common precision the number of players involved in a *Messiah* per/ formance—and a new scoring is apparent: twelve violins, three 'tenners,' three cellos, two double basses, four hautboys, four bassoons, two horns, two trumpets, kettledrums and organ. In *Esther* pro/ vision was made for flutes, hautboys, bassoons, theorbo, harp [1] and organ. In *Orlando* are used *violette marine, per gli Signori Castrucci.* *Alexander's Feast* has three bassoon parts, *Alexander Balus* a mando/ line, the *Fireworks* music a double bassoon, and *Saul* three trombones. In *Semele* there is a thrilling 'thunder' symphony for drums alone. Thus archaic and startlingly modern effects stand side by side. Handel, as will be seen, was a founder of modern orchestral music, and if we ignore his manipulation of different *ensembles* in performance we lose a great part of his music. With him each player or singer has a potentiality not to be disregarded in the working/out of his plot, and where his genius for transmuting the conventional into the extra/ ordinary appears most prominently is in his orchestration.

The prestige of an instrumentalist was lower than that of a successful singer; consequently the names of the majority of Handel's orchestral performers are lost in anonymity. Nevertheless some re/ main. Of violinists the most celebrated were William Corbett, Bannister, Carbonelli, Castrucci, Veracini, Pasquali, Michael Festing, John Clegg, Richard Charke, Defesch and Richard Collet. Caporale, Pasqualino, Filippo ('Pippo') Mattei—one of the *Muzio Scevola* collaborators—Abaco and the long/nosed and long/lived Cervetto established the cello. Caporale was a notably expressive player, Cervetto and Pasqualino technically finished but tonally raw. The great flautists were Lœillet, Jack Festing and Weide/ mann. Among oboists we hear of Kytsch, San Martini, Galliard and Richard Vincent, among bassoonists Karba, Lampe, Hebden and Miller, while the surpassing trumpeter was Valentine Snow,

[1] See Edward Jones, *Musical and Poetical Relicks,* 1784, p. 27.

sergeant trumpeter in the king's service. Most of these players performed on more than one instrument, so that, in the case of a special instrument being required for an exceptional effect, changes were made in performance in similar manner to that familiarized by the modern dance-band musician. Some of them were also composers. There could have been few complaints concerning lack of employ-ment. The king's band, the theatres, the pleasure gardens, Hickford's Music Rooms, the taverns and private clients gave as much work as most had time for.

Music which may be supposed to have been 'popular' is recorded in this programme of Carbonelli's benefit concert in 1722 [1] (the division into acts signifies the omnipotence of operatic design):

Act I. A new concerto for two trumpets, composed and performed by *Grano* and others; a new concerto by *Albinoni*, just brought over; song by Mrs. *Barbier*; concerto composed by Signor *Carbonelli*.

Act II. A concerto with two hautbois and two flutes, composed by *Dieupart*; a concerto on the base-violin by *Pippo*; song, Mrs. *Barbier*; by desire, the eighth concerto of *Arcangelo Corelli*.

Act III. Concerto by *Carbonelli*; solo on the arch-lute by Signor *Vebar*; song, Mrs. *Barbier*; a new concerto on the little flute, composed by *Wood-cock,* and performed by *Baston*; solo, Signor *Carbonelli*; and for *finale,* a concerto on two trumpets by *Grano*, etc.

It is not specified how long this concert lasted, but it is evident that the virtuosic and the bizarre were principal attractions. In 1729 the hearts of those who revelled in these qualities must have been gladdened by the appearance of one Joachim Frederic Creta, who at several concerts 'blew the first and second treble on two French-horns, in the same manner as is usually done by two persons.' It is to be regretted that this singular art died with its creator.

Handel dealt tactfully, from an artistic point of view, with singers, leaving them their exhibitionism but sublimating it to higher ends. In the same way he made use of the mechanical inventiveness of his instrumentalists while keeping in check their aptitude for music-hall display. And so their acrobatic feats fitted naturally into a more idealistic setting. Conspicuous examples are the trumpet parts, of which those to 'And the trumpet shall sound' and 'Let the bright

[1] Programme from the *Daily Courant,* quoted by Burney, *History,* iv. 648.

Seraphim' will be immediately familiar. Then there are the magnificent canonic entry at the beginning of the *Dettingen Te Deum* and the brief flourish which follows 'Thou shalt come to be our Judge':

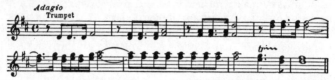

This latter is indicative of so many aspects of Handel that it merits closer attention. Obviously the trumpeters enjoyed it and so did the audience. On the other hand there is more to it than this simple equation of enjoyment. The passage is dramatically impressive. It halts the flow of *Te Deum* at the sombre and leaves the judicial vision of the hereafter poised in mid thought while by the association of ideas the crimson dignity of the assize court is evoked.

It will be remembered that Handel was a collector of pictures, that he had an eye as well as an ear. The conclusion drawn from his music at many points is that

whether life or nature be his subject . . . he has seen with his own eyes: he gives the image which he receives, not weakened or distorted by the intervention of any other mind: the ignorant feel his representations to be just, and the learned see that they are compleat.[1]

In music as in literature the classical theory of *mimesis* had particular validity in the eighteenth century. 'Every man's performance,' says Johnson, 'must be compared with the state of the age in which he lived, and with his own particular opportunities.' Therefore the response of Handel to the theory that music in general and orchestral music in particular held up the mirror to nature must now be considered.

There is, from our point of view, a naïveté in

[1] Johnson, *Preface to Shakespeare*.

in the bucolic

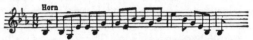

in the harp *obbligato* in 'Praise the Lord with cheerful noise' from *Esther*, in the murmurous insect life of *Israel in Egypt,* in the lute and flute dialogue of St. Cecilia's 'Soft complaining flute' and in countless similar descriptive passages. But such behaviour was part of the eighteenth-century stylistic convention. Avison, in summarizing contemporary thought, writes:

Thus Music, either by imitating these various Sounds (of Nature) in due Subordination to the Laws of *Air* and *Harmony*, or by any other Method of Association, bringing the Objects of our Passions before us (especially where those Objects are determined, and made as it were visibly, and intimately present to the Imagination by the Help of Words) does naturally raise a Variety of Passions in the human Breast, similar to the Sounds which are expressed. . . .[1]

By the side of this may be placed Mattheson's statement from *Der Musikalische Patriot*: 'All that produces an effect upon men is theatrical. . . . The whole world is a gigantic theatre.' The working out of this general theory brings us to the inevitable fact that 'there are various instruments suited to the different Kinds of musical Compositions.' Trumpets, horns, kettledrums are meet for 'the rough handling proper for Battles, Sieges, and whatever is great or terrible,'[2] while love, tenderness and beauty are the province of the lute or harp. Of descriptive sounds Avison comments first that

their Tendency is rather to fix the Hearer's Attention on the Similitude between the Sounds and the Things which they describe, and thereby to excite a reflex Act of the Understanding, than to affect the Heart and raise the Passions of the Soul.[3]

Yet such sounds are legitimate so long as the 'expression' is contained in the vocal line and the bird and allied noises are placed at a discreet distance in the accompanying parts. This was at Handel's expense. Handel could never refrain from giving his singers some share in the picturesque.

[1] Avison, op. cit., p. 4. [2] op. cit., pp. 30–1. [3] op. cit., p. 58.

It is difficult to see how the orchestra would have developed but for programmatic considerations, and Handel's large palette was in large measure, like those of Berlioz and Wagner, the result of the search for verisimilitudinous colour. Thus the little flute breaks into bird-song in *Riccardo I*; clarinets make tentative pastoral entry in *Tamerlano* (thirty years before, or thereabouts, Denner had produced the clarinet, although it was not until about 1770 that it became finally accepted as a member of the woodwind fraternity); the double bassoon, first made by Stanesby in 1739 and probably at Handel's suggestion, is introduced in *L'Allegro*; four horns exotically enhance the scoring of *Giulio Cesare*; three trumpets imperially add their ardour to the coronation music and to the *Dettingen Te Deum* (one marked 'Principal' indicates, according to Heinrich Christoph Koch,[1] a particular 'crashing (or martial) Style of performance, for which only the middle tones of this instrument are used'; three trombones are used majestically in *Saul*, a work which holds incredible fascination in its opulent instrumentation and the ready answer to those who ignorantly rail at the indifference of Handel's orchestral technique. Realism led Handel, who had a notable habit of following every idea to its logical conclusion, to anticipate Tchaikovsky in producing gun-fire as a musical climax. 'Handel,' wrote Mrs. Elizabeth Carter, 'has literally introduced firearms . . . and they have a good effect.' The reference was to *Judas Maccabaeus,* and the innovation was so startling as to provoke Sheridan at a later date to explain off-stage gun-shots thus: 'See, I borrowed this from Handel.'[2] It was not every one who approved these experiments: it was in fact a customary complaint that Handel made too much noise with his orchestra. Pope glances sidelong at the vogue for noisy theatrical effects in that passage in the *Dunciad* which begins:

> 'Tis yours to shake the soul
> With Thunder rumbling from the mustard bowl,
> With horns and trumpets now to madness swell,
> Now sink in sorrows with a tolling bell.

---

[1] Heinrich Christoph Koch, *Musikalisches Lexicon,* 1802. While on the subject of trumpets, it may be noted that in the *Rinaldo* march Handel uses four.

[2] In reference to *Jupiter*, a reworking of N. B. Halhed's *Ixion* (*c.* 1773).

This may or may not have some connection with Handel's zest for massive and unprecedented orchestral climaxes, but it does indicate how effects in drama and in music were of inspiring variety. The tendency towards extravagance was not confined to Handel, nor to England. 'One no longer hears the voice; the orchestra is deafening,' complained the conservatives in Germany.[1]

Before dismissing such criticism as unreasonable, it may be noted objectively that in general string tone was inadequate to cope with large additions of brass and woodwind: as a rule, about a dozen strings with harpsichord were expected to hold their own. Moreover, obscuration of the melodic line was regarded as an unpardonable offence against the canons of good taste, and without considerable augmentation of the string department such obscuration was at times inevitable.

The fact remains, however, that Handel was indicating progress in the employment of new combinations of colour. After directing attention to the mimetic a second factor supervenes. Avison laid down in brief that certain instruments were apt for certain forms of direct imitation; he also hinted at the attachment of other instruments to more indefinite and more philosophic ideas. Not that this represented anything new. In the Shakespearian theatre flutes made funereal impact on the mind; from the earliest times hautboys or their ancestors had stood for pastoral atmosphere; God, in the mystery plays, had been haloed by string tone. These ancient associations held point in the eighteenth century, as indeed they obviously do to-day; but Handel, with the keenest dramatic insight of his age, subtilized these general impressions. In so doing he urged romanticism from the wings.

'He was the first,' said Volbach, 'to assert the expressive personality of the violoncello.' Thus rich melancholy steals into *L'Allegro,* clad sombrely in cello and bassoon tone:

and sadness and virginity at a later point in the same work find sympathetic delineation in the voluptuous folds of a solo passage which any cellist would relish as an exercise in soulful dissertation. The viola was accepted in the eighteenth-century orchestra only on sufferance and it was the custom to insist on 'placing one of the worst hands to the Tenor,' much to Avison's annoyance. If Handel failed to raise this instrument to its true dignity, he did indicate the importance he attached to its particular timbre by withholding violins at the beginning of the second act of *Alexander's Feast* and by painting the ghostly with a dark combination of two violas, three bassoons, cello, basses and organ. In *Giulio Cesare* Caesar's 'Dall' ondoso periglio' is introduced with this dialogue in the strings:

Therein the viola receives more attention than was then common.

The gently suggestive use of woodwind colour is ubiquitous, and in such music as 'As steals the morn' in *L'Allegro*, where the oboe sings its own aubade, or 'Ferma l'ali' from *La Resurrezione*, where two flutes and muted violins undulate over a pedal, or in Oriane's 'Dolce vita' from *Amadigi*, where the picture of distressed beauty is thus delicately flavoured:

or in the colloquy between voice and oboe in Melissa's 'Ah! spietato!' from the same opera:

the delicacy of aquarelle invites an intimacy between performer and listener which is not apparent unless the fact that in Handel's day the orchestra had not left the domestic atmosphere of chamber music is realized.

At the opposite pole comes Handel's sense of tonal climax: instrument piled on instrument to achieve the golden enchantment of Parnassus in *Giulio Cesare*. Two orchestras are used with strings, oboes, harp, gamba, theorbo and bassoons. The music runs:

and then the second orchestra enters with answering phrase. The dramatic perfection of this movement lies less in the actual music than in the seductive colouring. Another point to be noted is that Handel was sensible that the numerical strength of the instruments employed was not necessarily in relation to the dynamic power intended. Mozart struck at the truth, even though by his supererogation he endeavoured to undermine it, when he observed 'Handel understands effect better than any of us—when he chooses, he strikes like a thunderbolt.' The last part of this has been remembered, the first part too often inconveniently forgotten. The mastery of effect was all-embracing.

As for the thunderbolts, we look for them chorally. But the massive trumpet climaxes which crown the full choral fury are overlooked, largely because they can never be heard. When they can they possess an Elgarian inevitability, as when they surprise the imagination in the Gloria of *Messiah* or when they anoint the regality of 'Thou hast set a crown of pure gold upon his head' in the first *Coronation Anthem,* or when, undarkened either by horns or trombones, they help the acclamation of 'God save the King.' With regard to his brass Handel had clear-cut ideas: trumpets were noble, horns—four of them at any rate—exotic, trombones priestly. The secret of their effectiveness lay in their rarity of appearance. When they did appear they were felt.

CHAPTER XI

CHAMBER MUSIC

THE essence of chamber music is domesticity. Handel wrote at a time when most music still retained something of its *camera* origins and for that reason, and because Handel was of amiable disposition in congenial company, his suites, sonatas and concertos are pleasantly evocative of fireside warmth. This is a great though often neglected quality, for when music loses its fraternal power to 'fetch out in smiles the mutual soul,' as Leigh Hunt wrote of it to Thomas Alsager, the graciousness of courteous hospitality is denuded of one of its chief agents. The proper setting for Handel's music, other than that obviously designed for public performance, was between Mrs. Delany's conversation and her mulled white wine: the two extremes of extemporaneous sagacity, wit and philosophy and discriminating hedonism. Music in the eighteenth century was disposed to stimulate pleasure, but an unwritten law decreed that pleasure should have such blend of intellectual and sensual appeal as became a set of comfortable eclectics. With the eclectics Handel was at home, and his music is monumental to his clubbableness; it is not esoteric like so much of Bach, nor shot with the febrile brilliance of Domenico Scarlatti, nor overrun with the tintinnabulations of the vulgar who, like the Rev. William Felton, had no more than 'a neat finger for common divisions and the rapid multiplication of notes,' but plainly pleasing.

It is symptomatic that the most eligible party piece for the not too precociously musical schoolgirl is the set of variations from the E major (No. 5) Suite (Set I, 1720), commonly miscalled *The Harmonious Blacksmith*. The long story of why this title and the attendant fable are mythical will do no good by repetition (a generation bred on Hollywood will be loth to believe that pretty inaptness in nomenclature is no great aid to musical appreciation), so let it simply be stated that there is no recorded instance of Handel's having had dealings with blacksmiths, harmonious or otherwise, at Edgware or anywhere else. The music of these variations is attractive to children, whose capacity for understanding Handel never underestimated. He worked hard to teach the Princesses Anne and Caroline the funda‚ mentals of musical practice and theory. Exercises to be worked by his royal pupils in a fairly rarefied harmonic and contrapuntal atmo‚ sphere are extant among Handel manuscripts in the Fitzwilliam Museum in Cambridge. Princess Louisa, youngest daughter of George II who married the King of Denmark and died tragically young in 1751, was also a favourite pupil, for whom Handel wrote the D minor and G minor harpsichord suites (nos. 6 and 7). As for the future George III, there is an anecdote from Southey relating how Handel, finding him when young a good listener, remarked, 'A good boy, a good boy, you shall protect my fame when I am dead.' This is what happened.

Some keyboard pieces betray a school‚room origin, but the majority have a strong personal quality. In the Prelude to the first Suite, in A major, the characteristic flourish of extemporization is represented in little more than a shorthand abstract. In the succeeding Allemande that gentle quality which, for want of a term of nearer precision, had best be defined as pastoral, demonstrates how much more musical thought meant to Handel than the implications of a set form. The suave counterpoint of the opening:

and the sinuosity of the last cadence:

have a cool French quality of rationalized whimsicality. The Courante has similar poise and recollects in its closing bars the particular note-disposition of the Allemande cadence. If inspiration fails, it is in the gigues of the harpsichord suites, which with their slickly tailored efficiency please once. An exception is the rum-bustiously percussive finale to the Suite in G minor (No. 6, Set II, 1733). This, unbuttoned and Beethovenian, is of more than normally generous proportion and elbows its rough way thus impulsively:

If this defeats the capacity of the harpsichord the same may be said of the Ouverture, also in G minor, to Suite VII (Set I). This intense prelude is too tragic for its context and suggests a sketch for some epic tale of high passion. Fuguing was a constant delight to Handel, but not as an exercise in academic rectitude. The purpose of a Handelian fugue was to demonstrate the personality of his subject. If students would learn how not to satisfy examiners they should model their counterpoint on that of Handel; if, however, they would realize the incentive to musical thought given by epigram they should study the suggestiveness of such themes as:

or the darkly anachronistic romanticism of the second movement of the Suite in F minor (No. 8, Set I). The third fugue in the set of six published in 1735, which also furnishes most of the Sinfonia to the Passion of 1716, gives further publicity to the St. Anne motif and, underlining the common sources of eighteenth-century musical diction, emphasizes the dangers of recognizing personal influence by fortuitous thematic coincidence.

Those who have looked at the suites will realize that often as between movement and movement there is some philosophic connection which imposes a sense of unity on what would otherwise be a collection of heterogeneous fragments. This is not simply a matter of key consistency, but an offshoot of Handel's fertile dramatic ability to present problems and situations with comprehension. An interest in the dramatic capacity of melody led inevitably to experiment with *Leitmotive*. The possibilities of this artificial aid to consistency were foreseen tentatively long before Handel's day, in fact the folksong⸝dependent mass⸝writers of the sixteenth century were first in this field; but Handel had a habit of anticipating Berlioz and Wagner in so many other respects that this practice, not fundamentally of the eighteenth century, cannot pass without notice. In Handel's case, however, it may often be attributed to accident rather than design. Thematic identity at the outset of successive movements, such as occurs in Suite 4 (Set I):

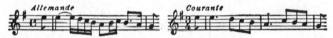

suggests the improviser calculating the future plan of development while automatically delivering what remains fresh in the mind. Sometimes, on the other hand, thematic reiteration comes as the result of deliberation: the most effective instance being in the 'Se mai turbo' duet in *Poro*, 'in which the lovers, Porus and Cleosilda, are ironically repeating the former promises which they had made to each other of fidelity and confidence.'[1]

In contrast to this subtlety lies the conservatism which generally pervades Handel's use of variations. Here too often the volant finger has little to proclaim except its own dexterity. Here and there, however, a masculine perversity recalls the acidulous flavour of the Elizabethan virginalists. The Chaconne in F is thus antiquely reminiscent, while elsewhere, and particularly in the organ concertos, monotony is relieved by Chippendale delicacy. Variations were to Handel a recreation. High seriousness he reserved for opera and oratorio, though accidents sometimes happened and let into the drawing⸝room an occasional glimpse of tragedy; and the ground basses which symbolize intensity of feeling in *Poro, Orlando, Hercules* and *Saul* demonstrate Handel's outlook on the relative functions of

[1] Burney, *History*, iv. 351.

opera and oratorio on the one hand and domestic music on the other.

This sense of fitness for purpose is one of the keys to Handel's omnipotence. It was not that opera and oratorio had a higher sanction than chamber music, but that when they were performed there was more likelihood of listening being more attentive than in the case of that homely music which entered the one ear not engaged in the absorption of whispered scandal. From all accounts Quin was a mighty Lear, but conversely he was a delicious raconteur. Handel had the same zest for rich expression, and the necessary complement to profundity may be discovered in the violin sonatas, supposedly written for Dubourg or his pupil, the Prince of Wales, or the flute or oboe sonatas, and in the various works for trio, most of which were grist to Walsh's mill. Of these works it may be said that they implicitly express approval of Telemann's 'Wer auf Instrumenten spielt muss des Singens kundig seyn.'[1] Otherwise they impress by high technical competence and by mellifluence which jointly predominate over imaginative adventure.

In the smaller chamber works there are many instances of recollection or anticipation of ideas familiarized in other settings. The 1735 collection of fugues presents those which fit horrifically into *Israel in Egypt* ('He smote all the first-born in Egypt' and 'They loathed to drink of the river'); the *Allegro* of the violin Sonata in D major appears symphonically in *Jephtha*; 'Why so full of grief' from the sixth Chandos anthem is reflected in the first of the 1733 trio sonatas and the fourth of the 1738 set remodels the overture to *Athalia*.

The organ concertos are properly to be regarded as among the chamber works, and it is now no longer necessary, perhaps, to indicate what effect this should have on their presentation. The largest organs of the eighteenth century, in England at any rate, where choral singing was well able to dispense with massive accompanimental support, were slight of build, clear-voiced, bright-eyed with mutation work, effective in contrast with the string ensemble and accordingly acceptable in theatre or house as well as in church. Pedal boards were rare in England; that they were not altogether unknown is shown by Handel's note that pedals should be

[1] Whoever plays an instrument must be conversant with singing.

used in Concerto I of the second (1740) set. In general, the style of writing for the organ was that proper for the harpsichord. In relation to modern interpretation this suggests a reduction of tone colour to near conformity with eighteenth century standards. This makes evident the integrity of the melodic line, the delicacy of contrast and ornamentation, the gentle persuasiveness of the orchestral scoring (how eloquently flutes and oboes can maintain silence!) and the intimate dialogue. The fifth concerto of Op. 4 was a transcription of a recorder sonata (Op. 1, no. 11) and it is helpful to bear this in mind in preparing a performance. The sixth concerto of the same set was the work popularized by the harpist Powell, a Welshman whose popularity at the court of George II and association with Handel were attested by Edward Jones in *Musical and Poetical Relicks of the Welsh Bards*. In both cases the quality of chamber music that characterizes the organ concertos is emphasized by origin and affiliation.

'Our Composers,' said Avison,[1] 'have run all their concertos into little else than tedious Divisions.' The unsympathetic may hold this generalization to Handel and suspect that it applies. But once again it is necessary to view the matter from an eighteenth century angle: then purpose will begin to appear. Concertos were an exhibition of skill (presumably they still are) into which the orchestra entered as a foil to pyrotechnic display. This display often stood out in a strong light because the concertos were, as Avison remarks, generally under rehearsed. Concertos in which the solo instrument was the organ and in which the soloist was Handel were different in one important respect. They were conceived as ancillary to a larger scheme, as intermissions in oratorio. Therefore while the concerto relieved the tension of the oratorio plot its technical flights were projected against a particular background. Thus the divisions never ran out of control.

The organ concertos were works of maturity. Op. 4 was published in 1738; Op. 7 in 1740.[2] They accordingly carry the flexibility conspicuous in all Handel's later music. Normally they possess four movements, but the length and character of each move-

---

[1] op. cit., p. 120.   [2] A third set appeared posthumously.

ment varies from work to work. A significant step in the direction of poetry is indicated by the frequent tendency to emphasize the slow movements at the expense of the more or less formal allegros. It is evident that these works were approved. Hawkins leaves this tribute:

When he gave a Concerto, his method in general was, to introduce it with a Voluntary movement on the Diapasons, which stole on the ear in a slow and solemn progression; the harmony close wrought, and as full as could possibly be expressed; the passages constructed with stupendous art; the whole, at the same time, being perfectly intelligible, and having the appearance of great simplicity. This kind of prelude was succeeded by the Concerto itself, which he executed with a degree of spirit and firmness that no one even pretended to equal. Such, in general, was the manner of his performance; but who shall describe its effects on his enraptured auditory? Silence, the truest applause, succeeded, the instant that he addressed himself to the instrument; and that was so profound, that it checked respiration, and seemed to controul the functions of nature [whatever that may mean!], while the magic of his touch kept the attention of his hearers awake only to those enchanting sounds to which it gave utterance.[1]

It remains to detail the enchantment. As for a 'slow and solemn progression,' there is none of greater beauty than the opening *Larghetto* of the concerto in F major (No. 5, Set I): here is the consummation of simplicity. Of almost equal simplicity, but of more profound feeling, is this enhanced repetition of the opening bars of the *Largo, e piano* from the B flat major concerto (No. 1, Set II), a movement which follows the sober optimism of the first *Andante* in the remoteness of D minor:

The preceding movement, in two sections, is a free fantasia on this commonly used bell motiv:

which serves as an impressive ground.   Another interesting ground⁄ bass treatment occurs in the G minor concerto (No. 5, Set II), where the Olympian tread of the octave⁄spacing continues from beginning to end of the *Andante larghetto, e staccato,* the only relief lying in the counterpoint in the organ.   That the orchestra was more than a sleeping partner becomes apparent when in the twelve⁄bar *Adagio* of the G minor concerto (No. 3, Set I) a *concertino* carries more or less extravagant modulations in contrast both to the organ and the *ripieno,* when in the D minor concerto (No. 4, Set II) veiled melan⁄ choly is enshrined thus:

or when in the last little concerto of the first set the organ is alterna⁄ tive to the harp, the violins are muted, the lower strings are *pizzicato* and flutes are added to a Botticellian atmosphere of fair⁄weather ingenuousness.   For the sake of completion it should be added that precisely what we most desire, Handel's extemporized cadenzas, are lost for ever.   A concerto without its embellishments and with sub⁄ sequent editorial accretions is as near the original as is a medieval church stripped of its wall paintings and made to look dismally religious by pitch pine and garish glass.

The surprising variety of orchestration suggested in the organ concertos is evident throughout Handel's larger⁄scale chamber works. The reason was the different conditions which prevailed when the works were written. The six *Concerti Grossi* (Op. 3), written *c.* 1716–22 but associated with the royal wedding celebrations of 1734, used flutes, oboes, bassoons and strings disposed in the normally contrasting arrangement of *concertino* and *ripieno*. The open-air music, that for the *Water Music* and the *Royal Fireworks,* naturally lays more insistence on the wind. More or less experimental combinations exist in various sketches. An organ concerto with choral termination, intended for the 1737 revival of *The Triumph of Time and Truth*; a concerto for two *concertini,* each consisting of two horns, two oboes and a bassoon, and supported with the customary string ensemble; concertos for trumpets and horns and for horns and side-drums. But the crowning works in concerto form are the great set written in 1739 and published as Op. 6.

In these works it is tempting to see the peak of Handel's creative genius. Elsewhere the flame of inspiration may leap momentarily higher, but nowhere else has consistency of imaginative thought so triumphal a progress. It is generally evident that Handel was on good terms with his orchestral players (it is encouraging to find no anecdotes to suggest the contrary). Understanding their point of view—after all, Handel started life as a fiddler at Hamburg—he was able to maintain that subtle balance between all departments which pleases the players and likewise the audience. With no more than strings and *continuo* a wealth of light and shade is achieved by the subtle interplay of *concertino* and *ripieno*. Elgar follows the pattern with magnificent fidelity to Handelian ideals in the *Introduction and Allegro* and underlines the lesson of the concertos that economy in material leads to amplification of musical thought. This economy imposes one sort of unity on the *Concerti grossi*: key relationship (in allowing the principal key to dominate all the movements Handel was following Corelli); and another, larger unity: that of action or idea. This is apparent in performance where any one of the concertos impresses as a complete essay and not, as in the case of so many suites, as a series of heterogeneous items thrown into accidental contiguity. It is not quite satisfactory to contain, as Romain Rolland does, the music within objective limits by the erection of somewhat arbitrary concrete imagery. More philosophically it may be suggested that each concerto concerns itself with one facet of the pattern of life, and that what variety is apparent rises from cognate impressions associated with the central idea.

This centrality of outlook, the capacity for representing largely and truthfully one aspect of the universal, is the supreme mark of greatness, and if Handel and Beethoven are to be in any way associated, as by Beethoven's admission they should,[1] it is by referring the concertos to Beethovenian standards of expression. Frequently in his overtures Handel leads us to suppose that the introductory slow movement is more than a conventional curtain-raiser: here are two quotations which contain in little space the conviction that the prelude was of parallel importance with its companion movements:

The tremendous rhythmic vigour here contained is urged insistently throughout the respective movements, the first declining into the mystery of this coda:

the second sweeping into spacious scale progressions cousinly to those in the first movement of Beethoven's seventh Symphony.

Writing fugues was not Handel's forte; writing fugally was. The contrapuntist who won early respect from Mattheson spreads himself throughout the *Concerti grossi*, although not in the construction of school fugues. In the last movement of the second Concerto the subject walks briskly through its exposition until halted by the ingenuousness of:

which the *concertino* projects against a plain chordal background in the accompanying parts. The two ideas eye each other like a couple of unintroduced mongrels and finally join together in boisterous merry-making which happens to involve double invertible counterpoint. The principal subject—Handel favoured fugues with two subjects—of the *Andante* of the third Concerto has Bachian tautness and resolves its dolours into a passionate climax of great power:

The whole of this Concerto is cast in severity, the prevailing darkness of the colouring being emphasized by the delicate detail of the *Polonaise*, the bright robe of which sets off the grief of the *mater dolorosa*. The *Allegro* shows the forward-looking Handel engaged in rough violation of all the accepted clauses relating to key change:

This ellipsis is characteristic, as in the eighth Concerto the *Andante* shows:

while the *Grave* proceeds with similar brusqueness from one scene to another:

This last passage contains the clue to the process. In choral music of the older schools such abruptness had grown naturally out of the juxtaposition of unrelated triads. Handel borrowed the idea, used it frequently and with majestic effect in his choral music, and translated it orchestrally. His harmonic sense led him to pursue courses which are effective by their unexpectedness. In the fifth Concerto the pedal-points of the second movement and the nine consecutive bars of tonic seventh, dangerously near the end, in the third movement speak with picturesque accent on romanticism. Students of elementary harmony may like to take up a set of consecutive fifths from the third bar of the *Minuet* in the ninth Concerto and inquire of their tutors wherein lies the crime.

Ingenuity in harmony and counterpoint should not blind us to the fact that Handel's chief blessing was a capacity for containing his text in a single line of melody. Apprenticeship to the theatre had taught that intensity of thought had more significance when memorably placed within the scope of the melodically minded listener. But melody gets pushed out to the limits. Wide intervals indicate mystery in the first movement of the ninth Concerto and wild spirits in the fifth movement of the fifth Concerto. In contradistinction, however, Handel can turn a one-note subject, as in the second section of the seventh Concerto, into a matter for jesting. This comic fugue terminates with cellos and basses wagging their bows over the diminution of minim to crotchet and crotchet to quaver.

The attention to landscape detail so familiar in the oratorios and the operas pervades the concertos, so that in the *Andante larghetto* of the eleventh Concerto this is placed after an opening of vigorous octave strides:

and a little later another corner is turned to reveal the insistent chatter of

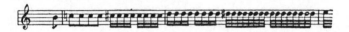

The truth is that tunes cropped up as if by accident, and where Handel had only meant a servant-boy episode he set a Sam Weller on an irresistible career.

CHAPTER XII

CHARACTERIZATION

FROM his biography it is clear that Handel was a realist. From his music a similar deduction, though with a certain difference in emphasis, may be drawn. In general his music had close association with the façade of life, being in seven cases out of ten concerned with more or less obvious description. From a Platonic point of view what we receive may be twice removed from reality, but despite that we conceive a fresh and vital reality of a new musical order. The purpose of music has defied the efforts of philosophy and theology to discover it. The most we may with certainty conclude is that it deals with the antithesis of ideas. In abstract music (this arbitrary term is here used on account of its relative convenience in definition), such as Bach's *Art of Fugue* or Mozart's G minor Symphony, the motivating ideas are of purely musical significance. It will be remembered that Berlioz to show his distaste for Handel dragged in a reference to a 'tub of pork and beer': a phrase which intends rudeness but points complimentarily to the *nihil humani alienum puto* thesis which is the substance of this chapter. The Russian writer referred to earlier claims Handel as a people's composer. The non-ideological side of this thought will be endorsed by the least musical, who will explain that the only music which for them has significance is Handel's. The incredible influence Handel holds, ruefully we must confess by means of the one or two fragments which duly pass from school hall to parish hall and from parish hall to town hall, is indicative of a particular capacity for understanding human nature. This came from an observation not of what people wanted, but of what people were, and are. Whether Handel succeeded in passing through the stages enumerated in the *Symposium* to arrive at ultimate goodness and beauty is a matter of opinion; what is certain is his shrewd observation of the world around him. Not only was he gifted in observation, but also in narrative expression, which being easeful and friendly breeds familiarity.

There were few crimes of greater magnitude in the eighteenth century than that of unsociability; therefore the easiest way to mis-understand Handel is to regard him as a detached creature addicted to supernal communion. Romantic anecdotes, in single setting assuming alarming significance, about the tears which accompanied the parturition of the Messianic Hallelujah disguise the fact that Handel was rarely at ease with God and sought general inspiration from what was epigrammatically considered the proper study of mankind.

It has already been indicated that music in the eighteenth century had greater relevance to everyday life than has been the case since. Thus in the most typical of eighteenth-century composers we should unravel part of the intelligence of the music by consideration of this point in its most graphic expression.

Handel left no diary and only a handful of polite letters, but a solitary inscription in one of his sketch-books to be found in the Fitzwilliam Museum has some compensatory value. The psycho-logist may care to enlarge on its significance: here it is sufficient to draw attention to the secret of well-oiled counterpoint, to the mental contiguity of work and play, and to the bachelorly preoccupation with details of hospitality (unless we accept Abram Brown's sugges-tion of addiction to secret drinking) which speak through this terse memorandum:

> 12 Gallons Port
> 12 Bottles French   Duke Street
>   Meels.

Handel engaged in decanting the port, in handing it round, in genial conversation, preludes the optimistic philosophy which imbues his music with infectious confidence, good nature and tolerance. And such convivial intimacy gave precisely those opportunities for observation which, from a wordly point of view, elude the more pietistic. And then supervenes the direction of Handel's education in opera and his own natural enthusiasm for that form of expression.

An opera is a story about people and their emotions intensified through the use of music. What people happen to be called on the stage is immaterial: what they are in fact are projections of the personality and emotional excitement of the audience which attends the opera. The heroic puffs up the manly breast; the villainous attracts anger or else that sneaking affection for daring wickedness which we all entertain; beauty provokes wonderment; distress draws tears; and so we might proceed through the gamut of conventional opera types. In more senses than one audience and actor were closer together in the eighteenth century than to-day, and Handelian audiences were fully competent to rival the players in histrionic endeavour. Thus, although the horseplay would have tried the patience of the earnest, there was a directness in approach to the project of opera which by-passed academic philosophies and took all that we may lecture about as read. The main requisites were colour, novelty, hot emotion and virtuosity: the requisites in fact of any popular art whose existence is dependent on satisfaction in the box office. Handel's triumph and failure were due to his practice of achieving more than was expected from him, but because he did this he rose above his environment and left for posterity an enlargement of the better attributes of contemporary outlook. This he did by avoiding writing with deliberation for posterity and by keeping his finger on the public pulse.

FitzGerald refers to Handel as 'a good old pagan at heart' and, in tacit agreement with Leigh Hunt, who makes kindly observation on his Theocritan aptitude for dropping milk and honey, puts a pen accurately on the side of truth when writing:

I think Handel never gets out of his wig, that is, out of his age: his Hallelujah Chorus is a chorus, not of angels, but of well-fed earthly choristers, ranged tier above tier in a Gothic cathedral, with princes for audience, and their military trumpets flourishing over the full volume of the organ. Handel's gods are like Homer's, and his sublime never reached beyond the region of the clouds.[1]

Bach invaded the *Himmelreich*; Handel found *Lebensraum* on earth. The fact is clear if Handel's music is regarded as a whole. Operas, oratorios and other works of cognate character form an immense

---

[1] FitzGerald wrote this after seeing Macready's stage revival of *Acis and Galatea* in 1847.

portrait gallery and an inexhaustible fund of carefully catalogued human emotion. For reasons which will in due course be made apparent oratorio provided a better framework for extended psycho‹ logical study, but opera was the first experimental laboratory. Unless the nature of Handel's operatic style is in some way understood the oratorios are lacking in point.

The people whom Handel was initially constrained to represent were of a conventional type. Kings and princes of a most excellent goodness, in the portrayal of whom a careful eye was cocked court‹ wards, for the seventeenth‹century habit of incidental flattery had not entirely passed out; bad kings and princes, who were possibly Jacobites in disguise; beauty in distress; sorcerers and sorceresses whose presence was often necessary for the smooth operation of the improbabilities which had to culminate in happy endings; occasional retainers, prophets, priests and warriors. It was the greatness of Handel to turn these vehicles of varied aria—*cantabile, di portamento, di mezzo carattere, parlante, di bravura* or *d'imitazione*—and recitative into people.

If Handel's characters sometimes stand stiff‹jointed and stylized, it is because such behaviour was expected and because had this connection with normality been ignored the operas would have suffered immediate relegation to the realm of impracticability. As it was, differences of opinion with singers and audience led to the ill acceptance of much of the finest music. But when Handel's people pose they do so with magnificent full‹blooded theatricality. The angel of *La Resurrezione* ends with Grinling Gibbons florescence the aria 'Disserratevi, oh porte d'Averno!' thus:

2 Trumpets & Strings

Almirena strikes the heroic in *Rinaldo* in what George Eliot would have called the 'mechanical dramatic' manner:

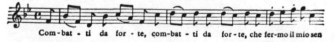

Com-bat - ti da for - te, com-bat - ti da for - te, che fer-mo il mio sen

and Galatea trails self-pity behind her like a representation of Rossettian charm.

The end-stopped theatrical presentation of personality was inevitable so long as Handel referred to the conventions by which recitative, although Keiser had educated him in the dramatic possibilities latent herein, and aria fulfilled the functions of plain narration on the one hand and onomatopoeic virtuosity on the other, while the incongruity of *da capo* provided a further handicap. But despite these obstacles Handel rarely leaves his characters solely mechanical. Into his arias he pours corpuscular energy, an achievement rare in the fluent Buononcini or in any other contemporary composer. For the most part it is possible to dislike Handel's feather-brained heroines—as helpless in the grip of circumstance as any of Hardy's—but, for all their supine resignation, they are attractive in lineament, and in their decorative subordination they reflect something of the eighteenth-century attitude towards women. Representative heroines of this order are the pallid Magdalena of *La Resurrezione,* the child-like Asteria of *Tamerlano,* the vapid Queen of *Solomon* and the obedient Merab of *Saul.* In depicting these women Handel seizes on the obvious, achieves skilful and apt portraiture, but hardly touches subtlety. On a first hearing this static quality may seem to define all Handelian characters: royalty has its vocabulary of apposite dignity: the hieratic, as in Valens in *Theodora* or that impressive song of the Levite in *Solomon,* 'Praise ye the Lord,' its Anglo-Catholic poise of cultured superiority; while braggarts storm in the same strain of cheerful anger from Argante to Harapha. To continue this catalogue is merely to indicate that, as all Handel's characters are in some measure self-projective, a family likeness is not to be unexpected.

The excuse of narrative, whether in drama, in literature or in dramatically conditioned music, is that emotional behaviour is naturally settled by the tendencies of plot. In the period under review the plot as such was subsidiary to the circumstances evolved by its often ductile meanderings. Sterne, Richardson, Fielding, Smollett and clearly Hogarth concerned themselves with the kaleidoscope of life, and in selecting incidents from their *milieu* endeavoured to portray faithfully what they saw, what was, rather than what they thought ought to be. This latter was left to the imagination of the beholder. Handel's music was complementary to the art of the above-mentioned, and his strength must lie in his capacity to express his sensibility to human passion. The moral purpose which he began to experience towards the end of his life was the natural outcome of extensive observation, a development of sympathy with what he described, and that attractive brotherliness which Leigh Hunt ascribed to Abou Ben Adhem.

What happened to Polissena in *Radamisto* is neither here nor there, but her anguish of soul, the result of her husband's attachment to Zenobia, is thus portrayed:

There is a universality about this which immediately makes the turgid plot development irrelevant and provokes sympathy with the victim of misfortune whoever she may be. Burney remarks somewhere that no one could use octave and unison passages with such effect as Handel. The rests, the melodic intervals, the ambiguous tonality of Polissena's opening are all symptomatic of the complex simplicity which Handel used in moments of strained emotion. In *Floridante* Orante similarly speaks agonizingly through the terseness of

This form of direct repetition links the Handelian style of musical development with that of twentieth-century practice: the fundamental

idea is represented in one short and pregnant theme which then
impresses the listener not by evolution in the academic way, but
by stark alliteration. Of this habit no more expressive example can
be found than in the accompaniment to the 'Monster Atheist' of
Saul. Accompaniment is the wrong term: the more intense Handel's
thought the more coalescently vocal and instrumental parts unite in
balanced symmetry. It was this insistence on the necessity for
orchestral partnership which led Handel into trouble with his contemporaries, but the truth is that his vision looked forward to a new
form of expression. Tolomeo's 'Stille amare,' for instance, is not so
much a song as a tone-poem the opening of which

leaves in the unsubstantial terms of pure music what Tolomeo endeavours, in inchoate mixture of recitative and aria and with death on
his lips, to put into coherence. On the side of tragedy Dejanira's
'Where shall I fly,' in *Hercules*, Samson's 'Total Eclipse' and
Orlando's mad scene are the most penetrating and awe-inspiring
examples of Handel's capacity for uncovering the raw nerve-centres
of mental agony. Sheer despair, haunting and spectral fear, mad
desires translate the personality from humanity to bestiality or to
primeval chaos. Dejanira expels her evil spirits. Orlando passes
the region of reclamation except for the intervention of magic. Once
again bare octaves suffice to carry the voice; once again the music is
peremptorily occupied in reiteration; and for the first time in history
the time-signature 5–8 appears. The catastrophic passage, so frequent
in reference and so rare in appearance, stands thus:

Was it prevision of personal misfortune or simply the observation of kindled imagination which prompted this anachronistic *scena*? The craft is superb. Mental affliction crosses recitative and aria, ebbs to exhaustion through the healing influence of the 'Vaghe pupille' gavotte and finally reposes Orlando in troubled sleep over the time-honoured motif of chromatically descending ground-bass. The return to sanity is achieved through the mediation of Zoroaster. Necromancy plays its superficial part, but the emotional picture is larger than the obvious limits of opera allow. Handel comes near, at this juncture, to the fundamental and unanswerable problems of life and death. Both in matter and manner there is an occasional tinting of Elgar. While Orlando is tossed into unhappy uncertainty the beneficent powers are arranging his release from suffering, the high priest officiates pontifically with solemn appeal to the unknown gods:

and supernatural agents bring restorative to the shadowy beauty of this soothing interlude:

The music for this scene is one of the more profound essays in characterization in the whole of Handel. But one point remains abundantly clear: Handel judged not his fellow men, but extended to them the full warmth of his sympathy. It is this sympathy, coupled with an abiding affection, which embraces all the moods in which we find the figures of opera and oratorio. Old age in mellowed serenity in the 'Nel riposo' of *Deidamia* or in the Manoah music of *Samson*; spirited chaperonage in the two Irenes of *Tamerlano* and *Theodora*; leafy amorousness in Dorinda's music at the beginning of the second act of *Orlando*; the bucolic jollity of Hercules; the apt representation of Ben Jonson's bluster in *L'Allegro*; even the *sic semper tyrannis* of Haman in *Esther* or of Tiridate in *Radamisto*; and the below-stairs comedy of *Serse* and *Almira*. The grateful antidote to the commonplace thesis that Handel principally enjoyed pious occupation in the production of endless Hallelujahs for the faithful is Elviro's Mozartian (albeit the cries of London exude in springtime vivacity) flower-selling song from *Serse*:

Ah! chi vo-le fior - a di bel - la giar-di - na chi vo-le fior - a di bel-la giar-di - na gia - cin-ta, in-di-an-a, tu-li- pa-na, gel-so-mi-na, gia-cin-ta, in-di-an-a, tu-li- -pa-na. Ah! —

The student of Handel will be readily able to add to this list of varied character studies and in so doing he will realize Handel's kinship with the diarist. But Handel was not only a diarist, he was a dramatist, and drama depends on the relationship evolved between one character and another. Because he was not satisfied in leaving his people in splendid isolation Handel proceeded to bring them into a psychological relationship typical of Mozart and to divest the opera of its more obvious function of providing a concert in fancy dress. Love-making, for the benefit of those who read autobiography in every bar, did not rouse Handel to considerable enthusiasm. But when jealous suspicion and possible infidelity appear the music warms up to the pitch of painful realism evident in the duets between Porus and Cleosida or Samson and Delilah. In *Rinaldo* and *Teseo* there are masterly contrasts between the two women in each opera, who respectively duel with each other over the possession of the men. In *Hercules* Iole and Dejanira are similarly brought together, but with greater subtlety, and their unsought rivalry is projected against a more significant background wherein the mutability of human nature and the vicious turns of inexorable fate are tragically intermingled. And at the climactic moment the shadow overhanging the scene takes recognizable shape as the chorus, that element which Handel required to fulfil his dramatic intentions with complete fidelity, after the foreboding of an octave introduction utters:

One more example of Handel's psychological insight must suffice. It is in that scene in *Solomon* where the two women appear: impudent harlotry and rich motherhood can rarely have had such representation.

This counterpoint of ideas is turned into triple counterpoint by the presence of Solomon, whose judicial behaviour at this point is perfect. To present three or more strands of thought simultaneously is the most involved problem in musical drama. Handel achieved the trio in *Acis and Galatea*, the quartets in *Radamisto, Semele* and *Jephtha*, all of which would appear superb at any period, but incredible in an age when such extravagantly truthful demonstrations of human frailty and perplexity were regarded as improper interpolations in an evening's enjoyment.

The libretti with which Handel had to deal were frequently of infuriating puerility, but they served as incentive to the composer to recreate from his imagination the types of personality there collected.

Characters and situations were so arranged in Handel's capacious and orderly mind that they were ready for any contingency: hence the speed of execution receives additional sanction. The operas were often episodic—the plots were to blame for this; the oratorios hardly ever. In general the texts on which he worked for oratorio composition possessed a singleness of direction never evident in the complex organization of the eighteenth-century opera; moreover, and this will receive amplification in a later chapter, the introduction of the chorus enabled additional matter relevant to the argument and impossible of mention by the principal characters to be adduced. The main difference between opera and oratorio lies in the capacity of the latter form to show not only isolated moments of inspired characterization but continuity in emotional development. Samson remains Samson through all vicissitudes and is musically recognizable at any given moment. Nicotris, like Storge in *Jephtha*, adjusts herself to whatever situation may arise, but stands perpetually fixed in an incredible pattern of grief, righteousness and forbearing motherhood. And in those late works *Theodora* and *Jephtha* Handel takes youth in hand with consummate understanding, leading Theodora and Iphis from the feckless innocence of newly awakened love through anxiety, bred of principle on the one hand and devotion on the other, to certainty in the value of values and to the uncommon climaxes of death in the one case and conventional immuration in the other.

So far as plot is concerned *Theodora* is a far remove from what oratorio is often thought to be. It is in fact from a novel. Morell acknowledged that he had taken the whole story from *The Martyrdom of Theodora and of Didymus*, 'by a Person of Honour' (1687). What Handel did was to restate the novel in terms of music. So it may be recognized from another angle how well Handel was attuned to the climate of his age.

CHAPTER XIII

'TONMALEREI'

IF there is one aspect of Handel which reveals him more than any other as sharing the traditional philosophy of the English it is his outlook on nature. The revival of romanticism belonged to his period, as the preoccupation of music with details of illustration—itself an inevitable outcome of the development of instrumental technique—the realistic essays in scenic adventure and the transition of poetic thought all indicate. 'What this increased interest in nature signified,' writes Professor Ifor Evans,

is difficult to record. Part of it was a delight in 'prospects,' in scenes which a painter might use. Now that roads were improving, gentlemen and ladies could look out from their carriages on the views, and many of them they found good. Some even constructed 'views' on their own estates and parklands. The delight was often not for the pretty and regular design, but for the more wild and rugged aspects of nature. It was as if the human mind were in revolt against the increasing rationalism of the century.[1]

In isolating Handel's approach to nature emphasis is once again laid on his genius for expressing the motions of eighteenth-century thought and equally on his genius for transcending the common-place and rising superior to his contemporaries by integrating fragmentary facets of imaginative exploration into unity. It is not uncommon to note that Handel conscribed a company of frogs, lice and locusts and that he brought down hailstones and fire from heaven for the discomfiture of Pharaoh's hosts, that he emulated Marvell's 'green thought in a green shade' in *Semele*, that he commanded thunder and lightning in *Riccardo I* and *Joshua*, that he shared with the Almighty the governance of the sea in the Chandos anthem 'The Lord is my Light' and in *Israel in Egypt*, and that in a hundred other instances he demonstrated powers of observation such as rarely find so adequate an expression. But it is less frequent to observe that Handel not only contemplated nature picturesquely, but also with a conviction that the mind of man and the operations of nature were of a piece in the universal design. Handel was by no means

[1] B. Ifor Evans, *A Short History of English Literature* (Pelican Books), p. 39.

lacking in religious faith, but his faith of an elementary and practical order left ample room for the expansion of a free will into those realms of speculation uncongenial to the theologically dogmatic.

From a technical point of view Handel invented nothing: he merely did what other people did, but generally better. Many eighteenth-century composers were exploring the possibilities of realism. Vivaldi had written seasonable music, in concerto form, to illustrate spring, summer, autumn and winter. Kuhnau had put sections of the Old Testament into sonatas. Werner had produced the detailed precio-sity of an *Instrumental-Kalender* and Telemann had invested opera and oratorio with some interesting naturalistic episodes. Such experiments served a double purpose: on the one hand the freedom of music was safeguarded against the encroachments of pedantry, and on the other the theatre was saved from operatic atrophy. In any form of drama continual adjustment of the scales is necessary for the preservation of true balance or rather, since drama has never fixed itself in absolute equipoise, for a semblance of true balance. Eliza-bethan drama accommodated itself to the inn-yard by expressing the scenic setting in the text. Eighteenth-century opera overcame the disadvantage of a tale told in an alien tongue by rendering narrative superfluous by elegance in back-cloths, by extravagance in properties, by conventional plot-arrangement (one opera being very much the same as any other in the number of persons employed and in the order and function of the various types of aria enumerated on page 131) and by the transference of antithesized ideas from the medium of words to that of music. In this latter respect the particular of verbal ex-pression was losing itself in the universal of musical exegesis. In the meantime, however, music was going half-way to meet the situation by embracing particularity. By nineteenth-century standards, which set opera religiously enthroned in the ultimate theories of Wagner, the eighteenth century was lacking in sense. Opera as an entertainment, opera as a diversified concert, opera without action (singers as a rule quitted the stage after each appearance) was all wrong, but only by the arbitrary standards of later generations. Viewed objectively the opera of Handel's day should be regarded as a necessary stage in the development of aesthetic perception. It was the training-ground of singers and orchestral musicians. It may be that, looking backwards,

Debussy, Mussorgsky, Wagner, Meyerbeer, Berlioz, Mozart and Gluck were chief agents in the evolution of opera; but what they in turn achieved was at least hinted at by Handel.

Handel's delineation of character was exact and meticulous. He threw on his canvas universal types of men and women such as we find elsewhere defined in the works of Memling. It happened that Memling's types were dressed as Flemish citizens, Handel's as heroes or heroines of classical or Hebraic tradition. Behind both sets was placed the background of nature. Memling's countryside shone in jewelled beauty and contrast; Handel's implied, Hardy-like, an influence over the characters it supported. Solomon, in the oratorio of that name, is not so much the ruler skilled in jurisprudence as the naturalist turning pantheist. *Acis and Galatea* is an essay less in personal than in landscape charm, and the metamorphosis of Acis into a river appears a proper sort of poetic justice. In the opening scene of *Orlando* Zoroaster stands majestically on his mountain-side, and whether the music directs attention to the one or on the other, is impossible to decide. Burney was sensitive to something strange and new when he referred to the scene as having 'a wild grandeur in it of a very uncommon kind.' [1]

In the second act of *Orlando* the summer lightness of Dorinda's 'Quando spieghi':

[1] Burney, *History*, iv. 363.

-men - ti a - mo - ro - so ro - si - gno - lo,

and the whole murmurous nature of the forest music exert an influence
on the musical progress of the opera by throwing Orlando's later mad-
ness into the most poignant relief. Wherever we look the presence
of nature as a separate, subtle and enveloping personality is evident.
The *Nachtmusik* of *Floridante* and *Amadigi* combines Schumann
and Weber in a sensuous blend of mingled starlight and feminine
charm; the garden path, up which most of us are led and beyond
whose end we seldom explore, presents the tree prospect of 'Ombra
mai fù'; moonshine reflects in the nocturnal intermezzo of *Ariodante*;
Susanna is a gossip piece interlaced with the sounds and sights of
village life; sunrise and sunset inspire the loveliest of the arias in
Theodora and *Samson*; *L'Allegro* has the vivacity of a seventeenth-
century *genre* painting, but also the more fragile poetry of Constable.

The intention of theoreticians was that music should, as Avison
suggests, depict nature; but the operations of emotional behaviour
were also considered to be susceptible of direct expression. Mattheson
wrote that

One can represent all the passions of the heart by simple harmonies and
their concatenation, without words, so that the hearer grasps and understands the development, the meaning and the ideas of the musical utterance
as though it were in actual spoken utterance.[1]

To this philosophy was linked the whole of Handel's achievement,
and viewed in this light his music dissolves into a profounder heart-
search than modern conditions of performance allow. The majestic,
leonine Handel is but part of an immeasurably greater whole. The
subtlety of theatrical chiaroscuro and the subtlety of life in general
drew from him a new orchestral technique. This has been discovered already in incidental music which reveals something more
than mere appositeness and suggests that the composer saw, in part

[1] See Mattheson, *Die neueste Untersuchung* and *Die musikalische Gesch-
macksprobe*, 1744.

at any rate, the substance which casts the shadow on the wall of the cave. This intensity of contemplation shows up again in the overtures which preface opera and oratorio. Starting from the original curtain-raising function of such music they proceeded to vary in outline (the outline bequeathed from Lully through Steffani) as the needs of the whole work decreed and even to summarize the emotional direction of the plot. The overture to *Messiah*, greyly contrasting its E minor with the E major of the first aria, holds Advent in its sober dignity and refrains from anticipating festivity by omitting the customary third movement in minuet form; that to *Saul* foretells the opening *epinicion* by turning into an organ concerto; that to *Deborah* presents Baalites and Israelites in immediate antipathy by quoting their particular thematic material from the later stages of the oratorio; that to *Esther* preludes obviously the tyranny, despair and triumph which furnish the life of the plot. The overture to the *Occasional Oratorio* is so familiar that its military zest needs no emphasis. In the overture to *Serse* the comedy is drawn out in the humour of the fugue subject:

and in the playfulness of its succeeding dialogue:

Alcina was a combination of opera and ballet and preludes its *élan* in an overture of fitting vivacity. The lines of the minuet:

epigrammatize the sparkling quality of this work and recall Mrs. Delany's exclamation that 'whilst Mr. Handel was playing his part I could not help thinking him a necromancer in the midst of his own enchantments.'

From orchestral we may turn to choral *Tonmalerei*. And here it would appear necessary to discuss the general principles which influenced Handel in his choral technique. This is always impeccable, and because the approach to the orchestra is at apparent variance with that of later schools and the balance of choir and orchestra has in large-scale performances altered to the disadvantage of the latter an undue emphasis is laid on the magnificence of those exceptional choral movements which appeared to justify their performance in the Crystal Palace. Handel himself was accustomed to small and relatively capable companies of singers for his choral movements which initially, except for works written for ecclesiastical use exclusively, were incidental. In opera and oratorio the eighteenth century followed in the wake of the seventeenth and aptly produced a chorus for the representation of crowd effects. Soldiers, sailors and attendants formed the basis of secular and observant congregations of faithful Christians of sacred choralism. Handel enjoyed crowds, appreciated the effectiveness of combined voices as an addition to orchestral colour, lived among people whose pleasure often led to the conviviality of collective singing, and accordingly expanded choral music into greater significance than hitherto. But the intention was not to exclude the orchestra at any time: it was to treat the one with the other on equal terms just as in later times the woodwind or the brass *ensemble* came to a reciprocal understanding with the strings. The Handelian view of the function of chorus is illustrated more simply in the operas than in the oratorios, where other considerations supervene.

In *Il pastor fido* may be noted the minuet pleasantry of the final chorus (choruses as finales were *de rigueur* in the system) 'Quel ch' il cielo' which, if not remarkable, is at all events fitted with the airy Arcadianism apt for pastoral drama. The Athenians have a cheerful welcome song for Theseus in the second act of *Teseo*. Burney observes of 'Ogn' un acclami' that it is not like the oratorio choruses, for an evident reason:

In these the subject being generally solemn, and in the church style, should partake of choral complication; whereas an opera chorus, being in action, and committed to memory, must necessarily be short, easy and dramatic.[1]

The importance of the choral writing, whether in opera or oratorio, lies not so much in complexity or in lack of complexity as in its dramatic situation. The short bursts of choral observation in *Messiah*, in *Israel in Egypt*, in the *Funeral Anthem* are simple in process but momentous in setting. In general this is true of Handel's music as a whole, and we cannot but deplore the practice of cutting amiable patterns for public offering while ignoring the texture to which the patterns belong. There is a chorus in *Alcina* which runs thus:

This was at one time put into the trimness of high-school uniform. It belongs to the naughty ravishment of Alcina's palace, Alcina being another of Handel's seductive heroines who combined the functions of princess and sorceress for the bewitchment of Ruggiero. There is no doubt that if some headmistresses were aware of Handel's mind-picture as he wrote 'Questo il cielo,' with what effectiveness can only properly be deduced from the score, the purified school song would be banned forthwith. This is not a complaint against the practice of encouraging the young to sing Handel so much as an objection lodged against the refusal, on the part of those who should know better, to take Handel seriously when he intended seriousness of artistic purpose. Of all the opera choruses that which is most telling is the 'Viva, viva il nostro Alcide,' with which *Giulio Cesare* opens. Here we have the tremendous exhilaration which infects the festive crowds of *Deborah*, *Solomon* and *Saul* and sets in immediate view the hot heroism of romanticized royalty. The oratorio choruses, possessed of a larger significance than those of the operas, will be

[1] Burney, *History*, iv. 241.

treated in greater detail, but it must be urged that they too had their origins in dramatic propriety.

Chromatic harmony is another weapon in the dramatic armoury, and reference must be made to Handel's dependence thereon in particular moments. The chromatic ground-bass usage, as in *Orlando, Poro* and in the magnificent petitionary pessimism of the Israelites' 'How long O Lord' in *Susanna,* follow familiar models: Purcell, in fact, is immediately recalled. Where, however, there is no ground-bass to impose a regulated course, Handel breaks the bonds of conformity and allows the urge of inspiration to dive into uncharted waters. In *Israel in Egypt* there is the 'He sent a thick darkness' chorus, of whose modulations Tovey has to say that

they are as expressive as the modulations in Bach's Chromatic Fantasia, inasmuch as they traverse most of harmonic space. On the other hand, they differ profoundly from the Chromatic Fantasia, and from Handel's own Passion recitatives in *The Messiah,* because they are not enharmonic—that is to say, each step is known as far as it goes, but there is no general aim and the end of the groping is incalculably remote.[1]

Herein we may emphasize 'each step is known as far as it goes'— a dictum applicable to the whole range of Handel's technical accomplishment and indicative of the perplexity in which we so frequently find ourselves, discovering how much we know of Handel and, at the same time, how little. As in the chorus of darkness Handel intrudes deep mystery into 'How are the mighty fallen' and 'Their bodies are buried in peace' in the *Funeral Anthem.* In twenty bars or so an immense profundity is stirred, by means which are perfectly obvious save in one respect. That is in the ellipticism of modulation already mentioned in connection with the *Concerti grossi* which takes us from key to key with this degree of suddenness:

The feeling is seventeenth-century [2] and on this form of behaviour

[1] Tovey, *Essays in Musical Analysis,* v. 97.   [2] See p. 98.

the eighteenth-century modernists no doubt looked deprecatingly. It savoured of archaism. When, however, school logic conflicted with emotional tension Handel preferred to follow the latter. In respect of this we may look at the second part of 'Tyrants now no more shall dread,' a chorus from *Hercules* which produces

> Horrid forms of monstrous birth
> Again shall vex the groaning earth;
> Fear of punishment is o'er,
> The World's avenger is no more.

These words, provoked by the death of Hercules under signally unfortunate circumstances, were sufficient to set Handel on a course symbolic of the bewilderment of the leaderless:

which terminates thus:

It is passages such as this to which we may like to think Cowper points.[1] It is in passages like this that Handel shows his complete

[1] Cowper, *The Task*, book vi:
> Remember Handel? Who, that was not born
> Deaf as the dead to harmony, forgets,
> Or can, the more than Homer of his age?

mastery of technique and his intellectual capacity for psychological interpretation.

We have all had our Handelian training in church, and the perfect church-going mood is one of pure abstract reverence. A mood of active intelligence would be scandalous. Thus we get broken in to the custom of singing Handel as if he meant nothing; and as it happens that he meant a great deal, and was tremendously in earnest about it, we know rather less about him in England than they do in the Andaman Islands, since the Andamans are only unconscious of him, whereas we are misconscious.[1]

The misconsciousness arises from a misconception that Handel was more interested in God than in man. The reverse is the truth. If this is by now established we may turn to the oratorios with clearer vision.

[1] Shaw, *Music in London 1890–4*, i. 110.

CHAPTER XIV

THE ORATORIOS

So involved are the motions of human thought that what is enter-tainment to some is instruction to others and what passes as amuse-ment to one generation serves the next with didactic purpose. In music the difficulty of appreciation lies in the fact that the component elements are of both orders simultaneously, so that the last quartets of Beethoven or the operas of Mozart are at once fit for philosophic scrutiny on the one hand and plain enjoyment on the other. Handel's purpose was primarily to amuse, to embellish life with leisurely occupation—how leisurely it was is clear from the inability of sub-sequent admirers to survive uncut masterpieces—but he also had in mind the enigmatic capacity of art for ethical interpretation and direction. He spoke out on this point to Lord Kinnoul. This being the case, sympathy may be extended both to those who treat *Messiah* sacramentally and to those who, ignoring doctrinal implications, sur-render themselves to an orgy of aural titillation. That the pious and the hedonistic sit side by side at such performances of Handel's 'sacred' music as are familiar is not, as they so often consider it, a tribute to them, but to Handel's vast instinct for universal com-panionship. This sense of fraternity would be better understood if the whole of Handel's output were known; even, if we accept the probability that the operas are likely to remain generally unknown, were the whole of the oratorios known.

If choral societies were filled with initiative and with versatile singers and took it upon themselves to produce works of such diver-sity as the Passion of 1716, *Saul, Theodora, Susanna* and *Jephtha—Israel in Egypt* is only here excluded because it is relatively familiar—it would be seen that Handel, so far from being among the Lord's anointed, which is where idolatry places him, is very mortal in his approach to immortality. At home with the elemental passions of men and women, he fails to get nearer to God than do most of us who have no

special claim to spiritual superiority. Bach imposes humility, seem
ing so frequently to see into eternity; Pergolesi inspires ardour because
he is burnt up with the heat of his Mariolatrous devotion; Palestrina
implies, almost Jesuitically, the logic of God; Byrd details philosophy.
Handel does none of these things. He stands before the unknown in
bewildered sorrow at suffering, in joy at virtue triumphant, in anger,
of a particular paternal and sympathetic order, at moral turpitude, in
simple wonder at whatever is incomprehensible. He shouts 'Halle
lujah' from pure *joie de vivre,* sings praises with the robust vigour of a
prosperous churchwarden and prays with the variable intensity of
those who look to the supernatural under stress of despair. The
Handelians may complain that this undervalues Handel. On the
contrary, it indicates his special claim to supremacy. He understands
human nature in its strength and in its weakness with more acuteness
than any other of the great composers. This is why there can be no
division between opera and oratorio in his case. The concern of both
is with human affairs.

The pedigree of oratorio takes us back inconveniently far to trace
in detail. In any case the normal encyclopaedists can present it
with ramified exactitude. Here it may be recapitulated that towards
the end of the sixteenth century opera, sanctified solely by verbal
indication, was impressed into the service of the Counter Reformation
with due caution by Filippo Neri, a priest whose behaviour matched
his birth in nobility and led to his canonization. Neri's intention
was to make intelligible to the illiterate youth of Rome the mysteries
of theology by their presentation in terms of drama and music. His
innovation, which in view of medieval religious drama was not really
an innovation, stimulated Italian composers of the seventeenth
century to issue many works of this kind. Thus from Cavalieri to
Scarlatti a steady flow of picturesque essays in dramatic musical form
appeared to grace varied episodes of ecclesiastical association, from
the *mater dolorosa* to the life story of St. Philip himself. Among the
vast array of oratorios and cantatas then composed those of Giacomo
Carissimi were particularly significant, blending recitative, aria and
chorus into narrative interest suitable for ecclesiastical perform
ance. Hawkins expresses an opinion which immediately directs
attention to the Handelian contact: 'Carissimi excelled in imitating

the inflexions of the human voice, and in uniting the charms of music with the powers of oratory.'[1] As the score of *Jephte* is easily accessible the Handelian student is urged to take the opportunity of making contact with this precursor of later oratorio. Handel knew his Carissimi sufficiently well to adapt 'Plorate filiae Israel' for the chorus 'Hear Jacob's God' in *Samson*.

The style of Carissimi was, however, outmoded when Handel lived in Italy. Its severity hardly commended itself to the worldlings who, opera having been prevented in the theatre by edict of Pope Innocent XII, dictated that oratorio should select such episodes from holy writ as would stimulate eroticism in the operatic tradition. Hence such pleasing subjects as Susanna and Bathsheba and the secularity of Handel's first contribution to oratorio in Italy.

It is to be regretted that *La Resurrezione* is no more than a library curiosity. Completely operatic, with a lovable Lucifer (Handel could never find the heart thoroughly to dislike villainy and shared the modern belief that sinners in general are victims of causality), a sweet-voiced little Magdalene, an agreeable—if somewhat Tennysonian—St. John, an angel of pleasant virtuosity, and with delicious water-coloured orchestration, this *oratorio sacro* imbues religious exercise with an easefulness which may be reprehensible to the austere, but which suggests a degree of comfort in heaven not to be despised by the world-weary. Renaissance painters believed less in heaven on earth than in earth, that well-fed and well-housed earth represented by the cardinals' standards of living, in heaven. The only improvements possible would be in sanitation.

Germany countered Italy with religious music of different significance. The social history of Reformation and Thirty Years War, together with the natural consequences of a northern climate, induced deeper reflection on the problems of suffering and of pain. Therefore there arose the tradition of setting the story of the Passion with its concentration of congregational interest in, and not merely on, the subject by the employment of chorales. Before Bach the representative names were Schütz and Keiser, but Handel wrote two Passions, of which one, that of 1716, deserves consideration. It is interesting

[1] Hawkins, iv. 92.

in that it demonstrates how de-germanized Handel had become by long residence abroad, yet, in contrast, how strongly he endeavoured to construct his music so as to be acceptable in the place of its presentation. The framework is German, but not the content. Chorales appear in severe unemotion. A daughter of Zion shows herself, but with little concern for the tragedy she witnesses. St. Peter is present in unseemly high spirits; Judas in obvious contrition which rings with little conviction in empty roulades:

Flames, chas-tize _____ me

and Christ. Here we may pause and consider in greater detail Handel's reaction to the central figure of the Crucifixion. The part of Christ redeems this Passion from the charge of complacency, which otherwise, and with propriety, might be directed at it. But Christ is the Man of Sorrows, with manhood as Handel's exclusive wonder. We view Him pictured with dignity, virility and affection as a companion of men sacrificed as a man on the altar of uncertain and extraneous circumstantial operation. The consecration of bread and wine is portrayed with massive simplicity:

and with a tenderness redolent of Handel's quick intensity of emotion before the shrine of friendship. 'Lo! I will smite the shepherd' is angry with the vigorous integrity which sweeps through 'Why do the nations' in the face of wilful disobedience and with the same breadth of arpeggio-fired inspiration. The Agony in the Garden produces the awe-laden sympathy of:

This is scrupulous portraiture, but lacking in the larger hope which sees not so much immolation of manhood as the triumph of the god-head. Thus Handel shows how his vision suffers general limitation in incomprehension of deep theology, but also he displays it limitless in human understanding.

It was fortunate for the subsequent history of oratorio that during his years of Burlington-Chandos patronage opportunities occurred for conversations with Pope, Gay and the surrounding constellation of wits and worthies. Human affairs are so frequently set in motion by accidents of companionship that it is safe to assume that had Handel not been on amiable terms with practitioners of arts other than his own *Esther* would not have appeared. Had this not happened, the possibilities of an English variant of *oratorio sacro* would have remained latent.

It may be imagined that Racine's *Esther* [1] came into conversation by chance, that Pope considered it an attractive proposition for translation, that Handel was sufficiently interested in what he had overheard to borrow a copy of the work, and that after reading it he suggested its further possibilities as a libretto. Here it may be interposed that he would have acknowledged in Racine a reflection of many of the ideas which were also his own. Racine was a drama-tist whose strength lay in humanizing the conventional figures of classical mythology. Therefore he emphasized matter at the expense of form and acquired a solidity of expression in the same way as did ultimately Handel. It is further worthy of mention that not only Racine's *Esther*, but also his *Athalie* prompted music by Handel.

[1] An English version of *Esther* was done in 1715 by Thomas Brereton, a graduate of Brasenose College, Oxford, and a 'gentleman of Cheshire.'

Esther (Handel's *Esther*) is an uneven work. Its principal defect is that it lacks the cohesion which marks the later oratorios. The solo music is tentative, except where Handel in Haman's cataclysmic opening looks prophetically forward through the years:

Let Jew-ish blood . dye ev-'ry hand, Let Jew-ish blood dye ev-'ry hand, Nor age, nor sex I spare

and much is in fact transferred from the Passion. The choruses similarly vary in quality so that the first with its ingenuous contra-puntal interjections and its anthem derivation carries not very much of personal conviction. The mannered use of the ♩ ♩ idiom in 'Shall we of servitude complain' is also symptomatic of conscious adapta-tion to English usage. Passing by 'Ye sons of Israel, mourn,' which has a histrionic plaintiveness akin to that of the coeval funereal chorus in *Acis and Galatea,* and the handsome jingle of 'Hallelujah' (an Italian 'Hallelujah'[1] whose coruscations are a relief from the lumber-ing of later choruses to this text) as possessing potentialities of extreme effectiveness in performance, we must draw up in astonishment at the final, cantata-like 'The Lord our enemy has slain,' which, with its *canto fermo* to crown the concluding 'for ever blessed,' is magnificent.

The years passed. Handel had forgotten *Haman and Mordecai.* In 1732 he had the chance to revise it into *Esther.* In that same year Aaron Hill inscribed his plea for opera in the vernacular. Handel witnessed the success of the revival, took note of his friend's admoni-tion and called Humphreys into consultation. It may be that further incentive to oratorio came from the publication four years earlier of John Ernest Galliard's *Morning Hymn of Adam and Eve,* a slender cantata, but a hint that Milton was a possible source of libretto inspiration. However, Milton does not just yet come into the Handel field. In 1733 it was Humphreys's version of the story of Deborah which called his attention. With the best will in the world it is difficult to arouse very much enthusiasm for this work, and the point of view of those who complained at the increased prices must

[1] Borrowed from the brilliantly attractive motet *Silete venti.*

be considered reasonable. In *Deborah*, however, Handel did discover the effectiveness of contrast between two choirs representing
different philosophies: his Israelites unfortunately are possessed of an
inapt docility which dulls their music and which enlists support for
the Baalites who, if obtuse, are spirited in utterance. Dramatically,
despite its apparent unification by the introduction of *Leitmotive*,
Deborah is a poor sequel to *Orlando* which appeared at about the same
time. It is seldom that Handel really touches banality, but when the
priests of Baal can do no better than this:

the palm for heathen exaltation must temporarily rest with
Mendelssohn.

In *Athalia* Handel reverts more happily to his operatic vein, and
while Baalites and Israelites again present a background of conflict,
with more subtlety defined in extravagances of languor and charm, the
personalities of Athalia, a character tied up with Storge and Dejanira in a primitive state of subjection to irrational projections from
the fearful dream-world, Josabeth, Joash and Joad (a knowledgeable
sort of person) play in the forefront parts of attractive individuality.
Up to this point there is, if one may ever say it of Handel, an immaturity in the disposition of oratorio: in each there is a specialized
interest but no real fusion of the disparate elements such as is met with,
after a space of two years, in *Saul*.

Saul is one of Handel's most extensive studies of human nature in
primitive form. It holds the stylized libretto in contempt and deals in
the same terms of epical eloquence with a story of heroic proportions
as does the writer of the book of Samuel. Jennens was neither
better nor worse than most of the poetasters who constructed libretti
to order, but the fiery clash of ancient arms defeated his decorous

transcription. However—and here a case may be made out for texts which in this way are incomplete—there was scope for Handel to revivify the dry bones. Handel went back to the Authorized Version and made an oratorio the music of which carried the same dignity, poetry and ripeness as the seventeenth-century words. Interest starts with the people of the plot, people delineated with the exactness of photogravure. But while we study the gnawing deceit of Saul, the pert independence of Merab (who puts ideas into her father's head by refusing to marry one 'of poor, plebeian parents born'), the pretty romanticism of Michal, the somewhat evirated mutual affection of Jonathan and David, the witch of Endor and the prophetic apparition of Samuel, the chorus saves itself for more or less abstract commentary. It is true that the chorus is also participant in the drama, with what effect is manifest in the opening chorus, but its detachment from the immediate scene is adroitly controlled so that the strictures laid on Saul by his subjects and in his presence have no incongruity. In this respect actionless oratorio has the advantage over opera, and *Saul* produces the choruses which are neither fit for opera, being too prodigious, nor for church, because too unkempt, but entirely proper to their intended setting: the theatre during Lent. 'Envy, eldest born of Hell' and 'O fatal consequence of rage' are terrible in their particular and in their universal application. The decadence of Saul as described in the latter is presented in terms which bear superficial resemblance to a not dissimilar mood survey in the *Schicksalslied* of Brahms. Thus the chorus follow the demented turmoil of the mind of Saul:

The affection possessed by Handel for Saul raises that monarch to the heroic stature of Aristotelean tragedy—'a man who is not eminently good and just, yet whose misfortune is brought about not by vice or depravity, but by some error or frailty.' Saul is kept free from exaggeration, and when he displays anger it is anger redolent of quick temper and free from unspoken malignity of thought. 'A serpent in my bosom warmed' is illustrative of this point and also of the further point that Handel treated formal considerations with scant courtesy when it suited his dramatic purpose. This aria terminates abruptly in G minor, without a *da capo*, as Saul hurls his javelin at a too agile David. The anger becomes uncontrollable, and as jealousy mingles with despair there comes the sudden impulse to invoke the powers of darkness. Thus Saul, whose recitatives are dramatically the most cumulative in tension in the whole range of oratorio, turns the corner to final moral dissolution:

If heav'n de nies you aid,   seek it from hell!

The soldierly death of Saul calls from David, hitherto an exemplar of sickly virtue, his best song, 'In sweetest harmony they lived,' and treachery passes out of the picture as the maids of Israel are reminded that it was to Saul's indulgent care they owed the scarlet and gold they wore. The oratorio should end with the chorus 'O fatal day,' but the necessity for a cheerful finale imposed on Handel the task of setting 'Go on,' many times repeated. This Panglossian termination is not the best of endings for a penetrating psycho-analytical work that suggests that this is not the best of all possible worlds.

The companion work to *Saul* was *Israel in Egypt*. Here is simply the story of a people in their progress from adversity to victory, epically related in what is to all intents and purposes a choral symphony. Whether Handel borrowed other men's ideas or not is not so important as the thankfulness to God, nowhere else so patent, which infuses the music, leads to the overwhelming impact of the ageless paean which prefaces the final chorus, and symbolizes the recovery of Handel himself from illness, the triumphant passage of the Children of Israel and, more than this, that of all peoples who have come through the darkness of oppression and subjugation. This is music of which it might truly be said that 'the touch of life has turned to truth.' The first chorus, in which the tremendous effect of the withheld bass part when it sets the earth rumbling with its cry to God should be noted as born of genius, is the representation of Europe as remembered from 1941.[1]

Why in 1741 Handel forsook his natural field of dramatic and heroic narrative for the solemn libretto of *Messiah* is difficult to decide. That it was entirely due to evangelistic zeal is improbable. The possibility is that the cause was more personal. At a period when disillusionment preyed on his mind his thoughts took flight to happier times, and the memory of his dead sister came back to him. And with memory came that of her favourite text—'I know that my Redeemer liveth.'[2] Therefrom possibly sprung the conception of a commemorative work—a *Trauerode*, which however should see death swallowed up in victory. Handel could see death in no other way.

The first triumph in *Messiah* is the text. Here one wonders at the felicity of extraction—in one detail the mixture of Job and Corinthians in the text above mentioned is so happy that it passes even the learned unnoticed—and whether Jennens really possessed the devotion

---

[1] A letter eulogizing *Israel in Egypt* appeared in the *London Daily Post*, dated 18th April 1739. The following extract indicates the writer's approval of my thesis. Catholic readers will judge the writer charitably and make allowances for the prejudices of the period:

'Did such a Taste prevail universally in a People, that People might expect on a like Occasion, if such Occasion should ever happen to them, the same Deliverance as those praises celebrate; and Protestant, free, virtuous, united, Christian England need little fear, at any time hereafter, the whole Force of slavish, bigotted, united, unchristian Popery, risen up against her should such a conjuncture ever hereafter happen.'

[2] This text was often set in motets and cantatas by German composers known to Handel in youth.

to Holy Writ to produce so masterly an abstract of Christian thought. It has reasonably been suggested [1] that the text owed to Nonjuror practice (Jennens being a Nonjuror), but one reflects also that Handel himself must have had a good deal to do with the textual compilation of *Messiah*. This is supported by the fact that the central figure of the work appears only in the background. Partly this may have been due to subservience to public feeling, but partly to Handel's lack of ease in the neighbourhood of divinity. Thus the music bears an imper-sonality, an eighteenth-century and Protestant quality as Handel throws aside, except for the 'He trusted in God' chorus, the intense passion and fire of *Saul* and *Israel in Egypt*. A Wren-like monument is the result: a temple of marble on which Mozart was later to hang stucco ornaments. A number of sections of the text were set by English composers of the period in anthems which preceded *Messiah* and which afford instructive comparisons.

Messiah is a careful and awe-inspired work. The scoring is indica-tive of this in its ferial nature. More thrilling choruses may be found in *Israel in Egypt* or in *Belshazzar*, finer arias in *Samson* or *Theodora*, recitative of greater musical significance in *Saul* or *Jephtha*, but no-where else is there a firmer homogeneity. This is due to Handel's evocation of ceremonial dignity. And this in turn explains the English affection for *Messiah*: it represents what, since the Reforma-tion, they have generally felt obliged to feel about God in public. Because it is representative of a nation's thought *Messiah* is a notable work, but also, inevitably, it is not Handel at his greatest. Jennens expressed an opinion that Handel might have done better with the subject. Jennens was wrong. Handel could have done no more with *Messiah*, but with a different text and with a less abstract theme he could have written music which, considered on its own merits and without the subtle influence of familiar words of acknowledged genius and specific religious association, was more intrinsically poetic.

The confirmation lies in the next oratorio—*Samson*, where music once again runs into the familiar channels of heroic narrative. Here we have an anthology of Milton, ingeniously doctored by Newburgh

---

[1] 'The Text of *Messiah*,' Geoffrey Cuming, in *Music and Letters*, July 1950, p. 226 et seq.

Hamilton,[1] running into the full tide of Handel's inspiration. The constant comparison of Handel with Homer has fullest significance in attachment to this oratorio, in which the clash of personalities is developed amid the tumult of many voices, both human and divine. There is also evident that particular capacity of Handel for living with the ancients and at the same time for placing both them and us, the listeners, in the same timeless pattern. Thus the priests of Dagon and those of Jehovah, well matched in strenuous earnestness, champion all the characters who immortalize the eternal struggle between the powers of darkness and of light. The choral writing which enshrines this meta-physical duality is sublime in picturesqueness and inflexibility. The voices move with the sinuous grace of strings, a quality not so con-sistently achieved by Handel until he wrote *Samson*, and yet in so doing lose nothing of the mountainous grandeur apparent twenty years before. The urgency of 'Awake the trumpet's lofty sound,' the expression of plea and counter-plea in 'Fix'd in His everlasting seat'—with this exalted exploitation of rests to suggest astonished contemplation:

the extension of *da capo* formality to 'With thunder arm'd,' with

[1] Newburgh Hamilton was related to the Duke of Hamilton. Before working with Handel his fame had precariously rested on *The Doating Lovers, or The Libertine Tamed* and *The Petticoat Plotter* (Thomas Winchop, *Scanderbeg*). It looks as though Handel selected his text for those works which had Hamilton's collaboration. In the first codicil to his will it is stated: 'I give to Mr. Newburgh Hamilton, of Old Bond Street, who has assisted me in adjusting words for some of my compositions, one hundred pounds.' Which was a hundred pounds less than Morell received. *Samson* borrows from *Samson Agonistes*, the odes 'On the Nativity,' 'On the Passion,' 'On Time,' 'At a solemn Musick,' the 'Epitaph on the Marchioness of Winchester' and the translations from the Psalms.

insight into the minds of those who reinforce the humility of prayer with more vigorous methods of advising the Almighty, the contrapuntal genius which contains a nation's grief in the twelve bars of 'Weep, Israel, weep' and the finality of the concluding hymn of praise are tokens of the complete mastery of choral technique.

In *Samson*, however, the emancipation of the chorus is not at the expense of the solo singers. Far from it. Each has his or her personality tightly packed into recitatives and arias in which untidy ends of virtuosity no longer trail about deprived of dramatic point. Samson with his tragic strength, Manoah with the virility of his paternal affection, Harapha, who stamps through the score with superb ὕβρις, and Dalila, whose truculent amorousness is implied as much as stated, are among the most heroic of all the persons of opera or oratorio.

The athletic quality of *Samson* leaves *Joseph and his Brethren* immobile and generally unattractive, but the old barbaric spirit returns in full glory in *Belshazzar*, an oratorio in which the contrast between vicious pleasure and God-inspired virtue, appropriately armed with effective weapons of offence, is demonstrated in the plain manner of an old morality play with keen emphasis on the inevitable wages of sin. Despite the coloured pageant of riotous living centred in the carousal music, *Belshazzar* holds a greater sense of personal obeisance before the divine will than do many of the other oratorios. The keynote is sounded initially by Nicotris, a tragic queen of immense power and courage on whom Handel lavished music of unsurpassable quality, in an extensive *recitativo accompagnato*, whose subject is the decline and fall of empires. The 'sprung rhythm' of Jennens's verse at this point momentarily attaches him to poets of greater fame. Handel's treatment of the closing bars of this recitative may be quoted as demonstrating the richer implications of his tone-painting faculty:

runs the same shad-ow-y round   of fan-cied

A further instance of this developed symbolism occurs in the scene during which Daniel interprets the writing on the wall:

The perfect dramatic setting of the chord of the diminished seventh.

The *Occasional Oratorio* served its ardent purpose by collecting contributions from earlier works: the overture survived the occasion and may still be enjoyed by those who like sublimated bellicosity. *Judas Maccabaeus* has little to commend it (Handel disliked a story devoid of love interest) and *Joshua* is fairly dull. 'See the conquering hero,' text by Morell out of Dryden,[1] provoked a dialogue which may be taken to heart by those who neglect the greater works of Handel. Sir John Hawkins was asked by Handel how he liked this chorus. 'Not so well as some things I have heard of yours.' Then said Handel: 'Nor I neither, but, young man, you will live to see it a greater favourite with the people than my other fine things.'

Alexander Balus, the third of the conscious tributes to Jewry, was less popular than either *Judas Maccabaeus* or *Joshua.* This may be

---

[1] Cf. *Alexander's Feast* :

> The jolly god in triumph comes !
> Sound the trumpets, beat the drums !

ascribed to the inability of the oratorio public, which by 1748 was setting up limited piety and prudery as standards of criticism, to reconcile themselves to a love story, albeit with biblical sanction, arrayed in the persuasive delicacy of Longus. Lest, however, it should be thought that Handel was indulging in unhealthy fancies, it should be duly noted that *Alexander Balus* is a bright celebration of conjugal fidelity and, while an influx of brigandage affords some excellent and dramatic relief, the central theme of matrimonial propriety is responsible for Cleopatra's sweet songs and for the cheerful connubiality of the epithalamium chorus 'Hymen fair,

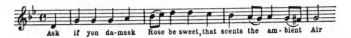

Ask   if yon da-mask   Rose be sweet, that scents the   am- bient   Air

Urania's son.' *Susanna,* the subject of a picture by Sebastiano Ricci, Burlington's favourite painter, is also a monument to chastity, its artlessness shown in this ballad strain which might have come from Somerset. The decline of the elders into maudlinity is consum-mately portrayed and the etching of 'Away, away, ye tempt me both in vain,' for Susanna and the two elders, is perfect. Behind the plot stands the awful severity of 'How long, O Lord,' a magnificently contrived prayer expanded over a ground-bass, the mystical union of the brute passions of man and of nature in 'The torrent that sweeps in its course,' and the rustic backchat of village gossips. The theme of the work is summarized hopefully in the final operatic and four-square chorus which emphasizes that

> A virtuous wife shall soften fortune's frown,
> She's far more precious than a golden crown.

Public morality, if affected at all by works of art, is less likely to be disturbed by *Susanna*, whose title has kept it immured for the private delectation of scholars, than by *Solomon*, in which the dalliance of Solomon with the Queen of Sheba contrasts violently with his relationship with his own vapid queen. *Solomon* has a considerable number of double choruses of great splendour, but their omnipresence is inclined to add an overplay of sententiousness to a work of uneven quality.

Regarding *Theodora* there remains evidence of Handel's private opinion. Handel possessed a rare perspicuity in self-criticism, and his judgment should be respected. He, so Morell wrote,

valued it more than any performance of the kind, and when I once asked him, whether he did not look upon the Grand Chorus in *The Messiah* as his masterpiece? 'No,' says he, 'I think the chorus at the end of the second part in *Theodora* far beyond it, "He saw the lovely Youth."'

Theodora has the maturity and the same mellowed courtesy that Shakespeare displays in *The Winter's Tale*. A Christian story, made into a novel, *Theodora* looses the gloom from eighteenth- and nineteenth-century religion by seizing on the attractiveness of the first Christians—which surely embraced courage. In the springtime of the faith the devout had not forgotten the pleasances of paganism. The geniality of 'Come, mighty Father' is worship of a more affectionate order than that to which the more ecclesiastical choruses in other oratorios admit us and springs in refinement from the rites of Venus and Flora, which also find eloquent expression in this work. There is in *Theodora* a contemplative quality and an intimacy revealing old Handel detached personally from the conflict of life, but in complete sympathy with the victims of catastrophe.

Finally there comes *Jephtha*: the *summa summarum*. The greatness of *Jephtha* reposes in Handel's philosophic absorption in the vast problem propounded by the plot—the obedience of man to the legislation of eternity. The abstract philosophy is carried by the chorus whose utterances, nine of them, lie rooted in the earthly actions of Jephtha, but offshoot towards the universal. The climactic, quadripartite 'How dark, O Lord, are Thy decrees,' placed (let it be noted) after Jephtha's desperate 'Deeper and deeper still,' contains the human acknowledgment of divine supremacy, achieved only after mystified and even angry protestation against the uncertainty of the pilgrimage. Handel, with blindness imminent (indeed, it was the above-mentioned chorus which suffered interruption on this account), had reason to follow his argument closely, for he knew himself to be in the inexorable grasp of destiny. The averting of a tragic denouement is accomplished in *Jephtha* by the intermission of an *angelus ex machina,* but the low-level drama of Jephtha, Iphis, Storge and Hamor is of small consequence beside that traced by the finger of God. Against the severity of the Almighty, however, Handel places a tranquillity in heaven which draws peace over the final stages of life. The opening of the 'Cherub and seraphim,' with its arpeggio-wrought effulgence, first cousin to the opening of *Zadok the Priest*, paints a picture which finds reflection in the lambent beauty of 'Waft her, angels,' the serene token of Jephtha's ultimate acceptance of the beneficence of divine governance, and in the music with which Iphis prepares to leave the world.

It is easy and natural to have talent at twenty; to have talent still at forty, that is the best; to keep it until old age, when it has been enriched by the experience of a lifetime, that is to be something more than a man of talent. Genius is always rare, and always admirable; but most admirable when it has matured into something that is uniquely personal.[1]

What Handel wrote at twenty and at forty may be easily discovered. What he wrote after the age of sixty reveals the unique genius of the man, and no work more than *Jephtha*, which secretes immortality in an awareness of spiritual adventure, in the hopefulness of perennial youth, and in the expression of the experience of a full life.

[1] R. C. Trevelyan, *Windfalls*.

CHAPTER XV

A MISCELLANY

BEYOND the pale of oratorio lies a sequence of works, neither opera nor oratorio, though related to both, which may only be ignored at the risk of falling victim to the Chadband-Handel myth. We move round the periphery which bounds the familiar terrain to discover a variety of entertainment reminiscent more of the spontaneity of the seventeenth than of the sophistication of the eighteenth century. The boundary between one age and another or between one form of art and another—Quiller-Couch's analogy with the limits which administratively settle where one county ends and the next begins may aptly be remembered—only assumes *raison d'être* when a certain distance from the arbitrary dividing line is covered on one side or the other. In respect of Handel rigid categorization, except where the cataloguer orders his lists, is impossible. Difficulties were early encountered. *Acis and Galatea* was variously described as a serenata (*Daily Journal*, 5th June 1732), which term also belonged to the earlier *Aci, Galatea e Polifemo*, as a pastoral (*Daily Journal*, 13th March 1731), as a pastoral opera (*Daily Post*, 2nd May 1732) and as a 'Mask' in Walsh's edition of 1730. Twenty-six years later the last term reappeared. The *Norwich Mercury* of Saturday, 28th February 1756 recorded:

Cambridge, Feb. 26. On Thursday night the Mask of Acis and Galatea was performed at Trinity Coll: Hall before a very numerous audience and was conducted by Dr. Randall, Professor of Music in this University.

From masque, the thoroughbred seventeenth-century stock, came the ideals of English opera. English opera, that is, as it was to develop under Purcell and receive its most extensive, elegant, odd and moving expression in *The Fairy Queen*. Masque entailed poetry—how exquisite may be judged from reference to the occasional offerings of Ben Jonson, Campion, William Browne of Tavistock and others of their courtly order. And it was poetry incapable of affiliation with the necessary music for the glamorous atmosphere of the public theatre. Masque also entailed dancing, the culmination of whose music was in *The Fairy Queen,* and the painting of scenery. The back-cloths of Inigo Jones are the finest things of this sort in the history of the English stage. The place for masque was at court on the occasion of a royal wedding, a coronation, the visit of a foreign potentate or a royal coming-of-age. Some pearls were produced, but as they were cast before swine they were disallowed by the Cromwell regime. To be fair to the Puritans it should be admitted that Inigo Jones's landscapes concealed many scenes of lechery. The idea of the masque, however, never died, so that Purcell depended on it, as later did Rich in his pantomimes (with music by Galliard) and Arne in *Alfred,* which properly fitted a garden party given by the Prince of Wales. Handel caught the spirit and when first presented with a piece of really lyrical poetry inscribed the music of *Acis and Galatea.*

Appropriateness, according to Dionysius of Halicarnassus, is the chief source of beauty. This thought may be applied justly to whatever Handel wrote, but in the particular instance of *Acis and Galatea* it will be seen that his appreciation of Gay's poetry—an echo of the whimsy of Jonson's *Oberon*[1] and a Jonsonian transmutation of classical into English country scenes—a feeling of affection for a legend which may at one time have impinged on a classical education, plus the knowledge that his finished work would adorn a *fête champêtre,* produced a masterpiece of Arcadianism, refined yet mixed with a natural zest which kept the music free from preciosity. The whole thing, excepting that voluminous 'Wretched lovers' chorus, catches at the heart like a memorable verse by Chaucer. *Acis and Galatea* is no oratorio, nor should it be performed like an oratorio. Put it on a sunny lawn on a summer's day.

Holst wrote of *Acis and Galatea* and that even sunnier companion work *L'Allegro*: 'Why didn't the old chap write more of that sort of thing?' He did. He wrote notably *Semele.* Congreve designed *Semele* as an opera libretto in 1710. The year is perhaps worth noting and it may be speculated whether Handel, possibly knowing Congreve through his other literary associates, was on the point of treating this promising theme when the Academy project came to monopolize his attentions. However that may be, *Semele* remained untouched

[1] Which masque was used by Arne in 1771 as the basis of *The Fairy Prince.*

until 1744. Then it served as an antidote to piety. It was, said Mainwaring, 'after the manner of an oratorio an English opera, but called an oratorio'—a pretty jugglery with nomenclature. But whatever *Semele* may be called it is, as the argument indicates in the word-book, a characteristic Renaissance flirtation with paganism.

After Jupiter's amour with Europa, the daughter of Agenor, king of Phoenicia, he again incenses Juno by a new affair in the same family, viz., with Semele, niece of Europa, and daughter to Cadmus, king of Thebes. Semele is on the point of marriage with Athamas, a prince of Boeotia; which marriage is about to be solemnized in the temple of Juno, goddess of marriages, when Jupiter, by ill omens, interrupts the ceremony, and afterwards transports Semele to a private abode prepared for her. Juno, after many contrivances, at length assumes the shape and voice of Ino, sister to Semele; by the help of which disguise, and artful insinuations, she prevails with Semele to make a request to Jupiter, which, being granted, must end in her ruin.

The surprise is that this was allowed in English, and in Lent.

Semele has its moments of tension, as in the lengthy recitative of Cadmus, 'Ah wretched Prince,' which culminates in the terse description of the seizure of Semele by Jupiter, with versatility appearing here as an eagle, and in the aerial ascent of raped and raper to the 'Waft her, angels' formula; in Juno's magnificent 'Awake Saturnia'; in the concluding scene which grows out of Semele's request and Jupiter's oath. But the same diversionary air overhangs the music as in *Acis and Galatea*. The story, indicates Handel, is a fable of no consequence, so what he allows to remain freshest in the memory is a distillation of nature's charms. 'Where'er you walk' in fact is the perfect summary.

A year later Handel once again retreated into classical antiquity. *Hercules,* done from Sophocles (*The Women of Trachis*) by the Rev. T. Broughton,[1] in contrast to *Semele,* is a work accurately described by its first advertisement as 'a new musical drama.' Like *Saul, Hercules* is a study in jealousy. It is also, like *Saul,* a commentary on human impotence. Dejanira's murder of her husband (one may agree with her in her judgment of Hercules's motives in bringing back captive the beautiful Iole from Oechalia) illustrates this impotence in simple

[1] Prebendary of Salisbury, who had been at Eton with Morell.

form. Hercules is finally done to death. A priestly recitative tells how an eagle lifts his body from a funeral pyre and takes it to a new life with senior deities and access to nectar and ambrosia. Dejanira, however, wins more sympathy than Saul. She is richer in portraiture, more heroic and defeated by a problem which might beset any woman passing the prime of her beauty and encountering an apparent rival of Iole's calibre. The whole of Dejanira is contained in the honest-to-goodness scolding of 'Resign thy club' (a title which should not be misinterpreted): an upright woman with a rasping tongue and a malignant impetuosity. Iole is a fitting foil to the older woman; graceful in movement, dignified in rebuttal of the false charges laid against her, sympathetic to Dejanira when she should have forfeited all claims to sympathy and courageous in grief. Iole is the ripest of Handel's young women, and marriage with Hyllus, son of Hercules, is (we may hope) a deserved reward for virtuous living under conditions of difficulty. Hercules himself is a bluff soldier with equal zest, if we read the music aright, for battle, murder and sudden death (provided that he is the dispenser) and bucolic sports. He also has a simplicity of character which places him immediately within the environs of sympathy.

The chorus appropriately holds a Greek position in abstract commentary. The quality of the individual choruses is uniformly high and, as in *Samson*, there is a pervasive flexibility. Thus a passage in doubled sixths illuminates the festivities which, at the end of Act 1 greet the returning Hercules:

And thus with subtle insinuation comment is made on the affection of Hyllus for Iole:

The uniqueness of *Hercules,* however, rests not so much on high technical competence as on the sensitive response of the music to changes of mood in the drama. Dejanira holds tragedy in mind in her first aria. Anxiety for her lord and master is the immediate source of melancholy, but deeper lies the intensity of the unknown grief. Notice the chromatic suspense—and Handel used such effects only rarely:

De - plore, in thick-est gloom_____ of grief,

Parallel with this is the acridity of Iole's lament for her father:

the sword in-flicts the dead - ly wound

with which dissonant discomfiture Handel points the despair which resolves itself in the anaesthetic resignation of 'Peaceful rest.' One more illustration must suffice to indicate the dramatic integrity of *Hercules*. During Act II Dejanira recalls that she has possession of a robe, dipped in the blood of Nessus which

> boasts a wondrous virtue, to revive
> The expiring flame of love: so Nessus told me,
> When dying to my hand he trusted it—
> I will prevail with Hercules to wear it,
> And prove its magic force—

So Dejanira in good faith endeavours to overcome her fears of infidelity (that her fears were groundless heightens the dramatic tension) and the chorus respond with delicious satisfaction at so happy a dénouement:

Love and Hy - men, hand in hand, Come, re - store the nup-tial band!

This completes the second act. From such a climax of contentment Act III immediately plunges us into disaster. The robe was poisoned.

Act III is a drama within a drama. Hercules dies in agony: Dejanira maddens as Handel lashes her with the snakes of Alecto, with the vision of 'Megaera fell, and black Tisiphone' in an aria which carries the unearthly impress of terror Blake understood. But from the trough of despair all are led by Jupiter, who sends his messenger to terminate the drama. An inevitable conclusion, but more appropriate to this excursion into antiquity than to the oratorios. That is if art and philosophy must be bounded by theology.

Another classical adaptation, the *Alcestis* (*Alcides* in the edition of Arnold), was arranged for Handel by Smollett. This English opera was metamorphosed into *The Choice of Hercules,* as for some reason or other Rich's projected performance never came off. With the minor works of attractive parts must be placed the incidental music to Ben Jonson's *The Alchymist* which, although reduced from *Rodrigo* in some part, has an antique simplicity in its airs and dances:

recalling the flavour of Lupo or Coperario, intimates of Jonson's and his particular composers, and pioneers whose honour has been neglected. Then there is the *Terpsichore* music which Arnold, with an eye unconsciously directed at the progenitors of so much music of the class, again designated 'A Masque.'

There are a hundred or so Italian cantatas and duets, whose composition at various times provided exercise in conventionality and ephemeral pleasure for the eclectic. The cantatas, after the manner of operatic scenes, and the duets, after the model of Steffani, were easy carriers of mellifluence. Their influence was ubiquitous.

The Independence of his Music

The genius of Handel was so pervasive that no work of his may entirely be ignored and we must be reluctant to draw the line at any point short of the complete pilgrimage. Yet here it must be done. This chapter was designed to segregate fine secularity and to free Handel from the eternal curse attached by the sentimental to a 'sacred' musician. The final conclusion is that in Handel there is neither Jew nor Gentile, neither bond nor free: there is a corpus of integrated membership, which, transcending critical definition, can only be comprehended by those who believe in the final independence of music and are willing to lay aside the dark glass of prejudice and pedantry to see the music—and the man—face to face.

CHAPTER XVI

L'ENVOI

'THERE, Sir, is the portrait of the inspired master of our art; when I open my eyes in the morning, I look upon him with reverential awe, and acknowledge him as such, and the highest praise is due to your country for having distinguished and cherished his gigantic genius.'[1]

So Gluck, in his bedroom, delivered his private thoughts to Michael Kelly as they stood before a rich-framed painting of Handel. A man may be judged from the quality of his friends, and Handel's represent a catholic assortment. The tributes of those who followed the same vocation may be considered, not because they are of necessity the most valuable, but because they display a degree of unanimity unusual in artists. The man commanded universal respect and indeed affection, but so too did his art. So much so that Handel was regarded by his greatest successors as the *fons et origo* of music and the tutelary genius of musicians. Intellectual genuflection was first made by Gluck. The gesture was impressive in that his reception by Handel in London—in 1747—was brusque and hardly encouraging.

'You have taken too much trouble over your opera,' said the old man, having eyed the score of *La caduta dei giganti*. 'Here in England that is mere waste of time. What the English like is something they can beat time to [Charles II was, according to Evelyn, the founder of the pulsatory school of appreciation], something that hits them straight on the drum of the ear.'[2] Which is, after all, a legitimate and homely interpretation of a fundamental of musical expression. If there was one lesson taught by Handel to posterity, and to Gluck according to Burney, it was that periphrasis is anathema.

[1] Kelly, *Reminiscences*, i. 255. One assumes that Gluck meant England and not Ireland, although it would be attractive to think that Gluck regarded an Irishman as an Irishman and not as an Englishman, and that he intended some tribute to the politeness of the generous nation which welcomed Handel in 1742.

[2] A. Schmid, *C. W. von Gluck*, p. 29.

An early and notable victim of Handel's straight-hitting faculty was Haydn. After hearing 'The nations tremble' from *Joshua* he told Shield that 'He had long been acquainted with the music, but never knew half its powers before he heard it, and he was perfectly certain that only one inspired author ever did, or ever could, pen so sublime a composition.' On another occasion Shield complimented Haydn on the quality of his recitatives in *Il ritorno di Tobia*. 'Ah!' exclaimed Haydn with that engaging habit of his of selfdenigration, '"Deeper and deeper," in *Jephtha,* is far beyond that.' The obvious influence of Handel on Haydn produced *The Creation,* the text for which had been lying about since before Handel's death. Haydn undertook this work after having experienced a Lenten season of Handel in 1794.

Mozart's counterpoint frequently reflected that of the master whose music he recollected having to read at sight under the critical eye of George III. An imitative fugue (the fugues of Handel were frequent companions to his studies) and the re-orchestration of *Acis and Galatea, Messiah, Alexander's Feast* and the *Ode for St. Cecilia's Day* betokened affection. It was these versions which started the canard about Handel's impotence in orchestration. The responsibility was van Swieten's, who in enthusiasm ordered the new scoring. Handel might have cursed van Swieten for his effrontery, but he would have complimented Mozart on his acceptance of a welcome commission. Handel, unlike many who profess to be Handelians, deplored indigence among artists and considered that it was the duty of a composer to undertake the particular tasks set by his patrons.[1]

Of his peers Beethoven was perhaps the most generous in his appraisal of Handel. 'He was the greatest composer that ever lived. I would uncover my head, and kneel before his tomb.' And again, when forty volumes of Arnold's edition, the gift of A. A. Stumpff, a German living in London, came to him in 1826: 'There is the truth.'

Handel was never so much alive as when he was dead. For this

---

[1] Samuel Wesley was the first to suggest keeping to Handel's orchestration in preference to Mozart's. See *Lectures* (B.M. Add. MS. 35015, f. 63), where he says that no other accompaniments are needed beyond 'what their immortal author deemed proper and necessary'.

there were two principal reasons. The first was George III; a discriminating music-lover and consistently generous in his promotion of Handel's posthumous fame. He supported the commemoration performances of 1784—that mammoth progenitor[1] of all musical festivals and choral constipation—encouraged Arnold's edition and was graciously pleased to accept from Christopher Smith those manuscripts which now glorify the royal collection. But with George III there was more to it than mere monarchic patronage. He could pen a critical memorandum to Burney's account of the commemoration:

Dr. Burney seems to forget the great merit of the choral fugue 'He trusted in God,' by asserting that the words would admit of no stroke of passion. Now the real truth is, that the words contain a manifest presumption and impertinence, which Handel has, in the most masterly manner, taken advantage of. And [this observation throws interesting light on Handel's methods of extemporization] he was so conscious of the moral merit of that movement, that, whenever he was desired to sit down to the harpsichord. if not instantly inclined to play, he used to take this subject; which ever got his inspiration at work, and made him produce wonderful capriccios.

It may be suspected that the court grew a little weary of the subject of Handel. When the king left off Mrs. Delany, a royal pensioner, would lapse into fond reminiscence.

On a memorable day in 1789 Fanny Burney ran into the king in the gardens at Kew. Fanny was terrified. The king was not well and under restraint. On this morning, however, an interval of tired sanity prevailed. The king called to Fanny, kissed her cheek, and 'What a conversation followed! When he saw me fearless, he grew more and more alive, and made me walk by his side. . . .' The conversation eventually turned to Dr. Burney and the *History*.

This brought him to his favourite theme, Handel; and he told me innumerable anecdotes of him, and particularly that celebrated tale of Handel's saying of himself, when a boy: 'While that boy lives, my music will never want a protector.' And this, he said, I might relate to my father.
Then he ran over most of his oratorios, attempting to sing the subjects

---

[1] Upwards of five hundred musicians participated.

of several airs and choruses, but so dreadfully hoarse that the sound was terrible.

The second principal to Handel's immortality in England was a revival of religious fervour. The Catholic church in its wisdom affords ample opportunity for emotional exultation, both in its liturgy and its furniture. The Protestant creeds, having renounced these riches, were obliged in the course of time to find compensation in other ways. Hence the inauguration of romantic hymnody in the eight-eenth century. Handel had written a chorus which had brought even a king to his feet. If it were necessary to summarize the religious character of the English people during the late eighteenth and early nineteenth centuries one word would suffice—Hallelujah. Hallelu-jah, which split the establishment, opened the eyes of the blind, brought sinners to tearful repentance, lit the ceremonial fires on Mow Cop, inspired the erection of a thousand conventicles and sent Handel rampaging the country like one of his Old Testament heroes. When a rich sequence of Hallelujahs was discovered to belong to a work entitled *Messiah* the terminology caught at the imagination of those whose spiritual pabulum was the Old Testament. It was part of Handel's misfortune, and part too of his glory, that his music should readily have become an integral part of the Englishman's religion. Anecdote was useful in supporting the position. There were memories of the aged and beloved Handel presiding in his latter days over performances for the benefit of the foundlings, of the constant worshipper at St. George's, Hanover Square, of the visionary who was reported to have seen the opened heavens in the white heat of inspira-tion, of the sublime deathbed and of the last wish that he might die on Good Friday 'in hopes of meeting his good God, his sweet Lord and Saviour on the Day of His Resurrection.' The Great (and Good) Mr. Handel was born in 1759. In that year *Messiah* began its pro-vincial course with a celebrated performance at Church Langton, Leicestershire.[1]

In the *Chester Courant* for 9th June 1772 appeared a notice which will serve to show what stimulus Handel gave to the provinces both in religious and in musical development. Many who remembered

[1] See Hanbury's *Charitable Foundations at Church Langton* (1767), pp. 80–7.

Handel's encounter with the saucy Johnson (precisely entered by one treasurer of the cathedral as Ap John) thirty years before would have been provoked to reminiscence by the following:

> On Tuesday, the 16th instant will be performed in the Broad Isle of the Cathedral, of this City, the Oratorio of
>
> ### 'MESSIAH'
>
> On Wednesday Evening, the 17th, will be performed in the Exchange,
> A Miscellaneous Concert of Select Pieces of Music, Vocal and Instrumental, the particulars of which will be expressed in the bills of the day.
> The principal vocal parts by Miss Linley, Miss M. Linley, Messrs. Norris, Price, Matthews, etc.
> The Instrumental by several of the most eminent performers from different parts of the Kingdom.
> On Thursday the 18th, will be performed, the Oratorio of
>
> ### 'SAMSON'
>
> And on Friday, the 19th, will be performed the Oratorio of 'JUDAS MACCHABAEUS.' No person to be admitted without tickets, which may be had at Messrs. Smith and Green's offices, opposite the White Lion, and all the Book Sellers' shops; where likewise may be had Books of the Several Oratorios.
> N.B. The South Door and the Cloister Door of the Cathedral will be opened each morning at Ten o'clock, and the performance will begin exactly at Eleven.[1]

And that, more or less, has been going on ever since. Occasionally the higher powers showed their approval by contributing to the orchestration. Once Jupiter capped Handel's thunderbolt. It was during a performance in 1791 at York of *Israel in Egypt* that a storm burst. Michael Kelly related how

> never before or since did I behold such a tremendous night,—such bursts of Heaven's artillery, and such sheets of fire, combined with the sacred words and the majestic music of the mighty master, were altogether appalling and magnificent.[2]

---

[1] The history of Handel at Chester is admirably told in Dr. J. C. Bridge's 'The Organists of Chester Cathedral': *Journal of the Architectural, Archaeological and Historic Society* (Chester), vol. xix, and in R. V. H. Burne's *Chester Cathedral*, London 1958, p. 200 et seq.   [2] Kelly, op. cit., ii. 8.

Religion and Handel were not confined to cathedral churches. There were the new foundations of the Methodists to which a hitherto musically disfranchized class were gradually drawn. Singing brought vision into the new squalor of industrial England and dignity to the singers. Handelian choruses levered latent talent into operation and became the priceless property (via the tonic sol-fa class) of the factory workers of Lancashire and Yorkshire, the potters of Staffordshire and the miners of Wales. Handel, who had among his early friends an unashamed coalman from Clerkenwell, would have been pleased. Here we may tread out of music into sociology to contemplate our grandparents escaping from the muck of Manchester to the vision of the glory of the Lord as revealed to them by Handel. Here the cynic stands dumb. We have heard what Gluck, Mozart, Haydn and Beethoven said about Handel. What they did in the Potteries may be remembered as a greater tribute. In 1892 the Hanley Glee and Madrigal Society received an invitation to sing Gaul's *Israel in the Wilderness* at the Crystal Palace. The invitation was declined because the choir preferred to stay at home to practise *Israel in Egypt*.

Almost without noticing it we have traversed a hundred years in a couple of paragraphs. A hundred years during which the settlement of oratorio left as well as its positive aspect a negative legacy. Under the impact of that newly cultivated vice of respectability—a quality which in the eighteenth century was literally laughed out of court—the Victorians lost the vivacity of Handel (nor has it yet been regained) and let choral singing deteriorate to the standards of community singing: they habituated themselves, as Bernard Shaw puts it, to 'lumbering along with Hallelujah as if it were a superior sort of family coach.' [1] Worse than that, they welcomed the fitful enlightenment of the twilight corybantic Christianity by the lucubrations of repressed academists. Israel went with Gaul to the Wilderness and stayed there for a long time. The enemies of sacred music are not the religious but the religiose.

Rejecting an excellent book a friend commented the other day: 'There's too much imagination about this. I like facts.' Which is a

[1] Shaw, op. cit., i. 110.

fair and concise exposition of the artistic creed mistakenly believed by the English to be the one they follow. The truth is that our imagination proceeds from a pragmatic terminus. But as we look at the world around us we allow a fertilization of fancy. Thus poetry exudes from common things. Unconsciously we take the validity of poetry for granted and therefore tend to deny its existence. Because he too starts from earthly phenomena and from commonplace actions and invests them with the imagery of poetic aspiration Handel finds house-room with us. This is the secret of his genius.

Matthew Arnold preached that poetry should be a criticism of life. It is not clear that he knew precisely what he meant himself. We may, however, approximate to his idealism if we contemplate the uniqueness of Handel. He was, above almost all other composers, lively because he was full of life. His music, moreover, is a part of life. The least literate among music-lovers will appreciate this. Epping Forest on a summer's day recalls a song from *Semele*, or perhaps from *Serse*; the Thames at Richmond the *Water Music*; civic or military festivity the march from *Rinaldo*; athletic victory a chorus from *Joshua*; surpliced choir-boys an air from *Theodora*; the burial of the dead a march from *Saul*. No other music serves in quite the same intimate and yet universal way. No other music, so far as we are concerned, is so oblivious of time. Handel, like Shakespeare and Dante, wrote for his audience:

their glory is that they have outlasted the conditions they observed. Yet it was by observing them that they gained the world's ear. Let us, who are less than they, beware of seeming to belong to our own time.[1]

Handel was a Londoner, the musician laureate of the *beau monde*. But into the stifling air of the city he brought the fragrance of the country. Not all his time was spent in Brook Street. This is too often forgotten. The eye of fancy follows the coach routes. Handel views the garden of Kent, stands on the spaciousness of Salisbury Plain, looks at the royal antiquities of Chester and dreams by the Dove. Did they tell him about Izaak Walton? At Calwich, in the freshest country in England, they put a monument to Handel—an eighteenth-century pavilion. They call it still—Bernard Granville's house is

[1] Quiller-Couch, *On the Art of Writing*, p. 44.

gone, but the pavilion remains in quiet testimony to the fragrance of a near-forgotten friendship—with divided dedication the Temple of Handel and of fishing.

Handel was a Londoner, but he loved England. He became an Englishman, but never forgot (for one cannot) the place where he had spent his youth. To the end, as his bequests show, he remained mindful of Halle, and a Hallenser. Although he was an expatriate, Handel was not ignored in Germany. As has been shown there were particular reasons why his music should be performed in Hamburg, and it was fitting that the first performance of *Messiah* in Germany should have been given there. It was also fitting that the performance, on 15th April, 1772, should have been directed by an Englishman— Michael Arne. The enthusiasm of C. P. E. Bach, then Director of Music in Hamburg, for Handel's choral works, and the development of choral societies as much devoted to them as were their British counterparts led to a wide appreciation of the talents of the most Anglo-Saxon of all Anglo-Saxons. Under the impulses of nine-teenth-century nationalism and the movement for German unity Handel was to some extent recovered for Germany and given the status of a national figure. In consequence of this Friedrich Chrysander undertook his researches, which are the foundation of all later scholar-ship. By the twentieth century Handel was as familiar and as loved in the country of his birth as in that of his adoption. And so, with a new race of musicologists making corporate genuflection, it is today.

But this is what remains transcendent. This is the record of a lover of humanity, of one who understood his fellow men and wrote their character with affection and optimism in the imperishable terms of great music. Manly music which springs from the contemplation of man. Is that not the source of the philosophy of the Augustans?

They wrote of him after his death:

Such was Handel, in whose character whatever there was wrong there was nothing mean; though he was proud his pride was uniform; he was not by turns a tyrant and a slave: a censor in one place and a sycophant in another; he maintained his liberty in a state in which others would have been vain of dependence: he was liberal even when he was poor, and remembered his former friends when he was rich. . . .[1]

---

[1] *Gentleman's Magazine,* May 1760.

APPENDICES

APPENDIX A

CALENDAR

(Figures in brackets denote the age reached by the person mentioned during the year in question.)

Year	Age	Life	Contemporary Musicians
1685		Georg Friedrich Händel born Feb. 23 in Halle (birthplace now museum, Grosse-Nikolaistrasse 5), son of Georg Händel, surgeon in Giebichenstein, and to the Duke of Sachsen-Weissenfels.	Bach born, March 21; Scarlatti (D). born, Oct. 26. Abaco aged 10; Albinoni 11; Ariosti *c.* 25; Blow 36; Böhm 24; Buononcini 13; Buxtehude 48; Caldara *c.* 15; Campra 25; Charpentier *c.* 50; Clarke *c.* 25; Corelli 33; Couperin 17; Croft 7; Desmarets 23; Destouches *c.* 13; Durante 1; Eccles *c.* 22; Fux 25; Geminiani 5; Keiser 11; Kerll 57; Kuhnau 25; Lalande 28; Legrenzi *c.* 60; Lotti 18; Lully 53; Muffat (sen.) *c.* 40; Pachelbel 32; Pasquini 48; Pepusch 18; Purcell 26; Rameau 2; Reinken 62; Scarlatti (A.) 26; Steffani 31; Telemann 4; Vivaldi *c.* 15.
1686	1		Marcello born, July 31/Aug. 1; Porpora born Aug. 19.
1687	2		Graupner born, Feb.; Lully (55) dies, March 22; Senaillé born, Nov. 23.
1688	3		Fasch (J. F.) born, April 15; Foggia (84) dies, Jan. 8.
1689	4		
1690	5		Carey born (approx.); Legrenzi (*c.* 65) dies, July 26;

184

Year	Age	Life	Contemporary Musicians
			Muffat (jun.) born, April; Vinci born.
1691	6		d'Anglebert (63) dies.
1692	7	Learning to play musical instruments.	Tartini born, April 8; Vitali (G. B.) (c. 48) dies, Oct. 12.
1693	8	In this, or the next, year taken to Weissenfels where it was advised he should have competent musical tuition.	Kerll (65) dies, Feb. 13; Locatelli born; Sammartini (G.) born (approx.).
1694	9	Pupil of Zachow (31) at Marienkirche near his home.	Daquin born, July 4; Leo born, Aug. 5.
1695	10	Having come under influence of local oboist, J. G. Hyntzsch, composes sonatas for 2 oboes and continuo (MS. in Brit. Mus.).	Greene born; Purcell (36) dies, Nov. 21.
1696	11	Visit to Berlin (?) and offer of assistance in respect of further musical training from Elector of Brandenburg, in whose jurisdiction Halle was.	
1697	12	Death of father (75) Feb. 11. Composition of church cantatas and organ music (lost).	Leclair born, May 10; Quantz born, Jan. 30.
1698	13	Student (until 1700) in Stadtgymnasium, where Rector Johann Praetorius is musical and where Singspiele are periodically performed.	Francœur born, Sept. 28.
1699	14		Hasse born, March 25.
1700	15		Strungk (60) dies, Sept. 23.
1701	16	Meets G. P. Telemann (20) for the first time.	Graun born, May 7; Sammartini (G. B.) born.
1702	17	Student in Law Faculty, Halle University. Succeeds intemperate Leporin as organist Calvinist cathedral, Mar. 13. Church music, including extant Laudate pueri, composed.	

Year	Age	*Life*	*Contemporary Musicians*
1703	18	Joins opera orchestra in Hamburg, directed by R. Keiser (29), as violinist and cembalist. Friendly with J. Mattheson (22), through whom he becomes music tutor to household of British Resident. Excursion with Mattheson to Lübeck where any idea of succeeding D. Buxtehude (66) is dispelled by contractual obligation on part of successor to marry Buxtehude's daughter.	Lampe born.
1704	19	Performance of *St. John Passion* (Postel). Quarrel with Mattheson over cembalo playing in Mattheson's *Cleopatra* on Dec. 5. Friendship resumed after cooling-off period.	Biber (60) dies, May 5; Charpentier (c. 69) dies, Feb. 24; Muffat (sen.) (c. 59) dies, Feb. 31.
1705	20	Success of *Almira* on Jan. 8. *Nero* performed on Feb. 25.	
1706	21	Uneasy relationship with Keiser, resignation from opera and concentration on teaching. Composition of pieces for pupils and *Florindo* and *Daphne,* and departure for Italy by way of Hanover and Halle. Meets A. Scarlatti (47) near Florence, Sept. (?).	Galuppi born, Oct. 18; Mattini born, April 24.
		From Florence to Rome where *Dixit Dominus* and (second setting of) *Laudate pueri* were composed. In Rome received by Cardinal Ottoboni and entertained at his private concerts. Guest of Prince Ruspoli. Meets Corelli (54), Marcello (21) and	H. Hall (52) dies, March 30. Buxtehude (70) dies, May 9; Clarke (c. 47) dies, Dec. 1.

Year	Age	Life	Contemporary Musicians
		Pasquini (70). Oratorios, *La Resurrezione* and *Il Trionfo del Tempo e del Disinganno* and other works composed in Rome. *Rodrigo,* his first Italian opera, successfully produced in Florence, July.	
1708	23	Serenata *Aci, Galatea e Polifemo* performed in Naples, July. Reputed meeting with an attractive lady—Donna Laura; attractive French cantata for another lady. Return to Rome. Hears Calabrian shepherds' music, including air as copied by English composer R. Valentine at this time and also used by Handel in 'Pastoral Symphony' (*Messiah*).	Blow (60) dies, Oct. 1.
1709	24	To Florence in spring. Meeting with D. Scarlatti (24), Lotti (42), Gasparini (41), and Earl of Manchester in Venice. Possibly renews acquaintance with Steffani (55) and Prince Ernst of Hanover. From Dec. 26, 27 performances of commissioned opera, *Agrippina,* in San Giovanni Crisostomo theatre.	Benda (F.) born, Nov. 25; Colasse (60) dies, July 17; Duni born, Feb. 9; Richter (F. X.) born, Dec.
1710	25	Succeeds Steffani as Court Director of Music in Hanover in June. After visiting Halle travels to Düsseldorf and thence to London. Here he is presented to Queen Anne (45), meets Heidegger (51)	Arne born, March 12; Avison born (date uncertain); Bach (W. F.) born, Nov. 22; Boyce born, Feb. 7; Pasquini (73) dies, Nov. 22; Pergolesi born, Jan. 3.

Year	*Age*	*Life*	*Contemporary Musicians*
		and Aaron Hill (25), and promises to compose *Rinaldo*.	
1711	26	*Rinaldo* (first perf., Feb. 24) a great success. Songs from the opera, 'composta dal Signor Hendel Maestro di Capella di Sua Altessa Elettorale d'Hannover', published by J. Walsh and J. Hare. *Rinaldo* draws enthusiastic houses and repeated fourteen times before end of opera season in June. Convivial musical evenings with celebrated coal-man, T. Britton (*c.* 67), in Clerkenwell, at which he becomes acquainted with much English music and some English musicians, amateurs as well as professional. Shows interest in M. Dubourg (8), boy prodigy violinist, and accomplished cembalist W. Babell (*c.* 21) who published harpsichord lessons on pieces from *Rinaldo*. Mary Granville (11), later Mrs. Delany, hero-worships Handel. Return to Hanover in summer, further visits to Düsseldorf and Halle. Composes chamber duets for Princess Caroline (28), as well as concertos and cantatas.	Holzbauer born.
1712	27	Arrival in London in autumn and production of *Il pastor fido* at King's Theatre, Nov. 22. Despite comparative failure Handel immediately offered *Teseo,* to a libretto by N. Haym	Zachow (49) dies, Aug. 14.

Year	Age	Life	Contemporary Musicians

(33) dedicated to Earl of Burlington (17).

1713 28 *Teseo* performed, Jan. 10, but manager of King's Theatre, O. MacSwiney (*d.* 1754) decamped with funds, leaving Handel and singers unpaid. Opera continued at artistes' and composer's risk. Handel composes *Te Deum*, belatedly to celebrate Peace of Utrecht, and Birthday Ode for Queen Anne. He follows models of ceremonial church music by H. Purcell and W. Croft (35) and of court music by J. Eccles (45). Queen Anne, delighted by performance of Ode on Feb. 7, and good reports of July 7 performance of *Te Deum* at St. Paul's Cathedral, arranges annual allowance of £200 for Handel.

Contemporary Musicians: Corelli (60) dies, Jan. 10; Dauvergne born, Oct. 4; Krebs born, Feb. 10; Terradellas born, Feb.

1714 29 Invited to stay at Burlington House, Piccadilly, where he meets Pope (26), Gay (29), and Arbuthnot (47). *Silla* performed, probably at Burlington House. Death of Queen Anne and accession of Georg Ludwig of Hanover as George I (54), who attends performance of *Utrecht Te Deum*, Oct. 28.

Contemporary Musicians: Bach (C. P. E.) born, March 8; Gluck born, July 2; Homilius born, Feb. 2; Jommelli born, Sept. 10.

1715 30 *Amadigi* produced at the King's Theatre, May 25, and acquaintance with Geminiani (*c.* 35), a former pupil of Corelli. Royal music master.

Contemporary Musicians: Wagenseil born, Jan. 15; Alcock born, April 11; Nares born, April; Doles born, April 23.

189

Year	Age	Life	Contemporary Musicians
1716	31	George I goes to his Electorate in July, and Handel to Hanover, Halle, Dresden, and Ansbach. A busy tour included arranging to compose a setting of Brockes's *Passion* for Hamburg, and to find singers for the London Opera in Dresden, and business in Ansbach possibly on Princess Caroline's account (she was from Ansbach). Return to London with J. C. Schmidt (Smith) engaged as secretary, amanuensis, etc.	
1717	32	Revivals of *Rinaldo* and *Amadigi*, but doubtful prospects for future of Italian opera at King's Theatre after end of season in June. Engaged by Earl of Carnarvon (cr. Duke of Chandos, 1719) as 'Composer in Residence' at Canons, where J. C. Pepusch (50) was also employed. A parttime job with a parttime group of musicians including wellknown singers from the Chapel Royal whose names were written in autographs of 'Chandos' Anthems.	Nichelmann born, Aug. 13; Purcell (Daniel) (*c.* 57) dies, Nov.; Stamitz (J. W.) born, June 19.
1718	33	Death of Handel's sister Dorothea Sophia Michaelsen. Collaboration with Gay in composition of masquestyle *Acis and Galatea*.	Vitali (T. A.) (*c.* 53) dies (approx.).
1719	34	Royal Academy of Music established by nobility for presentation of Italian opera under	

Year	Age	Life	Contemporary Musicians
		Handel's direction. Scouting expedition for singers takes Handel to Düsseldorf, Hanover, and Dresden. He spends much time in the Saxon capital and earns some money by playing the harpsichord to the Elector, and the envy of the Commandant of Dresden. Visit to Halle, but J. S. Bach is not able to arrange a desired meeting. Moves into house in Brook Street.	
1720	35	Opera season under Handel's direction opened on April 2. First performance of *Radamisto*, April 27. *Haman and Mordecai* (with Chapel Royal singers) performed at Canons, Aug. 29. Suites for harpsichord published, Nov. 14, because incorrect copies 'had got abroad.'	Agricola (J. F.) born, Jan. 4.
1721	36	As a gimmick *Muzio Scevola* (April 15) composed jointly by 'F. Mattei' (F. Amadei ?), Buononcini, Handel's chief rival in the affections of the London aristocracy, and Handel. Buononcini much in favour this year and Handel's *Floridante* (Dec. 9) does not go down well.	Kirnberger born, April.
1722	37	Despite diminishing interest in them in London, Handel's operas, somewhat roughly re-fashioned, taken into the Hamburg repertoire. At the end of the year Francesca	Benda (G.) born, June 30; Kuhnau (62) dies, June 25; Nardini born; Reinken (99) dies, Nov. 24.

Year	Age	Life	Contemporary Musicians
		Cuzzoni (*c.* 22), after some delay, arrives in London to sing in *Ottone*. Cuzzoni, tiresome in rehearsal, is threatened by Handel with defenestration.	
1723	38	*Ottone* produced at King's Theatre, Jan. 12. Appointed Composer to Chapel Royal in association with Croft (45) and Weldon (47). Scottish singer, Alexander Gordon, M.A. (Aberdeen) (*c.* 30), engaged for *Flavio* (first perf. May 14) and reported to have threatened jumping on the harpsichord, thus provoking a Handelian riposte that is probably apocryphal. The fifth season of Italian Opera opens, Nov. 27.	Gassmann born, May 4.
1724	39	Performance of Ariosti's (*c.* 64) *Vespasiano* proves disastrous. Handel completes *Giulio Cesare* which is performed on Feb. 20. Aug. 29, newspaper report of Handel playing organ at St. Paul's Cathedral to his pupils (exercises extant in Fitz. Mus. Cambridge), Princesses Anne and Caroline. *Tamerlano,* Oct. 31.	Theile (78) dies, June.
1725	40	*Rodelinda* (Feb. 13) successful as much on account of Cuzzoni's fashion-stimulating dress as the music. Handel helps in selection of T. Roseingrave (35) as organist of St. George's Church, Hanover	Krieger (J. P.) (76) dies, Feb. 6; Scarlatti (A.) (66) dies, Oct. 24.

Year	Age	Life	Contemporary Musicians
		Square, at which Handel was a worshipper.	
1726	41	New opera *Scipio* finished, Mar. 2, produced Mar. 12. Engagement of Bordoni (34) for Opera. Her appearing with Cuzzoni (*c.* 27) in *Alessandro* ensures full houses, but the two singers dislike each other. J. J. Quantz (29) visits London, and Handel tries to persuade him to remain.	Lalande (69) dies, June 18; Philidor born, Sept. 7.
1727	42	Eighth season of Italian opera. *Admeto* performed, Jan. 31. *Riccardo I* completed May 16 (first perf., Nov. 11). Cuzzoni and Bordoni come to blows during Buononcini opera in June, thus bringing season to precipitate end. Coronation of George II stimulates Handel (now British subject) to compose suitable anthems.	Croft (49) dies, Aug. 14; Traetta born, Mar. 30.
1728	43	*Siroe* (Feb. 17) and *Tolomeo* (April 30) produced for the Royal Academy, which, however, because of rising costs and diminishing returns, is obliged to close down. The *Beggar's Opera* (Gay-Pepusch), launched on Jan. 29, is an enormous success. In the summer Handel and Heidegger go into partnership and take a five-year lease of King's Theatre for production of operas.	Hiller (J. A.) born, Dec. 25; Lœillet (*c.* 53) dies; Marais (72) dies, Aug.; Piccinni born Jan. 16; Steffani (74) dies, Feb. 12.
1729	44	A European tour in seach of singers. Florence, Milan.	Monsigny born, Oct. 17; Sarti born. Dec. 1.

Year	Age	Life	Contemporary Musicians
		Venice, Rome; hears music by Porpora (42), Vinci (38), Hasse (29), and Pergolesi (18), and becomes acquainted with libretti by Metastasio (30). Visits his mother, now blind and infirm, in Halle. Wilhelm Friedemann Bach attempts to arrange meeting between his father and Handel, but is unsuccessful. Return to London at end of June. New opera undertaking opens with *Lotario* (Dec. 2) and without success.	
1730	45	*Partenope* on Feb. 24. Second season of Heidegger/Handel opera opens on Nov. 3 with revival of *Scipione*. Handel's mother (75) dies, Dec. 27.	Aylward born; Jackson born, May 29; Senaillé (43) dies, Oct. 15.
1731	46	*Poro* (libretto from Metastasio) performed, Feb. 2. Unauthorized revival of *Acis and Galatea*, with additions, and with Leveridge (c. 61) as Polyphemus, at Lincoln's Inn Fields Theatre, Mar. 26. Buononcini in disgrace having seemed to pass off a madrigal by Lotti as his own. Six sonatas for 2 vl., 2 ob., or 2 fl. and cont. (Op. 2) pub. Roger, Amsterdam.	Cannabich born.
1732	47	*Ezio*, Jan. 15. Revivals of *Haman and Mordecai* (renamed *Esther*), through B. Gates (c. 47), on Feb. 23, March 1, and March 3; and of *Acis and Galatea* (pirated version featur-	Haydn born, Mar. 31/April 1; T. Linley (sen.) born.

Year	Age	*Life*	*Contemporary Musicians*

ing Susanna Arne (18) at Lincoln's Inn Fields), May 17 and (directed by Handel and with additions from *Aci, Galatea e Polifemo*) at King's Theatre, June 10. Opening of new opera season in November, and *Orlando* completed on Nov. 20. Op. 2 pub. by Walsh.

1733 48 *Orlando* performed, Jan. 27, and (also at the King's Theatre) oratorio *Deborah,* Mar. 17. In June a rival opera company, set up by nobility in association with Prince of Wales, and Porpora (47) engaged as musical director. Handel visits Oxford to give concerts and (July 10) new oratorio *Athalia.* Italian visit to engage new singers in place of those who had deserted to Porpora's team. *Arianna* finished and new season opened at King's Theatre. Walsh publishes *Suites de Pièces* (2 vols.) which been composed as teaching material for the princesses.

Couperin (65) dies, Sept. 12.

1734 49 A tiresome year for Handel, whose opera season draws poor audiences, leading to cancellation of contract with Heidegger. H. arranges with Rich (*c.* 52) to put on performances at Covent Garden Theatre. For wedding of Princess Anne (24) composed anthem (as did M. Greene)

Ayrton born; Carter born; Cooke (B.) born; Gossec born, Jan. 17; Sacchini born, July 23.

Year	Age	Life	Contemporary Musicians
		and arranging *Parnasso in festa* from *Athalia*. 6 *Concerti Grossi* (Op. 3) issued on or before Dec. 7.	
1735	50	*Ariodante* and *Alcina* given at Covent Garden. Lenten series of oratorios for which H. composes and plays organ concertos. H. finds it difficult to maintain opera against diminishing interest and strong opposition. He closes season in July and goes into the country. At end of year considers oratorio proposal from Jennens (35) and begins work on N. Hamilton's edition of Dryden's *Alexander's Feast*. Six *Fugues or Voluntaries* (org. or harps.) (Op. 3) pub.	Bach (J. C.) born, Sept. 5; Eccles (c. 72) dies, Jan. 12; Krieger (J.) (83) dies, July 18.
1736	51	*Alexander's Feast*, completed Jan. 17, perf. Covent Garden, Feb. 19. Prince of Wales (29) marries Princess of Sachsen-Gotha. H. composes wedding anthem and produces *Atalanta* (May 10) in their honour. New opera season opens in November, with Hasse (37) replacing Porpora (50) at King's Theatre. H. subscribes to volume of songs by Gloucester organist, B. Gunn (c. 56).	Anfossi born (approx.); Caldara (c. 66) dies, Dec. 28; Fasch (C. F. C.) born, Nov. 18; Pergolesi (26) dies, Mar. 17.
1737	52	*Arminio* (Jan. 12) and *Giustino* (Feb. 16). Lenten oratorio season includes *Esther, Alexander's Feast*, and revision of *Il Trionfo del tempo* (1708). Serious illness causing tem-	Mysliveček born, Mar. 9. M. Haydn born, Sept. 14.

Year	Age	Life	Contemporary Musicians
		porary paralysis of right arm, April 13. After production of *Berenice,* May 18, goes to Aix-la-Chapelle for cure. Take-over of resources of two opera companies by Heidegger who invites H. to write new works for King's Theatre season. Death of Queen Caroline (54), Nov. 20. *Funeral Anthem* first perf. Dec. 17.	
1738	53	Performances of *Faramondo* (Jan. 7), *Alessandro Severo* (Feb. 25), *Serse* (April 15?). Vauxhall Gardens concert and unveiling of statue of H. by Roubiliac (42). Support for newly founded Society of Musicians, promoted by M. Festing (*c.* 58). Composition of *Saul* and *Israel in Egypt,* in autumn. Walsh publishes Six Concertos for org. or harps. (Op. 4).	Battishill born, May; Mursch-hauser (75) dies, Jan. 6.
1739	54	*Saul* at the King's Theatre, Jan. 16; *Israel in Egypt,* April 4 and 11. Italian opera and its nadir, H. produces miscellaneous works at Lincoln's Inn Fields, where the St. Cecilia's Day Ode perf. on St. Cecilia's Day. Seven sonatas for 2 vl., or 2 fl. and cont. (Op. 5) pub., and Twelve 'Grand Concertos' composed. *Alexander's Feast* performed at Gloucester Festival.	Dittersdorf born, Nov. 2; Keiser (65) dies, Sept. 12; Marcello (53) dies, July 24; Rust born, July 6; Wanhal born, May 12.

Handel

Year	Age	Life	Contemporary Musicians
1740	55	*L'Allegro, il Penseroso ed il Moderato* perf. at Lincoln's Inn, Feb. 27. Visits Haarlem and plays the organ. On his way to Berlin, according to German newspaper, possibly to investigate openings at the Court of the new King of Prussia, Frederick the Great (28). Return to London, last operas finished. *Imeneo* perf. Nov. 22, but without success. Publication of Twelve 'Grand Concertos' (Op. 6). Arne's (30) first Shakespeare songs published.	Arnold born, Aug. 10; Böhm (79) dies (approx.); Lotti (73) dies, Jan. 5; Webbe born.
1741	56	*Deidamia* produced, Jan. 10. Three performances of this mark the end of career as opera composer. A Farewell Concert, April 8, suggests depression and intention to retire. Invitation to Dublin from Lord Lieutenant spurs H. to further effort and *Messiah* begun Aug. 22 as a work to raise funds for Irish charities. Score completed Sept. 12. *Samson* virtually complete by Oct. 29. H. travels to Chester, where he is seen by C. Burney (15) and he runs through *Messiah* with help of local musicians. Welsh lay-clerk gains immortality by making errors in sight reading. After delay caused by bad weather H. and his party sail from Parkgate and reach Dublin,	Arne (Michael) born; Desmarets (79) dies, Sept. 7; Fux (81) dies, Feb. 13; Grétry born, Feb. 8; Naumann born, April 17; Paisiello born, May 9.

Year	Age	Life	Contemporary Musicians
		Nov. 18. Series of Subscription Concerts begins in Dublin, Dec. 23.	
1742	57	Handel lives in rooms in Abbey Street, Dublin while directing concerts and rehearsals. Public rehearsal of *Messiah*, Mar. 8; first performance in New Musick Hall, April 13. Reported stay outside Dublin and composition of *Forest Music* (based on older material). Return to London, August.	Abaco (67) dies, July 12.
1743	58	*Samson* at Covent Garden, Feb. 18, and first London perf. *Messiah,* Mar. 23. Completion of *Semele* (after Congreve) and *Joseph and his Brethren*. Defeat of French army at Dettingen (Bavaria) by English gave cause for composition of *Te Deum* (Chapel Royal, Nov. 27). Handel ill during the year, which caused his friends concern.	Boccherini born, Feb. 19; Carey (*c.* 53) dies, Oct. 4; Vivaldi (*c.* 73) dies.
1744	59	*Semele* (Feb. 10) and *Joseph and his Brethren* (Mar. 2) at Covent Garden. Mrs Delany (née Anne Granville) wants H. to compose an oratorio based on *Paradise Lost*. Because Lord Middlesex fails in running opera there the King's Theatre becomes again available. H. takes a lease of it.	Campra (84) dies. June 29; Leo (50) dies, Oct. 31.
1745	60	Performances of new works, *Hercules* (Jan. 5) and *Belshazzar* (Mar. 27) at King's	Albinoni (71) dies (approx.); Dibdin born, March 4.

Year	Age	Life	Contemporary Musicians
		Theatre. Indifferent reception for both, and H., again ill, withdraws from that theatre. Recurrence of illness. H. subscribes to T. Chilcot's Shakespeare songs. Gluck (31) meets H. in London.	
1746	61	*Occasional Oratorio,* celebrating failure of the campaign of Charles Edward Stuart (26) in England, perf. Covent Garden, Feb. 14. Massacre of Scots at Culloden (April 16) prompted composition of *Judas Maccabaeus* (completed Aug. 11).	Hook born, June 1; Stamitz (C.) born, May 7.
1747	62	Successful season of oratorio, *Judas Maccabaeus* being well liked.	
1748	63	*Joshua* and *Alexander Balus* novelties of this oratorio season. *Acis and Galatea* performed at Salisbury Festival (f. 1744), organised by J. Harris (39), and again in following year.	Shield born, Mar. 5.
1749	64	*Susanna* (Feb. 10) and *Solomon* (Mar. 17) performed at Covent Garden, the *Fireworks Music,* celebrating Peace of Aix-la-Chapelle, at Chapelle, at Vauxhall, April 27, and *Foundling Hospital Anthem* in Hospital Chapel, May 27.	Cimarosa born, Dec. 17; Destouches (*c.* 77) dies (approx.); Vogler born, Jan. 15.
1750	65	Music for Smollett's (29) *Alcestis* composed, but transferred to *The Choice of Hercules.* *Theodora* produced without	Stafford Smith born, April; Bach (65) dies, July 28; Buononcini (78) dies (approx.); Salieri born, Aug. 19;

Year	Age	Life	Contemporary Musicians
		attracting much enthusiasm on Mar. 16. H. elected Governor of Foundling Hospital, May 9, after his presentation of an organ and performance of *Messiah* there a week earlier. Last visit to Germany, and coach accident in Holland, during summer.	Sammartini (G.) (*c.* 57) dies (approx.); Veracini (*c.* 65) dies.
1751	66	*The Choice of Hercules,* Covent Garden, Mar. 1. H. takes cure in Cheltenham (during which plays organ in Tewkesbury Abbey) in May–June, returning to London on June 13. Troubled by failing eyesight.	Lampe (48) dies, July 25; Terradellas (38) dies, May 20.
1752	67	Last oratorio, *Jephtha,* performed at Covent Garden, Feb. 26. Operation for cataract (?) performed by S. Sharp (*c.* 52) unsuccessful. Chilcot organizes performances of H.'s music in Bath.	Clementi born, (?) Jan.; Pepusch (82) dies, July 20; Reichardt born, Nov. 25; Zingarelli born, April 4.
1753	68	H.'s plight excites general sympathy and his appearance at Covent Garden and the Foundling Hospital provided opportunity to express it. T. Linley names son after Handel.	Dalayrac born, June 13; Viotti born, May 23.
1754	69	With help of J. C. Smith (42) revises old works. Resumes correspondence with G. P. Telemann (73).	Kozeluch born.
1755	70	First performance of *Messiah* in Bath, conducted W. Hayes (49), May 17.	Harrer dies (52), July 9; Durante (71) dies, Aug. 13; Winter born.
1756	71	*Acis and Galatea,* conducted by J. Randall (*c.* 41), in Senate House, Cambridge; also perf. in Bath.	Mozart born, Jan. 27; T. Linley (jr.) born, May 5.

Year	Age	Life	Contemporary Musicians
1757	72	*The Triumph of Time and Truth*, from *Il Trionfo del tempo* (1708, 1737), with extra numbers dictated to Smith (45), at Covent Garden, Mar. 4.	R. J. S. Stevens born, April 27; Pleyel born, June 1; Scarlatti (D.) (62) dies; Stamitz (J.) (40) dies, Mar. 30.
1758	73	*Judas Maccabaeus*, *Alexander's Feast*, and *Messiah*, conducted by Elias Isaac (33), pupil of Greene and cathedral organist, Worcester Festival.	Dagincourt (74) dies, Zelter born, Dec. 11.
1759	74	Although in failing health H. as usual attends annual *Messiah* performance at Foundling Hospital (Mar. 30, April 6). Makes a codicil to his Will, April 11. Dies on April 14 and interred in Westminster Abbey on April 20.	Graun (58) dies, Aug. 8. Agricola (J. F.) aged 39; Alcock 44; Anfossi *c.* 23; Arne (T. A.) 49; Arne (M.) 18; Arnold 19; Avison *c.* 49; Aylward 29; Ayrton 25; Bach (W. F.) 49; Bach (C. P. E.) 45; Bach (J. C.) 24; Battishall 21; Bendi (F.) 50; Benda (G.) 37; Boccherini 16; Boyce 49; Cannabich, 28; Carter 25; Cimarosa 10; Clementi 7; Cook (B.) 25; Dalayrac 6; Daquin 65; Dauvergne 46; Dibdin 14; Dittersdorf 20; Duni 50; Fasch (J. F.) 71; Fasch (C. F. C.) 23; Francœur 61; Galuppi 53; Gassmann 36; Gazzaniga 16; Geminiani 79; Gluck 45; Gossec 25; Graun 58; Graupner 72; Grétry 18; Hasse 60; Haydn 27; Hiller (J. A.) 31; Holzbauer 48; Hook 13; Jackson 29; Jommelli 45; Kirnberger 38; Kozeluch 5; Krebs 46; Leclair 62; Linley 27; Locatelli 66; Martini 53; Mon-

Performances of *Messiah* and *Judas Maccabaeus*, for General Hospital, Bath, April 26, 27; *Messiah*, Cambridge, May 17, and Oxford, July 5; *Acis and Galatea*, Coventry, Sept. 18; and Handel Festival, Church Langton, Leicestershire, Sept. 26, 27.

Although Handel's works had figured at Three Choirs Festivals for twenty years, at Hereford, on Sept. 14, for the first time an oratorio, *Messiah*, was performed in the cathedral, thus setting a precedent followed ever since.

Year	Age	Life	Contemporary Musicians
			signy 30; Mozart 3; Muffat (jr.) 69; Mysliveček 22; Nardini 37; Nares 44; Naumann 18; Nichelmann 42; Paisiello 18; Philidor 33; Piccinni 31; Pleyel 2; Porpora 73; Quantz 62; Rameau 76; Reichardt 7; Richter (F. X.) 50; Rust 20; Sacchini 25; Salieri 9; Sammartini (G. B.) c. 58; Sarti 30; Shield 11; Stamitz (C.) 13; Stanley 46; Tartini 67; Telemann 78; Traetta 32; Umlauf 3; Viotti 6; Vogler 10; Wagenseil 44; Wanhal 20; Webbe 19; Winter 4; Zelter 1; Zingarelli 7.

APPENDIX B

CATALOGUE OF WORKS

(Dates in parentheses refer to those of first performance, or of first publication where known; in other cases the approximate time of composition is shown. MSS. in the British Museum, the Fitzwilliam Museum, Cambridge, and the Central Library, Manchester, are indicated respectively by B.M., Fitz. Mus., and Man. Volumes available in the Hallische Händel-Ausgabe are prefaced by H.H.-A. and in each case the editor's name is given in parentheses.)

ORATORIOS AND LARGE-SCALE CANTATAS

Aci, Galatea e Polifemo (version of 1708 and 1732), librettist anon. (Chrysander edition, Vol. 95.)

Acis and Galatea (1719), John Gay and others (3).

Alexander Balus (1748), Thomas Morell (33).

Alexander's Feast (1736), John Dryden (12); H.H.-A., I, 1 (K. Ameln)

Allegro, il Peneroso ed il Moderato, L' (1740), Charles Jennens, after John Milton (6); H.H.-A., I, 16 (J. S. & M. Hall).

Athalia (1733), Samuel Humphreys, after J. Racine (5).

Belshazzar (1745), Charles Jennens (19).

Choice of Hercules, The (1751), Thomas Morell, and/or Tobias Smollett (?) (18); H.H.-A., I, 31 (W. Siegmund-Schultze).

Deborah (1733). Samuel Humphreys (29)

Der für die Sünden der Welt gemartete und sterbende Jesus (1716), Barthold Heinrich Brockes (15); H.H.-A., I, 7 (F. Schröder).

Esther (*Haman and Mordecai*, 1732 version), Alexander Pope, John Arbuthnot, and Samuel Humphreys, based on J. Racine (41).

Haman and Mordecai (1720), first version of *Esther* (40).

Hercules (1745), Thomas Broughton, after Ovid and Sophocles (4).

Hymen (1742), anon., English concert version of *Imeneo*.

Israel in Egypt (1739), A.V. Bible (16).

Jephtha (1752), Thomas Morell (44).

Johannespassion (1704), Heinrich Postel (9); H.H.-A., I, 2 (G. Fellerer).

Joseph and his Brethren (1744), James Miller (42).

Joshua (1748), Thomas Morell (17).

Judas Maccabaeus (1747), Thomas Morell (22).

Appendix B—Catalogue of Works

Jupiter in Argos (apparently only once performed, in 1739); libretto from A.M. Lucchini (set by Lotti, Dresden 1717), for a 'Dramatical Composition ... intermix'd with Chorus's, and two Concerto's on the Organ'; MSS., B.M., Fitz. Mus., Man.

Messiah (1742), A.V. Bible, arr. Charles Jennens (45); H.H.✓A., I, 17 (J. Tobin).

Occasional Oratorio (1746), Thomas Morell (?), after Milton, Spenser, etc. (43).

Ode for the Birthday of Queen Anne (1713), anon. (46); H.H.✓A., I, 6 (W. Siegmund✓Schultze).

Ode for St. Cecilia's Day (1739), John Dryden (23).

Parnasso in Festa, Il (1734), English version by George Oldmixon; much of the music from *Athalia* (54).

Resurrezione, La (1708), Carlo Sigismondo Capece (39).

Samson (1743), Newburgh Hamilton, after John Milton (10).

Saul (1739), Charles Jennens (13); H.H.✓A., I, 13 (P. M. Young).

Semele (1744), William Congreve, with alterations and additions by Alexander Pope (?) (7).

Solomon (1749), Thomas Morell (26).

Susanna (1749), anon. (1); H.H.✓A., I, 28 (B. Rose).

Theodora (1750), Thomas Morell (8).

Trionfo del Tempo e del Disinganno, Il (1708 and 1737), Benedetto Pamphili (24).

Triumph of Time and Truth, The (1757), adaptation and translation of previous item, Thomas Morell (20).

OPERAS, INCIDENTAL MUSIC ETC.

Admeto (1727), Nicola F. Haym or Paolo A. Rolli, from Aurelio Aureli (73).

Agrippina (1709), Vincenzo Grimani (57).

Alceste (1750), for play by Tobias Smollett, but not performed and in part transferred to *The Choice of Hercules* (see above) (46b).

Alchimist, The (1732), for play by Ben Jonson (MS., B.M.) versions pub. J. Walsh, *c.* 1732, S. Arnold, *c.* 1790.

Alcina (1735), Antonio Marchi, from Ariosto (86).

Alessandro (1726), Paolo A. Rolli, from Ortensio Mauro (72).

Alessandro Severo (1738), pasticcio from various works of Handel with new overture, libretto Apostolo Zeno (?) (overture, 48).

Almira (1705), Friedrich C. Feustking after Giulio Pancieri (55).

Amadigi (1715), John J. Heidegger (?) (62); H.H.✓A., II, 8 (J. M. Knapp).

Arianna (1734), Francis Colman from Pietro Pariati (83).

Handel

Ariodante (1735), Antonio Salvi, from Ariosto (85); H.H.✓A., II, 32 (Fürth).

Arminio (1737), Antonio Salvi (89).

Atalanta (1736), from Belisario Valeriana (87).

Berenice (1737), Antonio Salvi (90).

Daphne (1708), Heinrich Hinsch (see *Florindo*) (music lost).

Deidamia (1741), Paolo A. Rolli (94).

Ezio (1732), Pietro Metastasio (English version by Samuel Humphreys) (80); H.H.A., II, 26 (Schneider).

Faramondo (1738), Apostolo Zeno (91).

Flavio (1723), Nicola F. Haym, after P. Corneille (67).

Flavio Olibrio (?), fragments based on Apostolo Zeno and Pietro Pariati (perf. Göttingen Handel Festival, 1969) (MSS. B.M., Fitz. Mus.).

Floridante (1721), Paolo A. Rolli (65).

Florindo (1708), Heinrich Hinsch, intended to form one *Singspiel* with *Daphne*; only one fragment of accompaniment for one aria extant (Man. MS. V, 11).

Giulio Cesare (1724), Nicola F. Haym (68); H.H.✓A., II, 14 (F. Zschoch).

Giustino (1737), Nicolo Beregani (88).

Imeneo (1740), anon. (93).

Lotario (1729), adapted from Antonio Salvi (77).

Muzio Scevola (1721), pasticcio with music of Act III only by Handel (64).

Nero (1705), Friedrich Feustking (music lost).

Oreste (1734), pasticcio from other works by Handel and some new material (see 48).

Orlando (1733), Grazio Braccioli, from Ariosto (82); H.H.✓A., II, 28 (S. Flesch).

Ottone (1723), Nicola F. Haym, from Stefano B. Pallavicino (66).

Partenope (1730), Silvio Stampiglia (78).

Pastor fido, Il (1712, 1734, 1734 with *Terpsicore* ballet and songs added), Giacomo Rossi, from Battista Guarini (59, 84).

Poro (1731), Pietro Metastasio (English version by Samuel Humphreys) (79).

Radamisto (1720), Nicola F. Haym, based on Tacitus (63).

Riccardo primo (1727), Paolo A. Rolli (74).

Rinaldo (1711, 1731), Giacomo Rossi from sketch by Aaron Hill, after Tasso (58, 58a).

Rodelinda (1725), Antonio Salvi adapted by Nicola F. Haym (70).

Rodrigo (1707/8?), anon. (56).

Scipione (1726), Paolo A. Rolli, from Apostolo Zeno (71).

Serse (1738), Niccolò Minato, altered by Silvio Stampiglia (92); H.H.-A., II, 39 (R. Steglich).

Silla (*c*. 1714), anon. (61).

Siroe (1728), Pietro Metastasio, altered by Nicola F. Haym (75).

Sosarme (1732), original title, *Fernando Re di Castiglione,* based on *Alfonso primo,* Matteo Noris (English version by Samuel Humphreys) (81).

Tamerlano (1724), Nicola F. Haym, from Agostino Piovene (69).

Teseo (1713), Nicola F. Haym (60).

Tolomeo (1728), Nicola F. Haym (76).

 Handel added recitatives to *Arbace,* J. A. Hasse (?) (1734), *Cajo Fabricio,* J. A. Hasse (?), (1733), *Catone,* J. A. Hasse (?), (1732), *Didone,* Leonardo Vinci (1737), *Ernelinda,* Francesco Silvani (1713), *Ormisda,* Francesco Conti (?), (1730), *Semiramide,* Antonio Vivaldi and others (1733), and *Venceslao,* several hands (1731), in his capacity as opera director.

CHURCH MUSIC

Ach Herr, mich armen Sünder (*c*. 1696), doubtful (see *Händel-Jahrbuch,* 1959, Leipzig, p. 100).

Lobe den Herrn meine Seele (B.M. MS. copy in unknown hand, dated 1719).

Dixit Dominus (1707) (38); H.H.-A., III, 1 (E. Wenzel).

Haec est Regina virginum (1707/8?) (see *The Musical Antiquary,* 1912, p. 116).

Laudate pueri (*c*. 1702) (38).

Laudate pueri (1707) (38).

Nisi Dominus (1707) (38).

Salve Regina (*c*. 1707/12) (38).

Seuiat tellus inter vigores (1707) (see J. S. Hall, 'Handel among the Carme-lites', *The Dublin Review,* 1959, p. 121) (MS. copy in B.M.).

Silete venti (1707?) (38).

Blessed are they that consider the poor (Foundling Hospital, 1749) (36).

'Chandos' Anthems (mainly 1717–20):

 1 *O be joyful in the Lord.*
 2 *In the Lord I put my trust.*
 3 *Have mercy upon me.*
 4 *O sing unto the Lord.*
 5 *I will magnify Thee.*
 6 *As pants the hart.*
 7 *My song shall be always.*
 8 *O come, let us sing.*
 9 *O praise the Lord with one consent.*
 10 *The Lord in my light.*

11 *Let God arise.*

12 *O praise the Lord, ye angels of His* (34, 35, 36); H.H.∕A., III, 6 (G. Hendrie).

Of these nos. 2–11 were for the first time published by Wright & Wilkinson in 1784 (in a different order), as anthems 'Composed Chiefly for the Chapel of his Grace the late James Duke of Chandos'. No. 1, being a version of the Utrecht *Jubilate,* was not published as being already available in a fuller form. No. 12, of doubtful authenticity, was added to the 'Chandos' set by Samuel Arnold in his 'collected edition' (1787–97) and was accepted by subsequent editors.

Coronation Anthems (1727):

   1 *Zadok the priest.*
   2 *The King shall rejoice.*
   3 *My heart is inditing.*
   4 *Let Thy hand be strengthened* (14).

Hymns (*c.* 1750), Words by Charles Wesley:

   1 *O Love divine.*
   2 *Rejoice the Lord is King.*
   3 *Sinners, obey the Gospel Word* (published Goulding & D'Almaine, *c.* 1827).

O praise the Lord (1714?)

Sing unto God (Wedding anthem, 1736) (36).

Te Deum, D major (*c.* 1714) (37).

Te Deum, B flat major (*c.* 1719) (37).

Te Deum, A major (reduction of previous, *c.* 1720/7) (37).

Te Deum ('*Dettingen Te Deum*', 1743) (36).

Te Deum and Jubilate ('*Utrecht Te Deum* . . .', 1713) (31).

The King shall rejoice ('*Dettingen Anthem*', 1743) (36).

The ways of Zion do mourn ('Funeral Anthem', 1737) (11).

This is the day which the Lord has made (Wedding Anthem, 1734) (36).

INSTRUMENTAL MUSIC FOR HARPSICHORD

Suites de Pièces (Lessons) (1720), in A major, D minor, E minor, E major, F sharp minor, G minor, F minor (2); H.H.∕A. IV, 1 (R. Steglich).

Suites de Pièces (Lessons) . . . Second Volume (1733), in B flat major, G major, D minor, D minor, E minor, G minor, B flat major, G major, G major (Chaconne and Variations)) (2); H.H.∕A. IV, 5 (P. Northway).

Appendix B—Catalogue of Works

Suites and Pieces (1):

Six fugues in G minor, G major, B flat major, B minor, A minor, C minor; Sonata, C major; Capriccio, F major; Preludio ed Allegro, G minor; Fantasia, C major; Suite, D minor; Suite, G minor; Allemande, A major; Allemande, F major; Gigue, F major; Prelude, D minor; Sonatina, G major; Sonatina, B flat major; Prelude, F sharp minor; Air, A major; Sonata, C major; Prelude, A minor; Lesson, A minor; Partita, A major; Prelude, G minor; Sonata, G major. H.H.-A. IV, 6 (T. Best).

Suites and Pieces (2):

Suite, C major; Partita, G major; Prelude, D minor; Prelude-Capriccio, G major; Ouverture, G minor; Entrée, G minor; Chaconne, G minor; Prelude, D minor; Allegro, C major; Chaconne, F major; Suite, D minor; Suite, D minor; Sonatina, D minor; Allemande, A minor; Fuga, F major; Chaconne, G minor; Partita, C minor; Suite, C major; Prelude-Allegro, A minor; Air, G minor; Toccata, G minor; Sonatine, G minor; Sonata, G minor; Courante, G major; Air, B flat major; Preludium, F major; Preludium, F minor; Prelude, G minor; Prelude, E major; Air, G minor; Air, B flat major; Impertinence, G minor; Air, F major; Allegro, D minor; Courante, B minor; [Supplementary] Air, C minor; Sonatina, A minor; Aria, C minor. H.H.-A. IV, 17 (T. Best).

Some works of doubtful authenticity and arrangements are in Chrysander 48 (see also Chrysander 2), and a supplementary volume of miscellaneous pieces will be issued (H.H.-A. IV/15).

For Chamber Ensemble

11 Sonatas for Flute and Continuo (Op. 1) (c. 1696–1730?) (27); H.H.-A., IV, 3 (H. P. Schmitz).

6 Sonatas for Violin and Continuo (Op. 1) (27); H.H.-A., IV, 4 (J.P. Hinnenthal).

9 Sonatas for 2 Violins, Oboes, or Flutes and Continuo, incl. 6 Sonatas (Op. 2) (c. 1731) and 3 Sonatas of which MSS. are in Dresden State Library (27); H.H.-A. IV, 10 (1) (S. Flesch).

7 Sonatas for 2 Violins, or German Flutes and Continuo (Op. 5) (1739) (27); H.H.-A. IV, 10 (2) (W. Serauky, S. Flesch).

6 Sonatas for 2 Oboes and Bass (c. 1696) (27).

3 Sonatas for Flute and Continuo (*c.* 1710) (48).

Sonata in B flat major for Oboe and Continuo, pub. Schott, 1948 (W. Bergmann, Thurston Dart).

Sonata in C major for 2 Violins and Continuo (from Fitz. Mus. MS., first form of Overture to *Saul*); H.H./A. I, 13, *Kritischer Bericht.*

FOR ORCHESTRA

6 Concerti Grossi for Flutes, Oboes, Bassoons, Strings, Continuo (Op. 3) (1734), in B flat major/G minor, B flat major, G major, F major, D minor, D major/minor (21); H.H./A. IV, 11 (F. Hudson).

6 organ Concertos, with Oboes and Strings (Op. 4) (1738), in G minor, B flat major, G minor, F major, F major, B flat major (28).

12 Concerti Grossi, for Strings (Op. 6) (1740), in G major, F major, E minor, A minor, D major, G minor, B flat major, C minor, F major, D minor, A major, B minor (30); H.H./A. IV, 14 (A. Hoffmann, H. F. Redlich).

6 Organ Concertos, with Oboes and Strings, Second Set (1740), in F major, A major, D minor, G major, G minor, G minor (48) Nos. 3–6 arr. from Op. 6 (nos. 10, 1, 5, 6).

6 Organ Concertos, with Oboes and Strings, Third Set (Op. 7) (1761), in B flat major, A major, B flat major, D minor, G minor, B flat major (28).

8 Concerti:

   (1) Oboe, Strings in G minor (1703?) (21).

   (2) Oboe, Strings in B flat major (1740) (21).

   (3) Solo Violin, Strings, in B flat major (21).

   (4) Oboe, Strings, in B flat major (21).

   (5) 2 Horns, Strings, in F major (21).

   (6) Organ, Strings, in D minor   } (see Organ Concertos,

   (7) 2 Organs, Strings, Bassoons, in D minor }   Second Set)

   (8) Oboes, Bassoons, Strings, a due chori

     (based on oratorio material) (47)

     H.H./A. IV, 12 (F. Hudson).

Other miscellaneous concertos, including material otherwise used in *Water Music* and *Fireworks Music* in Chrysander 47, 48.

Water Music (*c.* 1717) (47); H.H./A. IV, 13 (H.F. Redlich).

Fireworks Music (1749) (47); H.H./A. IV, 13 (H. F. Redlich).

Forest Music (1742, based on material in J. Walsh, *Forest Harmony,* 1733), reconstructed for Göttingen Handel Festival 1969, pub. Chappell, 1970 (P. M. Young).

Appendix B—Catalogue of Works

VOCAL CHAMBER MUSIC

72 Italian Cantatas for Voice and Continuo (50, 51).

28 Italian Cantatas for various Voices and Instuments (52a, b).

22 Italian Duets with Continuo (32).

2 Italian Trios with Continuo (32).

La Solitudine, Italian Cantata (MS. Cardiff Central Library), for Alto Voice and Continuo; pub. Bärenreiter 1970 (M. Boyd).

Il *Pianto di Maria: Cantata Sacra a Soprano da eseguirsi avanti il Santo Sepolcro*, with accompaniment for instruments; performed at Göttingen Handel Festival, 1972.

Neun deutsche Arien, for soprano, Violin and Continuo; pub. Breitkopf und Härtel 1931 (H. Roth).

Airs français (Cantate française) (c. 1708); pub. Bärenreiter, 1972 (P. M. Young).

Two Songs from an English Cantata, *Venus and Adonis (c.* 1711), John Hughes; pub. Augener, 1938 (W. C. Smith, Havergal Brian).

'I like the am'rous youth that's free'; sung by Mrs. Clive, 28 February 1737, in James Miller's *Universal Passion.*

'Love's but the frailty of the mind'; sung at· her Benefit, by Mrs. Clive, 17 March 1740, in Congreve's *The Way of the World.*

Comus, John Milton; 3 airs and chorus composed for Earl of Gainsborough (1745); (MS 130, Hd.4,v. 300 Man.).

Stand round my brave boys, for the Gentlemen Volunteers of London, *The London Magazine,* November 1745.

From scourging Rebellion, 'A Song on the Victory obtain'd over the Rebels by His Royal Highness the Duke of Cumberland. The words by Mr. [John] Lockman'; pub. J. Walsh, 26 May 1746.

The Morning is charming (1751), Charles Legh, Hunting song for the Legh family, Adlington Hall, Cheshire; facsimile pub. in Streatfeild.

Many songs were published in England bearing Handel's name, of which some were arrangements of instrumental tunes, and others were spurious.

In view of Handel's massive output, the posthumous attribution to him of works which he may or may not have composed, the dispersal and rediscovery of copies of sometimes doubtful authenticity, it is unlikely that a 'complete' catalogue of his works will ever exist. However, the *Ver-zeichnis der Werke G. F. Händels* (Leipzig, 1979) is the first volume of a definitive thematic catalogue. (See also *Händel-Jahrbuch* 1979 for HWV.)

APPENDIX C

Abaco, Giuseppe dall' (1709–1805), Italian cellist, born in Brussels, son of the violinist Evaristo dall' Abaco. He worked at Bonn, London, Vienna and elsewhere, and composed cello sonatas.

Albinoni, Tommaso (1674–1745), Venetian violinist and composer.

Ariosti, Attilio (born *c.* 1660), Italian operatic composer, who produced his first opera, *Dafne*, at Venice in 1686.

Arne, Cecilia. See Young.

Arne, Susanna Maria. See Cibber.

Avison, Charles (*c.* 1710–70), organist at Newcastle-on-Tyne. Pupil of Geminiani and author of *An Essay on Musical Expression*, in which Handel is sometimes adversely criticized.

Avolio (or *Avoglio*), *Signora,* Italian soprano singer of whose career nothing is known apart from its coincidence with that of Handel.

Baldassari, Benedetto, Italian tenor singer, in London 1720–2.

Banister, John (died 1735), English violinist and teacher of his instrument, composer for the theatre, son of John Banister (1630–79).

Beard, John (*c.* 1717–91), English tenor singer, chorister at the Chapel Royal under Gates (q.v.) in his boyhood, appeared first as a mature singer in works by Handel in 1736.

Bernacchi, Antonio (1685–1756), Italian male soprano singer and teacher, first heard in London in 1716.

Berselli, Matteo, Italian tenor singer, who came to London with Senesino (q.v.) in 1720.

Bertolli, Francesca, Italian contralto singer, first heard in London in 1729.

Bordoni, Faustina (1693–1783), Italian mezzo-soprano singer, made her first appearance in Venice in 1716 and came to London ten years later. Married Hasse (q.v.) in 1730.

Boschi, Giuseppe, Italian bass singer, member of St. Mark's, Venice; (?) sang Polyphemus in Handel's *Aci* in Naples, 1709. First appeared in London in 1711.

Boyce, William (1710–79), English composer and organist, boy chorister at St. Paul's Cathedral in London and later pupil of Greene (q.v.), whom he succeeded in 1755 as Master of the King's Band. Organist of the Chapel Royal from 1758. Published a collection of English *Cathedral Music*, 1760–78.

Brade, William (1560–1630), English string player and composer who worked in Germany. In 1618 he was in Halle and his daughter Magdalene married a surgeon to whom Handel's father was apprenticed.

Brockes, Barthold Heinrich (1680–1747), poet and important official in Hamburg.

Buononcini (or *Bononcini*), *Giovanni Battista* (born 1672), Italian opera composer, son of Giovanni Maria Buononcini (*c.* 1640–78), whose pupil he was and whom he succeeded as chapel-master of the church of San Giovanni in Monte at Modena, his birthplace. Attached to the court of Vienna in 1692 and of Berlin in 1696; produced his first operas in Rome in 1694. Vienna and Italy, 1706–20; London, 1720–32.

Burney, Charles (1726–1814), composer and historian. His Handel comments are valuable in that he had played the violin in Handel's orchestra.

Buxtehude, Dietrich (1637–1707), Swedish composer and organist, settled in Denmark and from 1668 organist of St. Mary's Church at Lübeck.

Campra, André (1660–1744), French composer of Italian descent. He became musical director at Notre-Dame in Paris, but was also famous as an opera composer.

Caporale, Andrea (died *c.* 1756), Italian violoncello player who came to London in 1734 and joined Handel's opera orchestra in 1740.

Carestini, Giovanni (*c.* 1705–*c.* 1759), Italian male soprano singer, afterwards a contralto. Came out in Rome in 1721 and made his first London appearance in 1733.

Carey, Henry (*c.* 1690–1743), English poet, composer and dramatist, pupil of Roseingrave (q.v.) and Geminiani (q.v.).

Carissimi, Giacomo (? 1604–74), Italian composer who cultivated the forms of oratorio and cantata in their early stages.

Castrucci, Pietro (1679–1752) and *Prospero* (died 1760), Italian violinists, who came to London in 1715, Pietro becoming leader of Handel's opera orchestra and Prospero a member of it.

Chilcot, Thomas (died 1766), English organist, champion of Handel's music in Bath, composer of delightful Shakespeare songs (1745).

Cibber, Susanna Maria (*nee Arne*) (1714–66), English contralto singer and actress, sister of Thomas Augustine Arne. She first appeared on the London stage in 1732 and married Theophilus Cibber in 1734.

Clari, Giovanni Carlo Maria (1677–1754), Italian composer. He was chapel-master in turn at Pistoia, Bologna and Pisa.

Clayton, Thomas (*c*. 1670–*c*. 1730), English composer and adapter, who set Addison's opera, *Rosamond*, in 1707, and for whom Pope wrote his *Ode for St. Cecilia's Day* in 1713.

Clegg, John (1714–*c*. 1750), English violinist of outstanding gifts, who became insane in 1744.

Clive, Catherine (Kitty) (1711–85), Anglo-Irish actress, versatile and successful, who sang in *L'Allegro* and *Samson*.

Croft, William (1678–1727), English organist and composer, pupil of John Blow at the Chapel Royal, organist at St. Anne's, Soho, from 1700 and organist with Jeremiah Clarke at the Chapel Royal from 1704; Master of the Children there from 1715.

Cuzzoni, Francesca (*c*. 1700–70), Italian soprano singer, first appeared in Venice in 1719 and in London in 1722; married Sandoni, singing teacher.

Defesch, William (died *c*. 1758), Flemish organist, violinist and composer, who settled in London in 1731, having been organist at Antwerp cathedral.

Dieupart, Charles (died *c*. 1740), French violinist, harpsichord player and composer settled in London.

Dubourg, Matthew (1703–67), English violinist, pupil of Geminiani (q.v.), for many years in Dublin and towards the end of his life in London, his birthplace.

Durastanti, Margherita (born *c*. 1695), Italian soprano singer, who came to London in 1720 and again in 1733. The text of a cantata sung by her at a benefit concert was by Alexander Pope.

Ebner, Wolfgang (*c*. 1610–65), German organist and composer who worked in Vienna, both at St. Stephen's Cathedral and in the court chapel.

Épine, Francesca Margherita de l' (died 1746), Italian or French singer, who first came to England in 1692, remaining there until her death and marrying Pepusch (q.v.) in 1718.

Erba, Dionigi, Italian composer, chapel-master at the church of San Francesco, Milan, in 1692.

Fabri, Annibale Pio (1697–1760), Italian tenor singer also known under the name of 'Balino,' who first came to England in 1729. He was also a composer.

Appendix C—Personalia

Farinelli (Carlo Broschi) (1705–82), Italian male soprano singer, made his first appearance in Rome in 1722, when he had already acquired some fame in southern Italy, and went to Vienna in 1724. His first appearance in London was in 1734.

Ferrabosco, Alfonso (c. 1575–1628), English composer of Italian descent, educated at Queen Elizabeth's expense. He became a musician at the court of James I.

Festing, Michael Christian (died 1752), English violinist and composer for his instrument in London, pupil of Geminiani (q.v.). Made his first appearance about 1724 and became a member of the king's private band in 1735. Musical director of Ranelagh Gardens from 1742.

Frasi, Giulia, Italian singer, who first appeared in London in 1743.

Froberger, Johann Jacob (c. 1617–67), German organist and composer. He was a pupil of his father at Halle, court organist in Vienna in 1637–57, visited Italy and England, and died in France.

Galliard, John Ernest (c. 1687–1749), German composer, settled in England c. 1706. Oboist, composer of pantomimes, anthems and cantatas.

Galuppi, Baldassare (1706–85), Venetian composer, who produced his first opera at Vicenza in 1722. He was in London in 1741–3, became vice chapel-master at St. Mark's in Venice in 1748 and chapel-master in 1762.

Gasparini, Francesco (1668–1727), Italian composer, pupil of Corelli and Pasquini (q.v.), chorus master at the Ospedale di Pietà in Venice, and appointed chapel-master of St. John Lateran in Rome in 1725.

Gates, Bernard (1685–1773), English theorist, singer and composer, Gentleman of the Chapel Royal from 1708 and Master of the Children some time before 1732.

Gaul, Alfred (1837–1913), English organist and composer, pupil of Zachariah Buck at Norwich Cathedral and later organist in Birmingham.

Geminiani, Francesco (1667–1762), Italian violinist and composer, pupil of Corelli in Rome, came to England in 1714 and lived in London, Dublin, Paris and again in Ireland until his death.

Giardini, Felice de (1716–96), Italian violinist and composer. He studied at Milan Cathedral and with Somis at Turin, played in various Italian opera orchestras, visited Germany and settled in London, where he succeeded Festing as leader of the opera orchestra in 1752.

Gordon, Alexander (c. 1692–c. 1754), Scottish scholar, writer, and musician, known as 'singing Sandie'; Handelian opera singer, author of *Itinerarium Septentrionale* (1726) and other works, and (finally) Secretary to Governor of S. Carolina.

Graun, Karl Heinrich (1704–59), German singer and composer. Studied at Dresden, went into the service of the court at Brunswick and later worked at that of Frederick, II of Prussia, first at Rheinsberg and after the king's accession at Potsdam and Berlin.

Greene, Maurice (1695–1755), English organist and composer in London, chorister at St. Paul's Cathedral as a boy, where he became organist in 1718. In 1727 he succeeded Croft (q.v.) as organist and composer to the Chapel Royal.

Harington, Henry (1727–1816), English physician and amateur musician at Bath.

Hasse, Johann Adolph (1699–1783), German composer of Italian operas, born near Hamburg, where he came out as tenor at Keiser's (q.v.) Opera. Afterwards sang at Brunswick, where he produced his first opera in 1721. Then went to Italy to study dramatic music under Porpora (q.v.) and Alessandro Scarlatti. Appointed musical director and manager of the royal opera at Dresden in 1731. Married Faustina Bordoni (q.v.) in 1730.

Haym, Nicola Francesco (*c.* 1679–1729), Italo-German cellist, librettist, composer, and concert director, active in London from 1702.

Hughes, John (1677–1720), English civil servant, essayist, dramatist, poet, translator, friend of T. Britton, at whose concerts he played the violin, author of Handel's first English libretto (*Venus and Adonis*).

Keiser, Reinhard (1674–1739), German composer, studied under Schelle at St. Thomas's School in Leipzig. Went to the court of Brunswick in 1692 and to Hamburg two years later, where he made the Opera the most distinguished in Germany for a time and composed 116 works for it. He also wrote church music, including oratorios and a Passion according to St. Mark.

Kelway, Joseph (died prob. 1782), organist of St. Martin's-in-the-Fields, harpsichordist to Queen Charlotte. Devoted to the music of Scarlatti.

Kerll, Johann Caspar (1627–93), German organist and composer, born in Saxony, but settled early in Vienna as a pupil of Valentini. Then studied in Rome under Carissimi (q.v.) and probably the organ under Frescobaldi.[1] In the service of the Elector of Bavaria in Munich, 1656–1674. Went to Vienna as private teacher and was appointed court organist there in 1677.

Krieger, Johann Philipp (1649–1725), German organist and composer. Studied at Venice and became chamber musician to the Duke of Saxe-Weissenfels.

Kuhnau, Johann (1660–1722), German organist, clavier player, composer and

---

[1] But Kerll was only sixteen when Frescobaldi died.

writer on music, cantor at Zittau, went to Leipzig in 1682, became organist at St. Thomas's Church in 1684 and cantor in 1701, in which post he preceded Bach.

Lampe, John Frederick (*Johann Friedrich*) (1703–51), German bassoon player and composer at Brunswick; came to England about 1725 and settled in London, but went to Dublin in 1748 and to Edinburgh in 1750.

Leveridge, Richard (*c.* 1670–1758), English bass singer in London, who made his first appearance before Purcell's death in 1695 and sang until a few years before that of Handel, his last recorded appearance being in 1751. He was also a composer of songs and theatre music.

Linley, Elizabeth Ann (1754–92), English soprano singer, daughter of Thomas Linley of Bath, where she sang as a child. She made her first important appearance at the Worcester Festival in 1770 and married Sheridan in 1773.

Linley, Mary (1759–87), English singer, sister of the preceding. She sang in oratorio and at festivals until her marriage to Richard Tickell.

Locke, Matthew (*c.* 1630–77), English composer. He was a choir-boy under Edward Gibbons at Exeter Cathedral and settled in London *c.* 1650, becoming an important stage and chamber composer.

Lœillet, Jean Baptiste (1680–1730), Flemish flautist, oboist and composer. He settled in London in 1705 and joined the orchestra at the King's Theatre. Later he went to Munich as chamber musician to the Elector of Bavaria, but returned to London some time after 1725.

Lotti, Antonio (*c.* 1667–1740), Venetian composer, singer in the Doge's chapel as a boy, produced his first opera at the age of sixteen. Became second organist at St. Mark's, Venice, in 1692 and first in 1704. He was at Dresden in 1717–19.

Lupo, Thomas (16th–17th century), English lutenist, singer and composer, member of a large family of musicians of Italian origin.

Mainwaring, Rev. John (1724–1807), rector of Church Stretton, Salop, and Professor of Divinity at Cambridge. Author of many theological works and (for no very obvious reason) Handel's first biographer. He was thirty-six and not, as is frequently stated, twenty-five, when he wrote his biography.

Mattei, Filippo, Italian violoncellist and composer at the Opera in London.

Mattheson, Johann (1681–1764), German writer on music, organist and composer, first sang female parts at the Hamburg Opera, then composed two operas (1699 and 1704), became cantor at Hamburg Cathedral in 1715, wrote several books on music, the most important being *Das neu eröffnete Orchester* (1713), *Der vollkommene Capellmeister* (1739) and *Grundlage einer Ehrenpforte* (1740).

Merighi, Antonia, Italian contralto singer, who first appeared in London in 1729.

Montagnana, Antonio, Italian bass singer, who first appeared in London in 1731.

Muffat, Gottlieb (1690–1770), German composer, pupil of Fux in Vienna, where he became court organist and music master to the imperial children.

Nicolini (Nicola Grimaldi) (born *c.* 1673), Italian male soprano singer, later a contralto, made his first appearance, in Rome, about 1694. First came to England in 1708.

Pasquali, Francesco (16th–17th century), Italian composer who studied and worked in Rome.

Pasquini, Bernardo (1637–1710), Italian composer, who as a young man became organist of Santa Maria Maggiore in Rome.

Pepusch, John Christopher (Johann Christoph) (1667–1752), German composer and theorist born in Berlin, appointed to the Prussian court at the age of fourteen, emigrated first to Holland and came to England about 1700, where he settled in London for the rest of his life. Married Margherita de l'Épine (q.v.) in 1718.

Pescetti, Giovanni Battista (*c.* 1704–*c.* 1766), Italian composer, pupil of Lotti at Venice. He lived in London from *c.* 1737 to shortly after 1750 and then worked at St. Mark's in Venice.

Porpora, Niccola Antonio (1686–1767), Italian composer, theorist and singing teacher, came to London as Handel's rival in 1729.

Porta, Giovanni (*c.* 1690–1755), Italian composer. Having been in the service of Cardinal Ottoboni in Rome, he lived in London in 1720–36 and then went to Munich.

Postel, Heinrich (1658–1705), Hamburg poet and librettist for the Opera House.

Quantz, Johann Joachim (1697–1773), German flautist and composer, who worked in Dresden, travelled in France and England, and taught the flute to Frederick II of Prussia.

Ramondon, Lewis (died *c.* 1720), English or French bass singer and composer, who sang in London until *c.* 1711 and then made a success as a song composer.

Randall, John (1715–99), English organist and composer, pupil of Gates (q.v.) at the Chapel Royal, organist of King's College, Cambridge, from 1743 and professor there in succession to Greene (q.v.) from 1755. Possibly encouraged Mainwaring (q.v.) to write a biography of Handel.

Appendix C—Personalia

Robinson, Anastasia (c. 1698–1755), English singer, made her first stage appearance in 1714 and retired ten years later, having married the Earl of Peterborough in 1722.

Roseingrave, Thomas (1690–1766), English or Irish composer and organist, son of Daniel Roseingrave (c. 1650–1727). Organist of St. George's, Hanover Square, London, 1725–38.

Scheidt, Samuel (1587–1654), organist and composer at Halle, and one of the important figures in German music. His acquaintance with English music is shown in variations on a theme of John Dowland. In Halle he was for a time a colleague of William Brade.

Schütz, Heinrich (1585–1672), German composer. Studied at Cassel and Marburg University, also with G. Gabrieli at Venice. He returned to the court of Hesse-Cassel, but in 1614 was appointed musical director to the Elector of Saxony at Dresden.

Senesino (Francesco Bernardi) (c. 1680–c. 1750), Italian male soprano singer, attached to the court opera at Dresden in 1719 and there invited by Handel to London, where he first appeared in 1720.

Shield, William (1748–1829), English violinist and composer. Pupil of his father and of Avison at Newcastle-on-Tyne. He went to London in 1772 to join the Opera orchestra as second violin and the following year became principal viola. He composed stage pieces and in 1817 became Master of the King's Music.

Smith, John Christopher (1712–95), English organist and composer of German descent, son of Johann Christoph Schmidt of Ansbach, who came to England as Handel's treasurer and copyist.

Snow, Valentine (died 1770), English trumpeter, appointed Trumpeter to the King in 1753 in succession to John Shore (died 1752).

Stanley, Charles John (1713–86), English organist, blind from the age of two, pupil of Greene (q.v.), later organist of several London churches.

Steffani, Agostino (1654–1728), Italian composer and diplomat, who spent much of his time in diplomatic missions at German courts, but was a remarkable composer as well as a scholar and priest.

Strada del Pò, Anna, Italian soprano singer, who first appeared in London in 1729.

Stradella, Alessandro (c. 1645–82), Italian composer of noble birth who appears to have held no regular musical appointments, and what is known of his career seems to be based more on legend than on fact.

Strungk, Nikolaus Adam (1640–1700), German violinist, organist and composer, who opened an opera-house at Leipzig in 1693.

Swieten, Gottfried van, Baron (1734–1803), Austrian diplomat, physician and musical amateur in Vienna.

Telemann, Georg Philipp (1681–1767), German composer, studied at the University of Leipzig 1700–4, was appointed organist to the New Church there and founded a Collegium musicum. After holding various posts at Sorau, Eisenach and Frankfort, he was appointed cantor of the Johan‚ neum and musical director to the five principal churches at Hamburg, posts which he held until his death.

Tesi‚ Tramontini, Vittoria (1700–75), Italian mezzo‚soprano singer, who made her first stage appearance at a very early age. In 1719 she was at Dresden, where Handel met her, but did not engage her.

Turini, Francesco (c. 1595–1656), Italian composer. He studied in Prague, Venice and Rome, became chamber musician to the Emperor Rudolph II in Prague and later cathedral organist at Brescia.

Urio, Francesco Antonio, Italian composer at Milan, whose first published work, a set of motets, appeared in 1690.

Valentini (Valentino Urbani), Italian male contralto singer, afterwards a counter‚tenor, who first came to London in 1707.

Veracini, Francesco Maria (1690–c. 1750), Italian violinist and composer. Studied with his uncle, Antonio Veracini, and with Tartini, lived in London in 1714–17, then worked at the Saxon court at Dresden, went to Prague in 1723 and returned to London c. 1735.

Vivaldi, Antonio (c. 1675–1741), Italian violinist and composer. Studied under his father and under Legrenzi at Venice, where he held various posts all his life, except for visits to Mantua and Vienna.

Waltz, Gustavus, German bass singer, who was (?) for a time Handel's cook.

Weideman, Charles (Carl Friedrich Weidemann), German flute player, settled in London about 1726.

Werner, Gregor Joseph (1695–1766), Austrian composer. He was ap‚ pointed director to the Esterházy family in 1728, being Haydn's pre‚ decessor at Eisenstadt.

Whichello, Abiel (died c. 1745), English organist and composer. He was organist at a London church, taught the harpsichord and appeared at Thomas Britton's concerts.

Young, Cecilia (1711–89), English singer, married Arne (1710–78) in 1736.

Zachow, Friedrich Wilhelm (1663–1712), German composer, theorist, and organist at Halle, first teacher of Handel.

APPENDIX D

BIBLIOGRAPHY

Arbuthnot, John, 'Harmony in an Uproar.' (London, 1732.)

Avison, Charles, 'An Essay on Musical Expression.' (London, 1752.)

Bayne-Powell, Rosamond, 'Eighteenth Century London Life.' (London, 1937.)

Best, Terence, 'Handels Solosonaten', *Händel-Jahrbuch* 23, pp.21–43. (Leipzig, 1977.)

Bishop, John, 'Brief Memoirs of George Frederick Händel.' (London, 1856.)

Bredenförder, Elisabeth, 'Die Texte der Händel-Oratorien: eine religions geschichtliche und literar-soziologische Studie.' (Leipzig, 1934.)

Brenet, Michel, 'Haendel.' (Paris, 1912.)

Burney, Charles, 'A General History of Music.' (London, 1776–89.)

—— 'An Account of the Musical Performances in Westminster Abbey and the Pantheon in Commemoration of Handel.' (London, 1785.)

Carse, Adam, 'The Orchestra in the XVIIIth Century.' (Cambridge, 1940.)

Chrysander, F., 'G. F. Händel.' 3 vols. (unfinished). (Leipzig, 1858–67.)

Cibber, Mrs. Susannah Maria, 'The Life of' (London, 1887.)

Clark, Richard, 'Reminiscences of Handel, the Duke of Chandos, etc.' (London, 1836.)

Cudworth, Charles, 'Handel, a biography; with a survey of books, editions and recordings.' (London, 1972.)

Dean, Winton, 'Handel and the Opera Seria.' (London, 1970.)

—— 'Handel's Dramatic Oratorios and Masques.' (London, 1959.)

Delany, Mary, 'Autobiography and Correspondence of Mary Granville, Mrs. Delany.' Edited by Lady Llanover. (London, 1861–2.)

Dent, Edward J., 'Handel' ('Great Lives' Series). (London, 1934.)

Deutsch, O.E., 'Handel—A Documentary Biography.' (London, 1955.)

Flower, Newman, 'George Frideric Handel: his Personality and his Times.' (London, 1922; new ed. 1948.)

Forstemann, Karl Eduard, 'G. E. Haendels Stammbaum, nach Original-quellen und authentischen Nachrichten.' (Leipzig, 1844).

Franz, Robert, 'Ueber Bearbeitungen älterer Tonwerke, namentlich Bach-scher und Händelscher Vokalmusik.' (Leipzig, 1871.)

—— 'Der Messias, unter Zugrundelegung der Mozartschen Partitur.' (Leipzig, 1884.)

Handel

Handel, G. F., Letters and Writings. Edited by Erich H. Müller. (London, 1935.)

Händel-Jahrbuch. Herausgegeben von Rudolf Steglich. (Leipzig, 1929, etc.)

Hawkins, John, 'A General History of the Science and Practice of Music.' (London, 1776 and 1853.)

Heinrich, E., 'G. F. Händel, ein deutscher Tonmeister.' (1884).

Hoyle, John, 'Dictionarium Musica.' (London, 1770.)

Ireland, John, 'Hogarth Illustrated.' (London, 1806.)

Jones, Edward, 'Musical and Poetical Relicks of the Welsh Bards.' (London, 1784.)

Johnstone, Diack H., 'The Chandos Anthems', The Musical Times, 117, July 1976, p. 601.

King, A. Hyatt, 'Handel and his Autographs.' (London, 1967.)

Kirkindale, Ursula, 'The Ruspoli documents on Handel', in Journal of the American Musicological Society XX no. 2, pp. 222–73.

Láng, Paul Henry, 'George Frideric Handel.' (New York, 1966.)

Leichtentritt, Hugo, 'Händel.' (Stuttgart, 1924.)

Loewenberg, A., 'Annals of Opera: 1597–1940.' (Cambridge, 1943.)

Lysons, Rev. D. (et al.), 'Annals of the Three Choirs.' (Gloucester, 1895.)

[Mainwaring, J.], 'Memoirs of the Life of the late G. F. Handel.' (London, 1760.)

Mattheson, Johann, 'Grundlage einer Ehrenpforte.' (Hamburg, 1740.)
—— 'G. F. Händels Lebesbeschreibung.' (Hamburg, 1761.)

Meyerhoff, Walter (ed.), '50 Jahre Göttinger Handel-Festspiele.' (Göttingen, 1970.)

Milnes, Keith, 'Memoir relating to the Portrait of Handel by Francis Kyte.' (London, 1829.)

[Morell, T.], 'Judas Maccabaeus . . . with remarks by W. Pole.' (London, 1857.)

Müller-Blattau, J., 'Georg Friedrich Händel.' (Potsdam, 1933.)

Nichols and Wray, 'The History of the Foundling Hospital.' (Oxford, 1935.)

Petzoldt, Richard, 'Georg Friedrich Händel. Sein Leben in Bildern.' (Leipzig, 1955.)

Prout, Ebenezer, 'The Orchestra of Handel.' (Proceedings of the Musical Association, Leeds, 1885–6.)

Reichardt, J. F., Georg Friedrich Händels Jugend.' (Berlin, 1785.)

Robinson, J. R., 'The Princely Chandos.' (London, 1893.)

Robinson, Percy, 'Handel and his Orbit.' (London, 1908.)

Rockstro, W. S., 'Life of Handel.' (London, 1883.)

Appendix D—Bibliography

Rolland, Romain, 'Haendel.' (Paris, 1910.)

Rosenberg, Alfred, 'Georg Friedrich Handel.' (Berlin, 1938.)

Rudolph, Johanna, 'Händel-Renaissance,' 2 vols. (Berlin, 1960, 1969.)

Sadie, Stanley, 'Handel.' (London, 1962.)

—— 'Handel Concertos'. (London, 1972.)

Sasse, Konrad, 'Händel Biographie.' (Leipzig, 1963.)

Schoelcher, Victor, 'The Life of Handel.' (London, 1857.)

Schultz, W. E., 'Gay's Beggar's Opera.' (New Haven, 1923.)

Serauky, Walter, 'Georg Friedrich Händel. Sein Leben—Sein Werk'. Vols. III, IV, V—uncompleted. (Leipzig, 1956–8.)

Shaw, Watkins, 'The Story of Handel's "Messiah".' London, 1963.)

—— 'A Textual and Historical Companion to Handel's "Messiah".' (London, 1965.)

Smith, William C., 'Concerning Handel.' (London, 1948.)

Squire, W. Barclay, 'Catalogue of the King's Music Library: Vol. I, Handel's MSS.' (London, British Museum, 1927.)

Stevens, D. H., 'Some Immediate Effects of the Beggar's Opera.' (Chicago, 1923.)

Streatfeild, R. A., 'Handel.' (London, 1909.)

—— 'The Case of the Handel Festival.' (London, 1897.)

Strohm, Reinhardt, 'Händel in Italia: Nuovi Contributi', in Rivista italiana di musicologia, IX (1974), pp. 152–74.

Taylor, Sedley, 'The Indebtedness of Handel to Works by Other Composers.' (Cambridge, 1906.)

Tobin, John, 'Handel at Work.' (London, 1964.)

—— '"Der Messias". Kritischer Bericht.' (Leipzig/Kassel, 1965.)

—— 'Handel's "Messiah". A Critical Account of the Manuscript Sources and Printed Editions.' (London, 1969.)

Townsend, Horatio, 'An Account of Handel's Visit to Dublin.' (1852.)

Uffenbach, Zachariasvon, 'London in 1710 from the Travels of.' Translated by W. H. Quennell and Margaret Mare. (London, 1934.)

Walker, Arthur D., 'George Frideric Handel. Catalogue of the Newman Flower Collection [Manchester Public Library.]' (Manchester, 1972).

Weissebeck, J. M., 'Der grosse Musikus Händel im Universalruhme.' (Nuremberg, 1809.)

Weissenborn, B., 'Das Händelhaus in Halle.' (Berlin, 1938.)

Young, Percy. M., Introduction to W. Coxe, 'Anecdotes of G. F. Handel and J. C. Smith'. (New York, 1979.)

APPENDIX E

HANDEL'S FINANCES

RECORDS relating to the banking account of 'George Frideric Handel [the signature in the Firm Book], in Brooke Street Hanover Square' are still extant in the Record Office of the Bank of England (fo. 97/2674). With the exception of a period from 28th March 1739 to 14th February 1743 a fairly complete statement is available from 2nd August 1732 until 21st March 1758. As details of payments are sparse ('By Cash' on the one side and 'To Cash Him' on the other have little helpful significance), an extract is only given to cover the alleged bankruptcies. It will be clear that Handel was not at any rate insolvent either in 1737 or 1745–6.

1734					1732		
June 26	To Cash Him		£1300		Aug. 2	By Cash	£2300
1735							
June 30	„	„	„	300			
Sep. 15	„	„	„	100			
Dec. 8	„	„	„	50			
1736							
Aug. 20	„	„	„	150			
Sep. 28	„	„	„	200			
1737							
Sep. 1	„	„	„	150			
1739							
Mar. 28	yᵉ balance		50				
			£2300				£2300

1743				1743			
Feb. 21	To Cash		650	Feb. 14	By Cash		650
	Chambers [1]			Mar. 6	„	„	250
1744				**1744**			
Apr. 5	„ do.	226.5.6		Nov. 3	„	„	500
17	„ Him	23.14.6		9	„	„	100
Jan. 19	„ do.	200		Dec. 11	„	„	50
May 4 [2]	„ Robinson [3]	210		Jan. 5	„	„	50
May 11	„ Francesina [4]	400		Feb. 1	„	„	150
13	„ Jordan [5]	140					
				1745			
				May 9	„	„	100
		£1850					£1850

1747				1746			
Apr. 29	To Cash Him	1000		Feb. 28	By Cash		400
				Mar. 7	„	„	100
				21	„	„	100
				1747			
				Apr. 9	„	„	250
				24	„	„	150
		1000					1000

These are the only payments specified in the whole of the banking account.

---

[1] Possibly Robert Chambers of Hackney (d. 1761), with whom Handel had dealings in 1752.

[2] Obviously 1745.

[3] Fees to Miss Robinson, daughter of John Robinson, organist of Westminster Abbey, and of Mrs. Turner Robinson. Miss Robinson (Hawkins, v. 182) sang in *Hercules* and other oratorios.

[4] Alias Mlle Duparc who, having left the opera, 'attached herself to Handel, was first woman in his oratorios for many years.' (Burney, *History*, iv. 667.)

[5] ? Abraham Jordan, the organ-builder.

In addition to this series of statements concerning his account at the Bank there are other documents indicative of Handel's shrewd financial sense.[1] Between 4th June 1728 and 22nd June 1732 he bought and sold South Sea Annuities [2] (1751) to the value of £4,622 (fo. 71/124). Between 6th May 1748 and 9th November 1749 his turnover in 4% Annuities (1748) (fo. 877) was £7,750 and between 10th April 1744 and 6th May 1748 3% Annuities (1743) (fo. D.1468) involved him to the extent of £3,000. By 2nd January 1753 he held £12,000 in 4% Annuities (1746) (fo. 874). Handel had commenced an interest in these on 22nd February 1749 with an investment of £7,700, which would appear to have come from the sale of the 1748 Annuities. On 2nd January 1753 the £12,000 were transferred to Reduced 3% Annuities. By 1759 these savings grew to £17,500. (fo. D.2646 M.2583).

In the Register Office Book A–K 1348 we read:

MEMORANDUM that GEORGE FRIDERIC HANDELL of Brooke Street Hanover Square, Esq. in the Probate late of the Parish of St. George Hanover Square In the County of Middx. Esq. died possessed of SEVENTEEN THOUSAND FIVE HUNDRED POUNDS Reduced Annuities at £3 per cent & by his last Will and Testament dated 1st June 1750 appointed JOHANNA FRIDERICA FLOERCKEN Sole Executrix with four Codicils respectively dated the 6th. Aug. 1756, 22nd. March 1757, 4th. Aug. 1757 & 11th. April 1759 wherein he appoints GEORGE AMYAND Esq. Co Executor making no mention of the said Anns. they are at the disposal of the said George Amyand Esq. he only having proved the Will.

Power reserved to make the like grant to Johann Friderica Floercken Wife of   Floercken the Neice of the said decd. & Executrix named in the said Will when she shall apply for the same.

Probate dated at Doctrs. Comm. 26 April 1759
Regd. 30th. April 1759

The final story of the dispersal of Handel's fortune in Reduced 3% Annuities is told in the following statement (D.2646 M.2583). It will be seen that the legatees mentioned hereunder did better than the terms of the will specify.

---

[1] Or that of his advisers.
[2] All these loans were managed by the Bank of England.

1759	£		£
2 May. To Christopher Smith [1] of Dean St. Soho, Gent.	2470	2 Jan. 1753. By Anns. 1746 Con'	12000
John Duburk of Hanover Sq., Gent. [2]	600	19 July 1754. Benjamin Jones of Bow, Gent.	1500
16 May. Peter Gallier, senior. Christian Reich of Westminster. Gents. Thomas Wood, Gent. of St. Giles in the Fields	1254	14 May 1755. Philip Hale of Basing Lane. Sugar Refiner	500
		23 June 1756. Stephen Gardes of Rathbone Place, Gent.	1000
25 May. To William Delacreuse of Castle Street, Esq.	400	19 May 1758. John Jones of St. Anns, Soho, Gent.	2500
Henry Monk of Dublin, Esq.	100		
8 June. William Prevost, jnr. of Shad., Thames, Gent.	500		
27 June. Edward Shewell of Lombard St. Goldsmith	500		
28 June. James Smyth [3] of New Bond St. Perfumer	700		
11 Oct. Johanna Friderica Floerken Wife of Johan Ernst Floerken. Director of the University of Halle in Saxony	9000		
31 Oct. To James Sinclair [4] of Shadwell. Mariner	500		
Lewis Morel of Fleet St. Goldsmith	876		
Edward Shewell of Lombard St. Goldsmith	600		
	17500		17500

[1] Was left £2,000 in the will.   [2] Was left £500 in the will.

[3] Was left £500 in the will.

[4] Died in 1789 *aetat.* 85, was a senior master in the Navy.

Other legacies included:

£1,000 to the Royal Society of Musicians.

£500 to James Hunter. [1]

£600 for his monument in Westminster Abbey.

£300 each to the five orphan children of his cousin Georg Taust, Pastor of Giebichenstein.

£300 each to his cousins Christiana Susanna Handelin, and Rachel Sophia; Thomas Harris [2] of Lincoln's Inn Fields; the widow of his cousin Magister Christian Roth.

£200 each to Dr. Morell; George Amyand; Reiche, Secretary of Affairs of Hanover.

£100 each to John Hetherington, of the Middle Temple; Matthew Dubourg, the violinist; Newburgh Hamilton; Mrs. Palmer, widow, of Chelsea; Thomas Bramwell, his servant.

Fifty guineas each to Benjamin Martyn, of New Bond Street; John Cowland, apothecary; John Belcher, surgeon; Mrs. Mayne, widow, of Kensington; Mrs. Downalan,[3] of Charles Street, Hanover Square.

The will and codicils are in Schoelcher and Rockstro in full.

---

[1] The scarlet-dyer of Old Ford.

[2] Of the Salisbury family and a master in Chancery.

[3] Or Donellan: an Irishwoman and an intimate of Mrs. Delany.

APPENDIX F

THE PROBLEM OF PLAGIARISM

THERE never was any doubt that Handel made fairly extensive use of other men's material. Explanations for his having done so have been various, and have led to a diversity of conclusions, from which have stemmed numerous essays in denigration or justification. It should be understood at the outset, however, that in the eighteenth century such conditions as now obtain in respect of an author's or a composer's rights were not operative, even though Handel and Arne may be seen to have been thinking in this direction. When he published his *Suite de Pièces I,* for instance, Handel protested about incorrect versions of his pieces being in circulation, while in 1741 Arne threatened with prosecution those who might pirate his Shake-speare songs published that year under Royal licence.

One of the reasons for a certain looseness in defining the limits of *meum* and *tuum* in Handel's day was the productivity required of any musical director. The prolificacy of composers then is now regarded with suspicious awe by those who are oblivious of the demands made on creative musicians. Handel was not only a great composer, he was in the entertainment industry and, according to contract, obliged to supply works of one sort or another at regular intervals. He frequently made pasticcios, and as often found himself being subjected to pasticcio treatment. Had he seen some of the versions of his operas presented in Hamburg he would have found it quite difficult to recognize them.

There never was any disguising the fact that Handel borrowed from other composers. Hawkins (iii, p. 92) notes that 'Hear, Jacob's God' (*Samson*) was taken from Carissimi's *Jephtha.* Burney (iii, p. 36) reports it as a generally held opinion that Handel 'availed himself of Clari's subjects, and some-sometimes more, in the choruses of Theodora'. J. A. Hiller, who in his edi-tion of Handel's *Ecce quomodo* gave comparative excerpts from the Funeral Anthem, observing, 'Ist es doch, als ob Händl die Stelle; er erit in pace—in Gedanken gehabt hätte, so ähnlich hat er die seinige gemacht.'

In a letter to Benjamin Jacob (19 October 1808) Samuel Wesley—anxious to promote the claims of J. S. Bach—put the matter in another light. '. . . We all know', he wrote, 'how he has pilfered from all manner of Authors whence he could filch anything like a Thought worth embodying . . .' It was a hundred years before the moral seed thus sowed began to fructify. Sedley Taylor published his *The Indebtedness of Handel . . .* in 1906, showing how Handel had used material from Muffat, Habermann, Clari, and

Graun. Percy Robinson, irked by the thought that Handel could be considered in any way culpable of misappropriation, and stimulated by the boys of Eton College finding a question on Handel's borrowings in an examination paper, wrote a remarkable book, *Handel and his orbit,* which was published in 1908. In this Robinson, commenting on Erba, Urio, and Stradella, from whose works *Israel in Egypt* appeared largely to be taken, ingeniously wished them away by saying that they were in fact all Handel.

Thus we find the matter of plagiarism being discussed in relation to a set of values that were not relevant to Handel's time. Even Edward Dent was led into some uncharacteristic opacity of thought when he argued (*Handel,* pp. 106–8) that while Handel's borrowings were connected with his mental condition in or about 1737, and were evidence of a state of deterioration, he could not do other than transfer whatever commonplace he took into a masterpiece.[1]

We should, I think, take particular note of Telemann's *Musique de Table,* which was published in 1733 and among whose subscribers was 'Mr. Hendel, Docteur en Musique, Londres'. The opening of the overture was quoted by Handel in that of *Alexander's Feast* (1736) in which material from the *Quatuor* of Telemann's work was also used. Contributions were received from the *Quatuor* into *Atalanta* (1736), while, rather more allusively, odd bars from the Flute Sonata in B minor of *Musique de Table* were worked into the sixth and seventh concertos of H.H.⁄A., IV, 12. Far from wishing, as Dent suggests, to cure some indecision in these instances Handel was surely intending to compliment one of his oldest friends.

Composers are not, as it used to be thought, themselves alone, but, whether consciously or unconsciously, members of a cooperative. It is recognized as proper that composers should borrow, and adapt, 'styles' and 'techniques', and many musicologists make a living out of demonstrating the ramifications of such adoptions and adaptations. The difficulty is that

---

[1] Handel's personality was discussed from a psychiatric standpoint by Eliot Slater and Alfred Meyer in 'Contributions to a Pathography of the Musicians: 2. Organic and Psychotic Disorders' (*Confinia Psychiatrica,* Vol. III, No. 3, pp. 129–45.

Dent, I suspect, at this point unconsciously took a hint from Handel as to the reproduction of existing ideas, for Burney (iii, p. 521) referred to a canon by F. Turini, 'upon the subject of which Handel has composed one of his finest instrumental fugues; but, *according to his usual practice* [italics P.M.Y.], whenever he adopted another man's thought, he has enlivened and embel⁄lished this theme, like a man of true genius, with a counter subject, and shewed that he saw farther into its latent fertility than the original inventor'.

the frontiers of legitimacy are always debatable. Handel was extraordinarily generous towards other men's brain-children. In addition to those taken from composers already named he entertained significant thoughts from (among others) Sebastian Knüpfer, at least one anonymous Thuringian motettist, Henry Hall, Thomas Roseingrave, William Croft, and Maurice Greene, from a compendium of whose works one could produce some substantial part of an alternative *Messiah*. Plagiarist or parodist? Handel, of course, was both.

Some things, however, were not done. In 1731 it seemed apparent that Buononcini, through Maurice Greene, had some three or four years earlier passed off Lotti's *In una siepe ombrosa* (*Book of Madrigals,* 1705) to the Academy of Ancient Music as a composition of his own. As a result of the deception being discovered Greene left the Academy, Buononcini left England, and Handel (it was said) was wryly amused.

INDEX

235

Index

Index

Index

Ward, Ned, 25, 48, 75
Ware, Mme, 28
Wass, singer, 87
Water Music, 28, 123, 182
Weber, 144
Wedding Anthem, 61
Wedgwood, Josiah, 87
Weely, singer, 33
Weidemann, C. F., 6, 42, 106, 220
Weldon, John, 43
Werner, G. J., 142, 220
Wesley, John, 73
Wesley, Samuel, 177
Westmorland, Lady, 73
Whichello, Abiel, 24 220
Wich, Cyril, 13, 32

Wich, John, 13, 43
William III, 7
Winchop, Thomas, 162
Wood, Thomas, 227
Woodcock, Robert, 107
Wollaston, John, 24
Wren, Christopher, 161

Young, Cecilia, 58, 220. *See also* Arne
Young, Esther, 58
Young, Isabella, 58

Zachow, Friedrich Wilhelm, 6, 7, 31, 220
Zoffany, John, 105, 106